TO BELÉM
& BACK

Also by Ben Batchelder

≈

Borderlands USA:
or, How to Protect the Country by Car

TO BELÉM
& BACK

*Backroads Brazil
with my Black Lab*

Ben Batchelder

EARTHDOG PRESS
MIAMI BEACH

For more: www.backroadsbrazil.com

Map design by Mary Rhinelander
Printed in the United States of America

ISBN: 0-9913372-2-0
ISBN-13: 978-0-9913372-2-4
Library of Congress Control Number: 2014914151
Library of Congress Cataloging-in-Publication
Data has been applied for.

Earthdog Press
Miami Beach, Florida
www.earthdogpress.com

To my mom and step-mom,
whose love of reading begat my own

≈

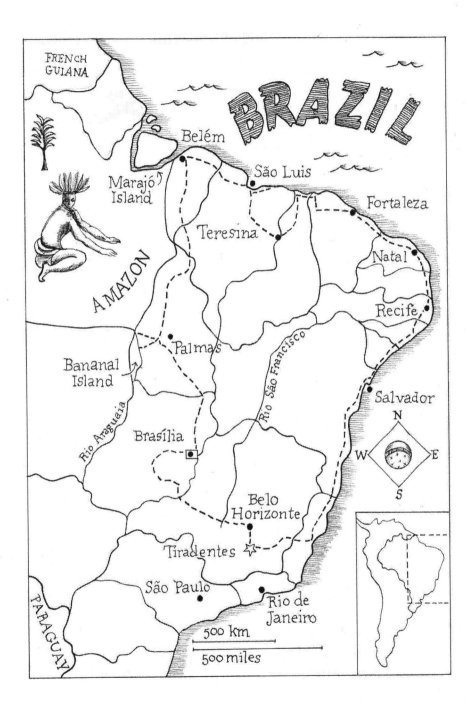

She complimented me
in a language I didn't know;
but when she blew cigar smoke
into my ears and nostrils
I understood, like a dog,
although I can't speak it yet.
They showed me room after room
and took me from here to Belém
and back again in a minute.

– Elizabeth Bishop, "Riverman," from
Questions of Travel

"– in these parts all men travel with fierce dogs."

– Richard F. Burton, *Explorations of the
Highlands of the Brazil, Vol. II*

~ 1 ~

TRAVEL IS OFTEN AN EXCUSE to accomplish something else. Call them exterior motives, but journeys are rich in metaphorical potential, driving the change catalysts, the line trajectories of one's path. Is your life stuck in a rut? Does your motor need a kick-start? Although the clichés are dated, recalling dirt carriage tracks and motorbikes, the parallels between life and travel are omnipresent, bordering on universal. So the allure continues, the desire and need to get out of one's self, one's routine, one's humdrum responsibilities, to chuck it all to the four winds and find a new potential at the crossroads within.

If Brazil is, famously, the country always of the future, what better place to discover your own glorious potentialities? A nation of endless summers, cheerful, attractive, and half-naked people – what more could you want? True, these are the perky postcards of a hard-won reputation for shimmering beachscapes, simmering Carnival, fruit-hatted Carmen Miranda, and a burning Amazon. Yet postcards are just that, subversive missives to the homeland of our banality, I Wish You Were Beautiful As It Is Here, now that I have been freed for a vacating while. To top it off, an old colonial saying from Brazil claims "beneath the Equator there is no sin."[1] Imagine that! A New World that is not puritanical, the un-Cola of the Americas, where sex-ed is unnecessary because it is redundant.

You may fault me with an over-zealous imagination, but then I am a prime candidate, a willing villain of circumstance, in the long parade of life's pratfalls. I had recently divorced and left an expatriate career of habit-forming perks: the corporate car, the company apartment, the trips home, the business boondoggles, and – for a brief but intensely pleasurable spell – a country club membership. I was even offered a *severance package*, or hush money after being de-limbed, which allowed me to contemplate a state of blissful unproductivity, at least for a pregnant while.

So if I was going to have an early mid-life crisis, why not, after a fashion, do it in style? I have traveled haphazardly before, hitchhiking from one country to the next, seeking the alpine highs of cultural rushes; so perhaps a roadtrip – a prolonged and even hazardous roadtrip – in one stupendously large country, a cultural, historical, and even geographical excavation rather than a peek-to-peek balloon ride, was not such a bad idea. Brazil is the size of Europe, after all, with far fewer foreign tourists – away from the coasts, almost none – and is therefore ripe for intrepid or just curious explorers, as it has been, languidly and patiently, for over five centuries.

But are there any roads?

I should confess up front that my ex-wife is Brazilian. And that I had already been living off and on in the country for seven years when the road urge overcame me. So I admit, I was and am a lot less brave than it sounds. Back when flying to Brazil for the first time, on a three month internship, I had in fact felt terrified, but that had more to do with the viral hepatitis picked up while slumming around India than any specific Brazilian reason for travel tremors. The multinational had given me two weeks notice and refused to pay for Portuguese classes, so after some language tapes I found myself on an overnight flight returning to the chaotic uncertainty so certain in the Third World. The plum overseas internship had been in London, complete with a plush company flat, so Rio de Janeiro didn't appear, at first blush, like much of a consolation prize. My body, not long recovered from several jaundiced months in bed, was in physical rebellion from the expected relapse and would have thrown itself out the night-filled porthole if given a chance. I don't recall sleeping at all. Then, as if to confirm my airborne fears, the local affiliate didn't meet me at the airport; the random taxi driver unkindly dropped me off with three months of luggage on the wrong side of a six-lane busy downtown thoroughfare; the cosmopolitan manager refused to speak in English even when welcoming me; and my first night was in a dark, stifling hotel room whose only window opened onto the kitchen air shaft. It could only get better from there – which it did.

One internship led to another and, then, after business school, to a long-term relocation to São Paulo, Latin America's juggernaut of business capital. Within a week I had met my wife-to-be, so while I came to Brazil to work I ended up getting married – the fate of untold foreigners since the days of Portuguese colonizers. She had one of the most beguiling smiles I've seen, one that could conquer, as did the *Bandeirantes*, much of a continent.

The work was good enough, while it lasted – including a stint in Costa Rica where, within the company at least, I was called *El Presidente* – but not sufficient. When a huge European corporation acquired our large American one, the Latin American president (from Argentina) told my Mexican boss that I would have to leave Costa Rica immediately – or else. Undeterred, the *else* still showed up two years later back in the same Brazil where my career had taken off, in the wake of the slow, corporeal torture called an *integration process*.

Regrettably, the integration of my marriage turned to disintegration as well. It was a multicultural marriage, fusing joys and challenges, but in the end only the challenges remained: different languages, differing cultures, confounding genders, confusing expectations. My wife refused to move to New York with me and, even then, was far from happy in quaintly provincial San José. The move from Costa Rica back to São Paulo, to familiar turf, was a relief in some ways, but at the same time the terms of our marriage contract were becoming clear: in the balance between America and Brazil, the former was in the past, the latter the future. My wife, apparently, could not be happy with me outside of Brazil, but was I ready to forsake my background, my history, my culture – even my English – to go native?

When I left São Paulo, our marriage, and the corporate cocoon of life support in an unfamiliar land, I moved to a small mountain retreat in the interior of Minas Gerais, a land-locked state the size of France. Out the window, then, went the all-in health and life insurance policies, the big-city comforts enjoyed with big-city friends, the imported products, the international foods, the bookstores, the newspapers, the cable television, the broadband internet and, missed most of all, the searingly beautiful day trips to the breathtaking beaches of the Brazilian Atlantic. It was like going cold turkey by taking a vow of Franciscan asceticism, some self-abnegation in the hope of starting a new, long-shot career, my third or fourth.

Brazil is not an obvious choice for a relaxing roadtrip. I see the difficulties that newly arrived foreigners, and many Brazilians, encounter all the time. Except in the tourist trap of Rio, road signs are only in Portuguese and place names often an indecipherable string of syllables in Tupi-Guarani, which complicates getting directions when you can't pronounce the destination. Worse, when road signs do exist – which is far from a given – they rarely confirm the highway or route number and instead simply list the next town or two ahead. Even with a good map, which itself is a challenge to find, driving is strictly a potluck affair, served up freshly each day with frequent stops, while getting lost, along the way.

Most Brazilians consider their national highways to be dangerous in the extreme. There are many solid reasons for such an opinion, which include: the deplorable state of the roads themselves, with frequent and unflagged potholes; a general lack of signage, reflectors, lane markings, or rail guards (which makes driving at night or in the rain nearly suicidal); and a mind-boggling proliferation of commercial trucks that clogs, pollutes, and tears up main roads with glee. Given the high rate of lethal accidents, many people drive only as a last resort. How else can you explain why so many travelers choose crowded and cramped all-night buses instead?*

---

* The high price of gasoline, for one.

Not that such a delightfully scandalous reputation dissuades everyone. I, for one, have always enjoyed the laissez-faire freedom of a car trip, and over the years have gotten used to the local hiccups. To be fair, things are gradually improving. Many years ago, during visits to a factory hours outside of São Paulo, I was puzzled to find the federal highway linking Brazil's first and third largest cities reduced to a lone, solitary lane for dozens of kilometers. While the Road Poobahs had gotten around to resurfacing the outgoing lane, the incoming one – somehow forgotten – was so impressively full of potholes no one used it. This created non-negligible problems when opposing traffic, including trucks and buses on blind curves, played chicken with your car, daring you to stay on the strip of blacktop that you had naively thought was yours. Such a valuable introduction to King-of-the-road, Brazilian-style, lasted for over a year until it was suddenly and superficially smoothed over, at least until the next rainy season.

So there I was, concerned about going native, but rather than returning to the U.S., like a normal re-pat, I moved six hours further inland. I had abandoned the busy Brazilian coast, yet instead of retrenching to the more familiar, predictable, and colossal Nook of the North was pressing into the largely backward, vast, and – to most outsiders – unexplored interior. Something about São Paulo – among my favorite cities anywhere – had gone sour. Despite being the one place in Brazil where things tend to work, the city had lost its manic allure and gritty romance for me. Not only is São Paulo much more expensive (of import to an out-of-work alien), it also prides itself on being different from, and better than, the rest of the country. Perhaps it was time to get closer to the more quietly yearning Brazil, the large and slowly changing country beyond the bustle of São Paulo and hustle of Rio, before giving up on the nation altogether. Maybe I could rediscover the desultory charm that had attracted me to Brazil in the first place, to relive some of the snake oil magic before a more permanent separation.

Unfolding a large map on the dining table of my small country house, I started to look for what could qualify, from my obscure base of operations, as the longest possible round-trip within Brazil. I calculated that driving down to Brazil's more European South would be short on distance – and drama as well. West was possible, but the roads just dotted or faded out among the headwaters of the Amazon. Which left north, reaching up to the mouth of the Amazon at the Equator before curving back south along the sun-stunned paradise of Brazil's never-ending Atlantic coast.

Perhaps such a long, circuitous roadtrip could teach me a thing or two about a country that, despite my seven year itch, still remained an enigma to me. How, you have to wonder, can such a fine people be so poorly governed? How can a country so rich in history and resources feel, at the same time, so backwards? Could an exploration of the nation's vast and less developed interior, teetering between past and future, give insight into the bewildered present? Most pressing, for an unmoored me, was the nagging doubt whether I belonged here any longer – that is, if I ever had.

You can learn many things from maps, so when I noticed that northwestern Brazil – whose entire Amazon region is larger than the Indian subcontinent – is all river systems with next to no roads, it got me wondering. Attempts have been made to beat back the wild, including the Trans-Amazonia roadway built by several military governments in the 1970's, but even that has reverted to jungle and is largely impassable. It just stumped me that the most westerly road you can take to Brazil's northernmost city of Belém, on BR-153 or the Belém-Brasília, runs up the middle of the country's bulbous head, bisecting it. Which is akin to discovering that the most westerly road to St. Paul, nearly midway across the United States, only reaches there east of the Mississippi.

I had also heard some enticing things about Belém, a decaying colonial city at the mouth of the monstrous Amazon River, the capital of Pará, and one of Brazil's oldest ports. I like places that time has passed by, for no better reason than I identify with them. All of which suggested I would particularly like Belém, for time has passed it by repeatedly – much as it has the country.

Why?

There is a *pardo*, or mixed-blood, friend of mine in town, originally from Rio de Janeiro, who runs our village's only bar with any charm – which is to say, that isn't fluorescent-bleached or cluttered with folding metal chairs. As Pedroca has driven twice down to South America's other extremity at Chile's Tierra del Fuego, once by motorcycle, he is invariably encouraging about what far-flung travel does for the soul. So one evening I brought by a good, large map (made in Portugal) to discuss routes and seek his advice, only to find him entertaining a distant cousin and her husband, a voluminously unpleasant consultant for the national petroleum company, Petrobras, who works in Mato Grosso just south of the Amazon. Not one to beat around the bush, cousin-in-law Marcos had this to say about my proposed itinerary:

"You're traveling alone?"

"Yes."

"Along the Belém-Brasília highway?"

"I'm thinking about it. Why?"

"Let's see: you're fair skinned, blondish, obviously a gringo; your Portuguese is OK but that foreign accent is unmistakable. And you plan to drive alone? On a highway famous for its assaults? I have only one word for it: suicidal."

Nothing Pedroca or I said could dissuade Marcos from his assessment, which he repeated several times for emphasis, evidently enjoying the slide of tongue, the quickening sluice of syllables punctuated with a bass finality: "Suicidal. Just su-i-ci-*dal*."

In his teens Pedroca had hitched around much of the country, but Marcos reminded him that Brazil has changed greatly since then, that thieves now kill not only for a watch but for the pleasure of it. And in places as remote as I planned to visit, that I would stick out like a sore thumb – or, more colorfully, like an armful of watches.

Marcos's dire warnings had the opposite of their intended effect, as a strangely familiar joy came over me, that began as a faint stirring in my legs and turned into a tremulous smile across my face. For some time I had been rummaging around for a crazy scheme to rattle me out of my lethargy – a debilitating sort of lethargy, born of a divorce and a career's end, that seemed to dog me no matter how long or hard I tried to shake it – and might have now, finally, stumbled upon one worthy of the name. How good, at last, to have a plan! The northern route it would be, then, along the profoundly uncertain and wondrously unpredictable Belém-Brasília, for the road chosen should be every bit as interesting as the destination, if not more so.

Around this time I approached my ex-wife and asked if I could take our Labrador Retriever along for the ride. "You're crazy!" was her immediate reply, and I knew better than to press further. So I let her think about it for a while, to be precise for a month, before broaching the subject again. The second time she relented, adding, "I'll let you take Atlas for one reason only: your safety."

As Atlas's Mom lives in São Paulo and has custody, she offered to help me find trip supplies for our black Lab that can only be found in the great, central distribution souk of Brazil – her home town. So we went to a pet superstore ("Your Animal's Shopping Mall") that would put many a *homo sapiens* supermarket to shame. It is huge and pleasant and well-lit and has dozens of high quality shopping carts that glide effortlessly up to one of fourteen check-outs. In fact, it's much nicer than any of my local food markets in the interior. Atlas had recently torn his bed to shreds (what would a dog Freudian say about that?), so I bought a new one from the "Boutique" section. Then there were the two fifteen kilo bags of special dog food just for Labs, with this and that essential mineral, which his veterinarian had recommended as added protection against all the nasties a vet-vacuumed dog can pick up in Brazil's backlands, as well as the new dog tags on which I planned to etch both my cell phone number and Mom's home phone, in case I died in an accident and Atlas survived. Not to mention the citronella bug spray found in the "Pharmacy" – yes, dogs can get malaria too – and four small rubberized booties to protect his pads from tropically scorching metal or sand, as well as from the invasive boring insect *bicho de pé* that burrows into paws on rustic farms. I also wanted to buy a cover for my station wagon's back seat, which came in two colors, black or light gray – causing a nostalgic flare-up down marriage row. I preferred black, she chose gray; fortunately Atlas didn't come shopping that day and had no say in the matter. After eyeing the "Bath & Brush" emporium through the picture windows, he would have mouthed most accessible temptations (Toys: Aisle 10) below knee level. Although nearly five years old according to his Costa Rican birth certificate, Atlas was a young five at that.

Purebred dogs, I've come to realize, are largely a phenomenon of the First World. Outside cities such as São Paulo and Rio or along the tourist-trampled coasts, they are practically unheard of in Brazil. Many developing nations show a lasting preference for hardscrabble mutts, the scrawny short-haired roof-top dogs tasked with security, who look the way most dogs did before anyone had the bright idea of selectively breeding them. Closer to their canine roots, Third World mutts are well adapted to survive deprivation, disease and, worse, two-legged contempt, to live incredibly long dog-lives against all odds. Pedigrees, on the other hand, are so little known in Brazil's interior swathes that I had to respond a half dozen times a day to children yelling, "Pitchy bull! Pitchy bull!" or less frequently, "Rottweiler!" – which must make the local news when one mauls someone a world away. In other words, Atlas was as strange and puzzling a sight as I was, which made us quite a pair.

When I loaded up the station wagon with his bare necessities and Atlas leapt onto the gray-covered back seat for the drive back to my mountain retreat, little did he know how many tasks I would give him in the months ahead, as we waved goodbye to Mom and pulled out of São Paulo for the six hour drive north, still within the mostly civilized patch of Brazil.

There are two major concerns about the Belém-Brasília highway, and the first, the abysmal condition of the road, is linked to the second, assaults, as it is much easier to rob cars when they are crawling among elephant-sized potholes and can't stampede. The one regularly updated Brazilian road map, called *Quatro Rodas* or Four Wheels (a somewhat optimistic claim about your car's integrity after a prolonged trip), includes a useful design for "Asphalt in precarious condition." The map key, in turn, is footnoted with an asterisk for those foolhardy enough to read on: "One defines the situation of the precariousness of a roadway based on the potholes in the pavement and by an average speed below 60km per hour." The officious language would be amusing if much of the country's road network were not lit up, like a Christmas tree, with so many red squarish dots. Even less encouraging was the discovery that over one third of the Belém-Brasília, for seven hundred plus kilometers, is so colored, much of it concentrated in the most remote and northern stretch within the Amazon. For if the worst road conditions are in the remotest areas, that's what you call double jeopardy.

The only person, Brazilian or not, I have ever met who has actually driven the infamous (and daily growing in stature) Highway from Hell runs a deli in town and – a kindred soul – professes to enjoy driving in Brazil. He recommended visiting truck stops to ask the long-haul drivers how safe things are ahead and, potentially, to convoy with them. (In the States this is called going "baby-in-the-sling," with your speeding car nestled between eighteen-wheelers, but here I wondered if my station wagon would be swallowed up by one of the craters that truckers simply skim over.) When I asked Renato, who once worked at a Thai-Brazilian restaurant in São Paulo, if I should stop for advice at the Federal Police stations sprinkled along all Brazilian national highways, he counseled against it out of fear the underpaid police could tip off local bandits that a lone gringo and his docile Pitchy Bull were loose and ripe for the plucking.

Brazilians tend to downplay risks that foreign media overplays – such as the far from remote possibility of getting robbed or maimed on Rio's beaches – so I was startled not only by Renato's warning, but also by a frank assessment in the Four Wheels travel directory for the last good-sized city before Belém, six hundred kilometers to the south: "Avoid traveling at night on the Belém-Brasília in the direction of Pará due to the risk of assaults, along with it being deserted." And this from the oldest touring guide in a country that bends over backwards to reassure tourists!

Others were equally discouraging. When I told some old friends in São Paulo about my planned trip, an energetic Brazilian couple who have lived in Portugal and the U.S. and are nothing if not cosmopolitan, their response was, "When are you going to grow up?," followed by a seconding of my ex's motion, "Are you crazy?"

"Do you realize how much traveling with a dog will complicate things?" my friend's wife added. "Where will you stay?"

They had a valid point, of course, but also lacked some of the come-as-it-may spirit of the open road where, as long as you maintain forward momentum – despite the usual hazards of bandits, potholes, overheating, and flats – you can come out all right. What is travel, after all, other than taking life to the next level, to a new intensity, where things begin to vibrate at the internal crossroads in growing harmony with an ever-expanding cosmos?

A small dose of ignorance can go a long way, after all, and a foreigner in a strange land has more bountiful access to such wells of blind optimism than most. So I was feeling pretty much on top of things until four savvy and level-headed Brazilians in a row, including the Japanese-Brazilian wife of a Scottish friend, asked if I would be carrying a gun. Me, carry a gun? I just couldn't picture myself armed and willing, fleeing from a crime scene of my own making, in the lawless interior of an already low-enforcement country. Yet the multiplying doubts had an impact. Beginning to feel less and less certain and not so sure of what I was getting into, I filled out my first will and testament on-line – and was off.

~ 2 ~

THIS IS REALLY ATLAS'S STORY more than my own. Or at least it should be, for he may well be the first of his kind to do what he did, making it all the way to Belém and back while pulling along the likes of me. It might also help to take the focus off of the humdrum and obvious and let it roam freely among God's creatures in one of God's biggest creations, The Land of the True Cross – that is, Brazil.

Some may note that Atlas is a purebred in a nation of mongrels – of beautiful mongrels I might add, for any place that mixes the races so thoroughly as does Brazil deserves a prize and that prize is a remarkably handsome people, which gives the rest of us some hope how the human experiment might end up. Despite the careful tweaking of his genes, Atlas could have been a show dog, with a fine, happy-go-lucky face that starts with two alert eyes, runs down a velvety nose that is not too sharp, not too snub, and ends in the gentle curve of his jowls and mouth that is a work of art itself, the jaw half open in expectation, tongue out, eyes up, ready for fun.

I shouldn't complicate too quickly, but this being the Americas where lineage is notional, Atlas's pedigree is in fact suspect. His mother bought him for me as a Christmas present the year we were in Costa Rica – an Indian gift if there ever was one – and found him at a shopping mall pet shop of all places, which may explain why his birth certificate, after claiming a Canadian and Spanish parentage, records his birthday on a date that, judging by his diminutive size, appeared to be off by a month or so. But as a citizen of the New World with a seafaring mix of Anglo and Hispanic, does it really matter what his papers say?

We never truly cared, as he turned out to be a prince among dogs, of such a sweet and even-tempered disposition that any mention of castration never crossed our lips. But then the only real input I had in his development was that we change his kennel name from *Atila*, which seemed too aggressive and deterministic by half, to Atlas, the hope of the world. I can't say if his new name played a part in his psychological development, but I like to think that it did, for all dogs – like the rest of us – need to have a purpose in life, even if a grandiose one.

Atlas soon lived up to his moniker and became a globe-trotter of sorts, precariously balanced on his mother's lap during car trips around town. During one weekend drive down from San José to the Atlantic coast, he swallowed so much sand and salt water in his enthusiasm to return to the (greater) Labrador Sea that thank Iemanjá, the Brazilian sea goddess, he had already been relegated to the back seat where he threw up impressive quantities of liquid sand. Labradors were first bred, some say, to help Newfoundland fishermen retrieve nets from the colder parts of the Atlantic – hence the useful webbing between toes and their maniacal love of water – so Atlas's first tussle with the elements didn't dissuade him. In fact when our small family, Mom, Dad, and dog, moved to Brazil and Atlas took his inaugural flight at the age of one, he did so with real panache. The local vet had recommended half a motion-sickness pill to calm his nerves inside the outsized travel cage, so when he emerged to take a piss break in Miami he proceeded to roll on his back, with paws flailing in the air, just like any other seasoned traveler on mind-altering drugs. Which is how Atlas came to Brazil and Brazil to Atlas.

Our trip dawned pleasantly – as they often do – on a lovely Saturday in mid-winter July. Atlas bounded into the car with greater enthusiasm than usual, not only glad to be going somewhere but relieved that days of packing had not foretold the greatly feared abandonment of His Dogness. Where I grew up on the streets of Cambridge, my older brother and his Lord of the Flies friends were experts at "ditching" younger me, leaving me to my fate which included sprinting from police and college bullies, but I would rather die than ditch Atlas. I think he understands, but the doubts persist.

It was a gloriously sunny day when we left mid-morning, and here in the tropical highlands, when the sun is out, even the shortest winter day is agreeable beyond belief. With windows down, spine straight, eyes ahead, I felt in full anticipation of what the journey might bring. After we turned off the road from town onto the two-lane highway signed BR-265, the freeway opened up and so did my station wagon's motor, warming up for the many thousands of kilometers of asphalt and dirt and gravel ahead. On the road at last!

Within minutes, however, we were stuck behind a procession of eight cars and two trucks, while sucking in diesel fumes rolling through the still air. As usual the culprit was an underpowered, overburdened truck chugging up the constant patchwork of Minas Gerais's hills, for here all but the most recent superhighways bob and weave with the earth's contours, up and down, snaking along old cattle trails only minimally widened. Not only does the lay of the land make it slow going for a veritable army of transport trucks, but for passing as well, as straightaways are infrequent, the sight-distances short. My speedometer read the minimum ten kilometers per hour, and then the polluted conga-line shuddered to a stop, as the lead truck swung out far into the oncoming lane to avoid the first major sand pit of the day. Welcome to Brazilian highways, where driving is a slow, cursive calligraphy on the earth's surface, wobbly and with few direct lines.

For Atlas it was much the same, having little sense of pace or progress, much less for our far-off destination of Belém. Pleasantly surprised by his promotion from the wayback to the newly covered back seat, he preened with pleasure, paws tapping seat, head bobbing up. While the wayback has the advantage of flatness, making it easier to distribute legs and balance weight during curves, it suffers from the major drawback of no downable windows. From car-Siberia only the nostril-tip of a nose can, with effort, try cupping the slippery air just beyond reach. Now, as master-of-the-back-seat, Atlas could fully sample the weather from either side and then press a cold nose against my shoulder to say hello. His upgrade to this-means-business class had practical advantages as well. Not only could trip supplies and baggage hide under a foldable cover in the back, but Atlas's proximity meant we could more closely keep an eye on each other and the developments ahead.

Our itinerary that first day out was a reassuring route into the past called the Estrada Real. It is Brazil's Camino Real, an old royal road established to facilitate and control the 18ᵗʰ century gold rush – more than a century before California's – that forever changed Brazil's fortunes and forged a Brazilian, versus a colonial Portuguese, identity. (Although founded at the start of the 16ᵗʰ century, Brazil only gained independence three centuries later, kindness of the Portuguese emperor's son.) To build any road other than the Estrada Real, at the time, was treasonous, and to travel its length, from the port of Paraty to mountainous Ouro Preto, took three months by mule and required a permit.[2] Long neglected and almost forgotten, the Royal Road lays hidden in the bushes or buried beneath, here along state road MG-383, a curvaceous two-laner barely wider than Oz's yellow brick road.

But first we had to pass through São João del-Rei, as ring roads are rare in the interior, making it all but obligatory to lose your way through town centers cleverly designed to entrap virgin visitors. Luckily I know St. John the King – the town nearest to mine with a good-sized supermarket – well enough that I didn't need to keep one eye on dodging bicyclists or stray dogs and the other on spotting reticent road signs, pointing the way out.

There is nothing like the prospect of a long journey to key up the senses, to strip away the tyranny of the quotidian, to slow you down long enough to absorb the revelations of everyday life. Today I was especially glad to see the Radio Man, a local eccentric who pedals around on his all-season carnival bike, a cacophony of colors, playing his sturdy radio perched on his sturdy handlebars. His musicycle is but a more whimsical version of the loudspeaker cars that crawl through most Brazilian towns, the downtrodden Chevy Impalas laboring under

Whoville-sized loudspeakers, whose advertising decibels are inversely proportional to the motor's ponypower. Atlas, who has an equal-opportunity reaction to clowns, costumed ducks, and salesmen festooned with jangling inflatables, barked.

As we passed a newly renovated square decorated with a half life-sized Smoking Mary locomotive, we caught sight of a small circle of youngsters, from tween to teen, dressed in white martial arts pajamas, practicing the *capoeira* dance that originated among African slaves in Bahia. (Bahia, of course, is the equally large state just northeast of Minas Gerais, which due to the clockwise nature of our journey was slated for last, but whose subversive influence can be felt throughout Brazil.) Here, while some troupe members lay out the rhythm by plucking on the bow-like *berimbau* and others clap, a changing pair of street dancers spin and crouch in a fluid, ritualistic mating spar once mistaken for fighting. True to the cultural kaleidoscope that is Brazil, whose elements are as ever-changing as the dance's, I realized that not one among the dozen *capoeristas* was black, even though Minas used to have more African descendants, proportionally, than any state save for Bahia.[3]

After clearing São João, the Estrada Real turns into an enchantingly sinuous road, whose path skims along ridges with roly-poly fields falling from each side to earth's end. Minas is a land-locked state which, despite its mineral wealth-in-waiting, was protected for centuries behind the Serra da Mantiqueira, an inland range that abuts São Paulo to the south and Rio de Janeiro to the east. It is an undulating terrain, with gracefully rolling hills that visually unite yet physically separate, on high plains under a steady procession of tropically robust clouds. At valleys and hilltops, but especially near rivers and veins of gold, small hamlets developed under the big Mineiro sky with names such as Archangel, Mother of God, and St. John the King, like cries of faith out of the hills.

Minas is also a bloody-minded state with a disproportionate share of Brazilian revolutionaries – which may be what attracted me in the first place. The most famous is named Tiradentes, a republican-spirited dentist – hence the nickname "Pull-Tooth" – who was the lone *Inconfidente* to be drawn and quartered for his crimes by the Portuguese crown, as he was the only one who wouldn't rat on his more highly born "co-conspirators." (My colonial gold mining town, near his birthplace, is named after him.) Much like Bonnie Prince Charlie of Scotland, it is not only for his bravery but for his tragic incompetence that he is revered, honored by one more national holiday in Brazil's already crowded field of leisure.

We pass a lone figure walking along the highway's frayed edge, an old man with a gray trim beard, a white rakish cap, and high-tide cotton pants over bare shins and flip-flops: he could be a sailor were we not four hundred kilometers – and counting – from the sea. His fleeting, incongruous presence reminds me that I, too, am more and more out of place, a fugitive from my own sea-like past.

In truth, I was feeling out of sorts myself. The beginning of a long trip is always unsettling for me, beyond the usual sense of dislocation, but something this day filled me with more anxiety than before, even foreboding. The practicalities of the journey had consumed weeks and months, distracting me from the enormity of the task itself. Atlas and I, despite countless warnings, were turning away from the routine of the more or less familiar and taking a running leap into a large, trembling unknown.

This may explain why I found the Estrada Real so reassuring, even comforting, that first tumbled day on the road. The continuity of history can do that, underlining the belief that not all actions, deeds, or follies are paved over and forever buried by the march of time. This seemed particularly true on a Royal Road that reverberates with echoes from long ago, when Brazil was still a struggling colony and not yet an ever-young nation.

One such echo, not long after São João del-Rei, is Lagoa Dourada, whose name reflects the colonial era fantasy of Eldorado with its lakes rimmed by gold. It is a one-lane town, as many are in the interior, whose physical drabness of helter-skelter concrete and brick buildings is enmeshed by webs of crazy wiring and jumbled signage, that betrays few hints of a distinguished past other than a lonely baroque church here or there. But Golden Lake is different, proclaiming a fame well beyond its ramshackle municipality, due to a long and daft Pastry War over *rocamboles*, a French specialty – so they aver – brought here by the Lebanese immigrant Miguel Youseff do Líbano over a hundred years ago. A faded billboard sign ten kilometers from town for *O Legítimo Rocambole* boasts of over ninety years of tradition. Only three kilometers away, one for the King of Rocambole differentiates itself with "Various Flavors!" The corner store Rocambole & Company brags of over sixty years of service and the original location, next to the main bus stop, where the culinary craze exploded. Not to mention *O Delicioso Rocambole* or, before that, the Emperor's Fig Tree which advertises "the traditional Rocambole" as though the others have innovated the poor thing to death. It is too early to sample, but I have already tried the delicacy which most closely resembles a rolled-up exercise mat. When sliced and served, the layers of fluffy cake-bread wedged between *doce-de-leite* of varying infusions, including chocolate and guava, spiral hypnotically inwards. Rocambole is a serious matter in Lagoa Dourada, where the venerable O Legítimo boasts of having "projected the name of Golden Lake to national renown." For only here are the lakes lined with rocambole.

Like the Santa Fe trail, the Royal Road was less a fixed road than a series of roughly parallel tracks, a few of which still climb through the mountain range next to my town, on durable stone and boulder pathways laid down by slaves. Most traffic on the Estrada Real went south, carrying gold bricks stamped with the Royal seal after payment of the Royal fifth, for export by sea. On northing return trips, the mule carts freshly filled with price-gouged goods climbed back up the barrier mountains, accompanied by a constant supply of slaves and laborers – semi-immigrants, like myself. Now and then came visits from the only emperor to have been born and ruled in the New World, Dom Pedro II, whose stopovers in Golden Lake are still mentioned with reverence to this day.

Revived in recent years after a long slumber, the Estrada Real is a delight of a road, full of inviting detours. After the rocambole wars there are signs promising shiitake mushrooms and ostrich farms and ostrich parks, if only you turn down this side road a short ways. Another labeled *Casa Grande*, for an old plantation house, serves as a reminder that slavery wasn't localized in colonial Brazil, it was everywhere, permeating the national psyche. Highway vistas are framed intermittently by the invasive eucalyptus, the country's favorite harvesting tree; by feathery yellow-green bamboo; and with the noble *jacarandá mimosa*, the Brazilian rosewood, which bursts into purple flower in the fall and was once called Saints' wood by the Spanish, because of its medicinal properties against dysentery.[4]

Ridge-driving has its surprises, as when a line of railroad tracks breaks out below, birthed in more than historical terms by the Estrada Real. A sign indicates an iron ore mine fifty kilometers ahead, which the rail line most likely serves to the exclusion of passengers or all else, as Brazil's once-grand railroad network long ago rusted away with neglect, forcing nearly all commercial transport onto the country's current beasts of burden, those overloaded and underpowered trucks.[*]

Turkey vultures swirl overhead and a whiff of carrion, likely from a stranded cow, lingers until cleansed by the bracing smell of skunk.

Before leaving the old road short of Congonhas, if you look down the left-hand side you'll see the pipeline terminal BR *Transpetro*, which is a Petrobras natural gas pipeline slated to fuel the regional operations of the world's largest iron ore miner called Companhia Vale do Rio Doce,[5] now Vale for short, whose interests would follow much of our journey into Brazil's export-driven future. In such a manner the evolution of an old transport road can be gauged, from mule cart to trucks, from Emperor to tourists, from railroad to pipelines. The only constant is the mining, now carried on by the semi-privatized Vale,

---

[*] Trucks carry 60% of Brazil's freight, compared to 16% in the U.S., per *The Economist's* Feb. 2006 São Paulo briefing, "A long, bumpy road."

whose full name translates to the saccharin-sounding Sweet River Valley Company.

I had some mining to do myself, of course. Such a long, itinerant drive around Brazil would be ideal for just that: to rediscover the land's layers of meaning for me, buried under seven years of experience. What else is purposeful travel about, after all, other than to deepen the ruts of understanding, to plow the lines, to leave your mark?

Despite spending only a few hours together that morning, I would soon miss the old road's company. We parted at Congonhas, where the Estrada Real rambles off through Ouro Branco to Ouro Preto, from White to Black Gold, after MG-383 dead-ends at the large federal highway that connects the capitals of Minas and Rio. Unlike the playful and meandering Royal Road, it is an old-style expressway where the asphalt is plentiful and the only road marking is a lone, center dividing line, more of a guideline than a hard or fast rule.

Sure enough, as we approach the outskirts of Belo Horizonte a massive iron ore mine opens up to the east, one of Vale's originals, and the highway between the nation's second and third largest cities becomes dust covered from a never-ending fleet of mining trucks. So constant is the mine's flow that trees and bushes to the sides have turned reddish-brown from the dust-up; if it weren't for the heavy rains it would be hard to imagine how they survive, as we entered what felt like a muffled, still forest, after a blizzard of atomic-ash. At the administrative office turnoff, by contrast, the highway curbs are splashed with whitewash and the grassy entrance and exit triangles perky green from watering.

Yet the army of trucks pushes forward, their numbers so great that each truck is identified with meter-high numerals stamped in white. When turning onto the ring road around Belo Horizonte, I am surprised to see Truck 475 plunge onwards, towards the heart of the Mineiro capital whose name translates no less lyrically than Beautiful Horizon. To the gullible foreigner all of this can appear unsettling, but to most Brazilians it is called progress. At times like these, you realize that Brazil is still in the intimate throes of its own personal industrial revolution.

~ 3 ~

A ROADTRIP FROM southern Minas Gerais all the way to
northernmost Belém, I slowly came to realize, is also an
exploration into Brazil's gently receding past. It is a past not so much
backwards – though, at times, it is that too – but out-of-date, as Lévi-
Strauss generalizes in *Tristes Tropiques*. This out-datedness, which
accumulates the further you wander from Brazil's southeastern coast
towards the Equator, this sense of being a decade or more behind the
times, is an enduring part of the country's atmospheric charm –
especially when you slow down enough to breathe it.

Accentuating such a visceral past is a cultural geography deeply
grooved by human happenstance. For Brazil is a vast canvas which, if
broadly brushed, forms an inverted triangle of distinct hues: from a
southern cone characterized by European immigration; to a
northeastern bulge that, due to the massive trading of slaves, is
spiritually, and geographically, closer to Africa; to the Northwest's
Amazon region, the highwater and last bastion of indigenous culture.

History is a dry subject, but in a country as waterlogged as Brazil
could it be key to understanding the place? My quixotic plans,
apparently, were shaping into a journey of fitful discovery, an
excavation in time. For an itinerary starting in the original melting pot
of Minas, heading northwest a thousand kilometers to the modernist
fantasy of Brasília, then another few thousand north to Belém, before
the long coastal return, would potentially tap into three colonial fluents
that course widely below the surface of contemporary Brazil – namely,
the colonial apogee of Minas Gerais, as well as the markedly different
tales of Indian and African slavery.

When I first moved to Brazil and lived in São Paulo, I was largely ignorant of such historical forces, but the longer I stay in the country the more I sense how much its past overflows the present, like the Amazonian floods which subsume huge trees that survive for months, stoically, under water. (During the rainy season you can actually swim among tree tops, like a childhood dream of hovering flight come true.)

So while the notoriety of the Belém-Brasília highway and the desultory decadence of the old port city of Belém first drew me to the itinerary, other factors came to play when I realized that such a journey, almost archaeological in its roughness, could shed light on some of the country's shadows.

But why, you might wonder, should it matter? The New World continues to supply many lessons to the Old and Even Older, yet it is the Colossus of the North that grabs most of the world's attention. Brazil, the continental blur south of the Equator's steamy prism, is in many ways a reflection of its northern neighbor, an enormous, multiracial, and above all creative nation – the America, of the Southern Hemisphere, that could have been. On first blush, I had felt immensely attracted to the country and its youthful optimism, and still am despite its abundant lawlessness and overheated opportunity, its awful governance, and the childishness (the downside of youthfulness) bred by generations of patriarchal rule. In some ways it feels like the New World newly-discovered, a far-off land hovering somewhere in our collective past, just over the ocean's refractive edge. It is a paradise found, lost, and then long forgotten – a living parable for both man and the land.

It is also a large enough country to get lost in, a characteristic which attracted me from the start.

The region of Minas Gerais where I live and didn't leave that first day's drive is called the Vertentes, or Watershed, for the number of river systems that originate here. It lays up in the southern reaches of the Serra do Espinhaço, which as Brazil's "spinal column" contains the country's, and some of the world's, oldest rock and geological formations. The most famous river basin is the São Francisco, whose main source starts in Minas near Ouro Preto and loops up north, passing four northeastern states before disgorging in the Atlantic. (If all went well, it would bookend our trip from the headwaters here to its northeastern delta on our return.) At over three thousand kilometers, the São Francisco is the longest entirely Brazilian river and, given its life-giving properties in the arid interior of the Northeast, one of the country's dearest, nicknamed Old Chico. Rocks and water are the Brazilian dialectic over time, characterized like all riverine places by steady erosion. So what better place than the Vertentes, an old-stone watershed, to consider the nation's historical sources as well?

The dawn of colonial Brazil broke in 1500 when the Portuguese navigator, Pedro Álvares Cabral, was blown off course on his way to the Indies and first sighted Mt. Easter in southern Bahia. There are doubts about this official version, but, if true, then Brazil was discovered by mistake. Most of the rest of the Americas are content to trace their collective discovery to Columbus's arrival in the Caribbean eight years earlier, but not Brazil, which has long inhabited a metaphorical island unto itself. Cabral christened his find the Island of the True Cross, an awkward mouthful that gave way to the more melodious *Brasil* – from the brazilwood whose red dye made it the first highly successful export to Europe, even though the abundant supply, in the first of many exploitative frenzies, was plundered within a few decades.[6] A more suggestive etymology traces the country's name back to Celtic legends commented upon by William Blake and James Joyce, and shows up in maps as early as 1325 by a Genovese cartographer, which places a large island, a Paradise on Earth, off the west coast of Ireland and labels it "Brasil" (instead of, say, America).[7]

In the year following Cabral's landfall, the same Florentine, Amerigo Vespucci, who modestly lent his name to the New World, came upon the wide delta of the São Francisco and baptized it, following tradition, after the Catholic saint of the day: St. Francis. The river became so important to the settling of the colony's interior, largely inaccessible behind the high coastal range called the Great Escarpment, that it came to be known as the country's Mississippi and still runs a few old paddle-wheel steamers floated all the way down from there.

Fortuitously Atlas and I slept near the banks of Old Chico's main tributary, Rio das Velhas, our first night on the road. The prior evening I had dropped by to say goodbye to some neighbors, an elderly couple who run our town's best inn. When I mentioned I hadn't decided where to stop that first day out, and asked for advice, Anna Maria immediately rang up a friend and fellow innkeeper north of Belo Horizonte and made a reservation for me at a *pousada* near Jaboticatubas. So efficient was her energetic succor that I didn't have time to ask how much it cost, or if they accepted dogs.

Fazenda das Minhocas, or Farm of the Worms, is a grand plantation house dating from the early 18th century at the end of a long, bougainvillea-lined gravel road – our first of many dirt roads, though certainly the most colorful. Atlas is not easily intimidated by such places and, relieved to be free after the long drive, confidently sniffed his way to the reception cottage to announce our arrival.

My general strategy with Atlas, rather than subterfuge, is to be direct. He is such a bewitching specimen of a dog that I fully expect him to charm his way through doors that otherwise would slam shut. It helps, surely, that he is clean and generally well groomed and, when in a good mood, obeys the simpler commands, such as Sit and Stay. After practicing all of the above within the eye-lines of the startled receptionist, I explained that I had meant to inquire about their dog policy and hoped that Atlas's presence would not create insurmountable difficulties. Well-trained in dealing with the unexpected, the receptionist was the model of calm. She took down our particulars and suggested a late lunch while they settled on the appropriate arrangements.

In the end, Atlas and I were offered the presidential suite whose private entrance includes a long, covered veranda overlooking a garden courtyard from the second floor. The veranda would be for Atlas and his accouterments, including his new bed, bowl, and various toys, while the three interior rooms were mine, overlooking the placid yet quick moving Old Squaws' River, whose embankments were a bright watercolor of green and chest high grass.

Accepting fate, even if dear, I felt grateful for the special treatment that comes with being a friend of a friend, for everything in Brazil works better with connections. And what if it was a splurge? In general I prefer to take to the open road, head in the desired direction, and stumble upon accommodation along the way, but then I am often on pins and needles the first night out, torn away from the predictability of near and dear creature comforts – just when a reservation can help smooth the transition.

After claiming our master-of-the-plantation suite, Atlas and I took a walk in the forty hectare "ecological" reserve, a forested area that encompasses the Worm Creek for which the inn is named and whose flow, in colonial times, was diverted for gold panning. Like the stone fences that wander aimlessly through New England woods, echoing an agricultural past, traces of gold mining long abandoned can be detected in many a Mineiro landscape.

As for the gold itself, it is difficult to overestimate its importance to the development of Spanish and Portuguese America, whose latter focal point was Minas Gerais. For integral to the Paradise on Earth paradigm was the terrestrial nugget, which obsessed many an otherwise lucid European at the time and drove many a conquistador to serial madness. While it would take several centuries to reveal the extent of Brazil's gold riches, indications of where to look were accurate from as early as 1570 when the Portuguese author of the (rather short) *History of the True Cross Province* wrote:

> Principally it was spoken publically among them [the Indians] about a very large lake in the land's interior, from whence proceeds the São Francisco River...within whose confines it is said there are many islands, and on them many villages, some of them quite large, where there is much gold, in greater quantity, according to what is affirmed, than in any other part of the Province.[8]

Things take time in Brazil, or in this case about a hundred and thirty

years to discover the fountain of gold nuggets, as most rivers including
the upper reaches of the São Francisco were unnavigable, the Indians
less than welcoming. But the precious metals weren't going anywhere,
and soon after the gold rush began in Minas Gerais, or General Mines,
at the start of the 18ᵗʰ century, slaves were digging up half the world's
total production. At long last the development of the near-frontier was
on, with cities such as Ouro Preto growing to rival, for a time, New
York and Rio.[9]

More importantly, what developed was a distinctly Brazilian (as
opposed to Portuguese colonial) culture, based on the rigid hierarchy
of a slave plantation system that also incorporated a few flexible and
adaptive aspects. The uniqueness of what evolved, like a land-bound
Galapagos Islands, was encouraged by the interior's isolation, an inland
incubator away from the coast and most of its foreign influences.

Following Worm Creek down an old gold vein, whose damp, green
walls rose precipitously to both sides, I let Atlas off the leash for a
good run until realizing, too late, that the rut was about to submerge
itself into the murky duck soup of a pond. Knowing well the result of
Atlas's free interaction with water – and fearing for our reputation
upon returning to the presidential suite with his coat as slippery as an
otter's – I yelled out, "Atlas, come! COME!" followed by one of the
simpler commands, "Good boy: SIT!" which he did, a meter from the
dark, mineral-rich water.

Dona Sonia is a severe-looking woman whose sharp profile and thin
mouth make her look even more exacting than our mutual friend, Anna
Maria, herself a perspicacious professor of Mineiro history. I was
invited to join her and husband Netto for dinner served buffet-style in
the stone-encased dining room that, coolly tucked halfway into a
sloping hill, may have once served for food storage or, perhaps, as a
morgue. During the meal I learned that innkeeping is not easy in Brazil,
especially with colonial accommodations that offer more historical
curiosities than contemporary distractions. While the manor house, as
was the habit during pioneering days, has its own baroque chapel,

restored and open to all in need, the rooms lack television, that steady filler of the *ennui* cracks of time.

"Each year the world is with less and less taste," Dona Sonia proclaimed after Netto had gotten up to chat with some other guests. When asked why, she ascribed the general coarsening to commerce and the need to sell products, push images, and publicize in false and misleading ways to get ahead – in other words, marketing. Evidently she was having a tough time selling the inn to prospective guests, and had recently dabbled in advertising on the internet, "ninety-five percent of which is garbage," she dismissed. Yet Brazilians, in particular, were hesitant, unsatisfied with an arid bath in colonial history and often bemoaning the lack of satellite hook-up or in-room mini-fridges.

"Look at the youngest generation," she continued, "and how hooked they are on products. It is one and the same thing. They masochistically hurt themselves with body-piercings and tattoos, thinking it both rebellious and fashionable. It is all part of the greater commercial culture, whose advertising and mass media penetrate their craniums and make them both slaves to the commercial creed and alienated from themselves, the culture, their bodies. Everything is a fashion model."

She had some good points there, but after the spent fuel of my trip's lift-off I was in no condition to defend popular capitalism, the real object of her ridicule. As for fashion models, I am tickled that Brazil sports more than her fair share, even though I never seem to meet them. What could I say? That I am both a culture vulture and a philistine, who revels in high and pop culture at the same time? By dwelling on the alienation of well-to-do Brazilian youth, she seemed to be hinting at her own.

The conversation turned momentarily to my life's peripatetic nature, prompting the comment that Brazilians are family-oriented and rarely leave their hometowns. It is mostly outsiders, she hazarded while eyeing me, who shift about from town to town, country to country.

Yet when Dona Sonia learned of my far northern destination, she positively brimmed with advice. "You know that the Belém-Brasília is quite dangerous?"

"Yes, I've been told."

"Full of potholes, with frequent assaults?"

"That, especially."

"Well, to know about conditions ahead you should talk to the long-distance truckers from São Paulo – they're the ones with radios, they'll know what's up." Advice, I noted, which seconded the deli owner's in Tiradentes.

"And once you get there, be careful. The state of Pará is full of bandits, did you know?" After a beat, she added, "Many of them are foreigners, of course."

"Oh, really?"

"Yes, it has always been the most lawless state in Brazil, so it attracts all sorts from the area: the Andes, Central America, the Caribbean. You know, my daughter hitchhiked up to another region, to the Northeast, when she was only seventeen, and had to depend on strangers for all sorts of help and counsel. She found it safer to seek advice from adults who have children. Not any old children, mind you. Street children, no, for many of them are informants."

"How interesting."

"In the end, the best people to ask for help or directions are people of roots, you know, the people of the region no matter what class. They can be as poor as they get, but if they grew up in the place they're most likely decent, kind people. If they're alone – without family, that is – or from another place or town, watch out!" (Her warning, wisely, was to avoid depending on people like myself.)

"That's interesting advice," I reiterated, running out of things to say. "And it reminds me: you mentioned earlier how family-oriented Brazilians are. Which, in another way, you just repeated, by saying that someone without local roots is not to be trusted. And so our conversation has come full circle."

Minas Gerais was settled, of course, by such untrustworthy transients, who were called Bandeirantes, or "flag bearers," for the tough, warrior bands – looting parties, really – which came up from São Paulo to settle the wild interior. Looming behind the coastal Great Escarpment, the long, inland Serra da Mantiqueira had protected the high plains Indians for centuries until the Bandeirantes conquered all. They were ruthlessly efficient during repeated missions to capture indigenous slaves, plant the Portuguese flag, and eventually uncover precious metals. Although the discovery of gold beyond the conquerors' most ravenous dreams took many generations, Indian laborers to build the thinly populated coastal outposts were found and enslaved by the thousands.

Even with such a surfeit of forced labor, Portugal had a rough time claiming, settling, and controlling a colony whose size, nearly from the get-go, equaled all of the continental United States-to-be. Their empire already over-extended, the beleaguered Portuguese repeatedly had to fight off foreign interlopers, including the Spanish, the French, and the Dutch, but especially the last two. Foreseeing a problematic rivalry in the New World's southern hemisphere, Pope Alexander VI issued a series of papal bulls, codified in the Treaty of Tordesillas at the end of the 15th century, which divided opposing rights along an arbitrary north-south line near the 50th meridian, with Spanish dominance ceded to the west, Portuguese to the east.[10] This did not dissuade the French, despite fealty to the Pope, from numerous incursions throughout the 16th century, from Maranhão in the North to the Southeast's Rio de Janeiro, which they settled until they were unceremoniously tossed out. And so it was for the first several hundred years – Rio was attacked and succumbed, once again, to French advances in 1711 – the Portuguese surrendering control of large chunks of Brazil to Holland, France, and Spain for decades at a time, before bloodily recapturing them.

Yet even during periods of truce among the mad-dog Europeans, colonization proved an overwhelming task which the Portuguese crown essentially contracted out. Without sufficient resources itself – and to be fair, Portugal was in the process of extending a lucrative trading empire all the way to Asia after Vasco da Gama's famous sea-journey to India in 1497 – the crown granted captaincies to favored nobles who were expected to make the requisite investments. Although the coasts were still largely unexplored, the hereditary land grants extended along parallel latitudes well west, as far as the demarcation line of the Tordesillas Treaty, like long, thin banners of land, well frayed on the wild, inland side. But the challenges were so daunting, even along the accessible coast, that of the original fourteen captaincies only two survived, São Vincente in the Southeast (including São Paulo) and Pernambuco in the Northeast. Desperate to kick-start development, the crown scrapped the captaincies in 1550 and dispatched the first governor-general of the Colony, Tomé de Souza, who founded Salvador, Bahia, the colonial capital for several long, languorous centuries to come.[11]

Setting aside the intoxicating ambrosia of gold dust, the Paradise on Earth utopia had other, livelier origins. They were, of course, the people found there.

The coastal Indians, known as the Tupi-Guarani due to a common language group, were surprisingly welcoming to the Portuguese who, in turn, were enchanted by the first encounters. Pero Vaz de Caminha, the scribe for the Cabral expedition, called the Indians "tough, healthy and innocent," while Portuguese King Manuel later wrote to his Spanish counterpart: "My captain reached a land...where he found humans as if in their first innocence, mild and peace-loving."[12] The parallels with the Garden of Eden were numerous, and early reports from the Brazilian paradise – where the weather was always temperate and diseases were unknown – inflamed the imaginations of European authors for decades to come, including Jean-Jacques Rousseau's eulogizing of the "noble savage."

Such "first innocence" was also evidenced in a most natural nakedness, which would have otherwise shocked the devout Portuguese. As the scribe Vaz de Caminha wrote:

> There walked among them three or four maidens, young

and gracious, with very black, shoulder length hair, and
their shameful parts so high, so tight and so free of hair
that, though we looked at them well, we felt no shame....
And one of those maidens was completely dyed, both
below and above her waist, and surely was so well made up
and so round, and her shameful part (that had no shame)
so gracious, that many women from our land, seeing her
countenance, will feel shame in not having theirs like
hers.[13]

In other words: the first fashion models, jauntingly immodest!

But what began so swimmingly could not continue, as the natives'
less savory habits – including rampant adultery, easy incest, and graphic
cannibalism – inevitably disillusioned the Portuguese who, feeling the
economic imperatives of colonization, began to enslave the hitherto
"mild and peace-loving" Indians. Their involuntary servitude was used
to harvest the dyewood so highly valued in Europe, and then to
cultivate the sugar cane that flourished, after introduction, in the
coastal tropics of the Northeast. Yet how could two peoples so
different – one splendidly clean and naked, the other hirsute, dirty, and
heavily clothed – meet? (A question that still arises with frequency at
the arrivals' lounge of Rio's international airport.) Disenchantment, that
old and reliable binder of the cultural dialectic, inevitably set in. Worse,
as hunter-gatherers, the Tupi-Guarani were ill suited to forced labor –
not to mention unused to European diseases – and so either died off
or melted into the dense jungles of the interior, fleeing as far as the
Amazon along a route approximating our own.

I found that to be cold comfort, following the path of bewildered
and despairing Indians, who in trying to lose their pursuers often
became lost themselves. The rootless following the uprooted. Their
flight, however distant, lent a historical precedent to our journey, while
paralleling another, into an internal land of retreat and disenchantment.

$\sim 4 \sim$

EVEN IN THE GARDEN OF EDEN one has to pay attention to
the food – perhaps especially so. One of the first surprises when
I moved from São Paulo to Minas Gerais was the distinct and
unchangeable fare. Like a *bandeira* foraging party through wild and
unfamiliar territory, Brazilian cooking is essentially fusion cuisine, with
every major region offering its own mix of culinary rootage. Mineiro
cooking, true to form, is more of a melting pot than most, for it is
based in the Bandeirante forays, when Indian-guided *Paulistas* brought
African cooks who catered to Portuguese culinary tastes while making
due with local ingredients. Hence the chicken stews cooked in
earthenware pots show the African influence, while the Indian
flavorings make the dish. (One example is the wild jungle leaf called
ora-pro-nóbis, Latin for "pray for us" – though not particularly lethal.)
Also widely available are pork and bean recipes named after the
tropeiros, the long-distance mule-drivers. What startles is that these
dishes, each more thickly tasteful than the last, have not only descended
unchanged over three centuries, but still rule the roost, as Mineiros
overwhelmingly prefer the same barely modified slave and muleteer
fare of their ancestors. There is something oddly comforting about this
stubborn continuity, of the past bubbling into the present, akin to the
enduring solace of the Estrada Real.

During our first roadside meal, I got an idea of what it may have
been like for the ever-moving tropeiros, themselves a rambling cross
of cowboy and nomad. For it was at a place called Yellow Forest,
occupying a precarious strip between ridge edge and asphalt lanes
dusted by dry eucalyptus leaves, that I sensed Atlas's and my status as

curiosities – almost as freaks – in the traveling road circus of the modern-day mule train.

When the tropeiros were moving large herds of mules and cattle across the expanse of Brazil, one saying goes, the short-legged pigs and chickens got tired and stayed put in Minas Gerais. This may explain why Minas takes a particular shine to swine, and specializes in pork dishes more than any other region. The Yellow Forest, like most Mineiro roadside eateries, obligingly serves *linguiça* pork sausage inside a puffy roll called "French bread," all the better to soak up the grease.

Atlas's and my entrance caused a stir behind the balcony, even though the place was open air and sparsely populated, with a few plastic tables and chairs for outside seating. I wrapped Atlas's leash around a fence post next to an open table and, while ordering at the balcony, discovered that a small group had spontaneously formed a semi-circle around him. If I hadn't already known the object of their curiosity, I would have thought someone was injured, spread-eagle on the floor and attracting the usual gawkers. Approaching the scrum, I saw one grown-up playing to the crowd by pushing a food morsel with his foot, tentatively, as if the beast could nip his leg at any moment.

"It is not a good idea to give food to my dog," I counseled, just as the man, fearful for his toes, skipped backwards and stepped on mine.

"It just fell to the ground," he replied with an impish grin.

"I know," I sympathized. "But it is still not a good idea to give food to my dog."

After the spectators scattered, a Brazilian couple of Japanese extract came over to sit down and drink their coffee. Given that the largest population of ethnic Japanese outside of Japan lives in São Paulo, they were probably Paulistas on vacation. They looked at our (even greater) foreignness and didn't bother to ask if they could join us, instead smiling and gesturing to the table, to which I replied with a nod and a smile.

"Look at that, traveling alone. Isn't that dangerous?" the man asked no one in particular.

"Sure," his wife replied, taking up the conversational gambit, "but with the internet these days and how independent young people are, I wouldn't be surprised if our daughter, when she's 17 or 18, does the same thing. They research the trip on-line and then just do it by themselves."

The husband looked skeptical. "But would you let her do it? Alone? With a dog?"

"Yes, I think we'll have to."

"No, not me. It is too dangerous, too many things can happen. She can go alone, but only if I accompany her."

So began our unaccompanied voyage westwards in what used to be the Holy Spirit captaincy of Epírito Santo. Our path, on the usual two-laner here numbered BR-262, would take us over the westernmost tributary of the São Francisco on the way to Araxá. We were about to leave the São Francisco basin and all of its assuring, if roundabout, ties to the Atlantic. With each day's drive we were departing the more established Southeast and venturing into Brazil's rough and tumble hinterlands, where the roadways labor under heavy harvest loads year-round and, consequently, are full of surprises. To supplement my various Quatro Rodas road maps, I had taken the extra precaution of researching updated road conditions for the first few days out on the federal highway system's website. "Condition Red," the equivalent of the map's "precarious" advisory, would be encountered for the first time between kilometer markings 352-365, 401-413 and 686-730, which were thudderingly accurate. The starting numbers, of particular use, helped us to prepare (i.e. de-accelerate) for the viral outbreak of potholes that is rarely, if ever, signed.

Araxá, part of the Mineiro Triangle of agricultural lands in the western beak of Minas Gerais, is a hot springs town. With the gold long depleted, Minas is known nowadays for its colonial cuisine, baroque architecture, and bountiful hot springs which still percolate up through the relentlessly mined mineral formations. I felt especially drawn to Araxá by the legend of Dona Beja, an early 19th century courtesan of the Imperial court, at a time when the Portuguese King, fleeing from Napoleon's invasion of the Iberian peninsula, had installed himself in Rio (the one instance of a European empire ruled from the New World). Local lore has it that the adolescent Beja was seduced by an Imperial magistrate, with whom she eventually lived, but in the end – so the story goes – it was she who captivated the Imperial court and, despite remaining unmarried all her life, garnered much prestige. Her story, of a beautiful and independent woman at a time when most were outwardly submissive, has been taken up twice by samba schools for Rio's Carnival – the perfect vehicle, one for the other, as the parades' enduring allure is scantily-clad women posturing with elaborately decorated floats. Rumor has it that the secret of Dona Beja's physical charm was daily mineral baths in Araxá – so why not give one a try?

The imposing Grande Hotel, built next to the springs during World War II and a favorite of native son and subsequent President Juscelino Kubitschek, has an approach every bit as impressive as the Biltmore's in Coral Gables; although here, the large city block of buildings sprouts out of a tropical tangle of jungle, lakes, and fountains. Recently renovated, the renamed Tropical Araxá contains nearly three hundred rooms, three pools, and two bars, one by the double-vision name of "Bar Scotch Bar." While I had no doubt Atlas would gladly take a dip in one of the mildly radioactive tubs, I was less sure if the town's famed hospitality extends to dogs.

After beaching myself on the reception's high and wide marble slab, I took my chances with the young woman with a friendly smile behind, hoping that the thought of two foreigners lost so far from the coast would lead her to take pity on us. It almost worked, as Alessandra visibly softened under a barrage of witty, charming, and increasingly desperate pleadings, but an exception to the policy of no dogs could only be made by the front desk manager who, despite Alessandra's whispered entreaties, flatly said no. Clearly my power of seduction is a good deal less than Dona Beja's. I felt skeptical about the kennel associated with the hotel until Alessandra, a dog-lover herself, assured me I could trust her.

She offered for the kennel to pick up Atlas, but I opted to visit the place myself. It was back in town, seven kilometers away, and turned out to be no more than the simple home, with a concrete-encased backyard, of a dog-besotted family with no less than seven of their own. While excited by the plethora of dog scents as we took a tour, Atlas soon enough sensed his unceremonial abandonment when his bowl and bed followed quickly on his heels.

A premature darkness fell as I returned to my hotel room overlooking the gigantic, multi-leveled pools. I tried to forget my betrayal by visiting the cavernous Thermal Baths, whose enclosed central courtyard can only be called Fascist Grand – appropriately enough, as it was inaugurated by the dictator of the day, Getúlio Vargas. There I learned that the eight major bath entrances, eight frescos, eight stained glass designs, eight paintings, and eight columns reflect the eight lessons of Buddha, with the integer itself – at least lying on its back, like most clients – the symbol for the infinite. If you think that the 1940's was a precocious time to be building with such New Age concepts as Buddhist numerology, you're right, but then Brazil has always been in the New World's spiritual vanguard.

The long entrance from the hotel was so daunting that I felt disoriented and, at day's waning, had a hard time finding anyone to tell me about the finite here and now. It was too late for any of the sulfurous baths (with petals, herbs, wheat and honey; or, the most transformative, "infantile"), so I had to make due with a surprisingly surly bath attendant who recommended a Finnish dry sauna ("used for relaxing and re-generative disintoxications"), followed by one of two showers. The choices were the Circular shower, whose sensurround water jets are "greatly sought after for [their] tranquilizing capacity and for treatment of central nervous system dysfunction," or the Scottish shower, a 200 year old process of hot and cold water flashes that "stimulates, is agreeable, induces euphoria, while providing relief for depleted energies and mental exhaustion" and is "utilized for the treatment of irritability and insomnia" – the twin ailments of any Scot beyond the reach of a Bar Scotch Bar. How to resist?

Yet as comeuppance, the "relaxing" Finnish sauna was so hot it left red lash marks on my shoulder blades and calves, augmenting the irritability which the Scottish shower, with only the cold water working, deepened.

Feeling guilty for abandoning Atlas and even less becoming than upon arrival, I slept poorly that night, dreaming of dognapings. Urban Brazil is now famous for what are called "lightening" kidnapings, when a thief carjacks the victim and forces him or her to drive from one cash machine to another, withdrawing the maximum at each stop. Dognapings, lightening or not, are certainly less common, but what if Atlas had broken away while on a walk in hot pursuit of a mutt in heat? I felt bathed in a shame-like doubt, for in truth it wasn't the first time I left a loved one in the lurch. Besides marooning a younger brother in the middle of an extended family crisis to travel around the world on ten dollars a day, in the end it was I who left my young Brazilian wife – young, but not as young as when I had met her seven years previously. Our marriage counselor pointed out that both my parents had moved on to second marriages, implying that my first tying of the knot was destined to unravel, but I am not a fan of such head-shrinking determinism. Still, a sticky film of guilt, like the thin layer of sweat under long-sleeved jungle attire, stayed with me that long night at the Tropical Araxá.

The next morning, while preparing for an early start, I received a message relayed by the front desk that the hotel manager would like to speak to me. This was the consequence, I surmised, of yet another contact of a contact – Minas Gerais is geographically loose yet socially tight – and that I was being mistaken as the representative of my elderly friends, the Tiradentes innkeepers, who had recommended the hotel in the first place.

When ushered into the manager's office by a fixed-grin secretary, I had no idea what to expect. There, behind a big desk, sat Alfredo, a middle-aged man with a streamlined hairline and a friction-free smile. Without delay, and after a few formalities during which I learned that Alfredo is energetic and from São Paulo, he told me emphatically that service is his passion and yet, regrettably, the hotel has a long way to go. Expressed this way it was hard not to demur, which I did by praising the friendly and professional front desk staff. At the same time I had to wonder if the Thermal Baths were under his purview, after noting that the customer satisfaction form omitted them. The manager replied smoothly that he was working on better integrating the two operations and left it at that – that service is his passion, period.

Alfredo, whether aware of it or not, is part of a large reverse migration trend – of which I may qualify as an honorary member. For years Brazil's poor and destitute, mostly from the drought-decimated Northeast, have fled to São Paulo, doubling the city's population within the last two decades and stretching its already torn social fabric. Now the tides have turned, as many *Paulistanos* (the confusing term for Paulistas from the capital itself) return to their ancestral lands, bringing with them new habits of efficiency, or as skilled managers, like Alfredo, who fan out throughout Brazil. They are the new Bandeirantes, carrying the flag from the only place in Brazil that mostly works, once again conquering all in their path.

When Alfredo discovered that I intended to drive all the way to Belém, he asked, "You're driving alone, just you and your dog?"

"Yes."

"Well, you're more courageous than I am. I would never do that, with or without a dog."

Paulistanos are, contrary to the urban myth and their Bandeirante heritage, not always the bravest of souls, much in the way that New Yorkers can be touchingly provincial and petrified of bugs in the wild. But Alfredo had already worked at exotic hotels in Belo Horizonte, Manaus, and off the Atlantic coast, so it could hardly be said that he lacked exposure.

"As for Pará, it is a rough state where you should definitely steer clear of three things: wood, women and gold." I didn't ask him how he knew – though Manaus, in a neighboring state, is only a several day boat-ride away – or if the prohibitions were necessarily in that order.

"Here's my card," Alfredo offered in parting and, with a knowing smile, added, "Drop me a line afterwards to let me know you survived."

He said it in a pleasant, half-joking way, but what did Alfredo know that I didn't? Could it be I had taken too big a bite of local fare to swallow? I didn't linger to ask, even as it became clearer and clearer that ditching Atlas for a night in Araxá would be the least of it, and that we could only expect trouble ahead.

~ 5 ~

W HEN WE DEPARTED Minas Gerais for Goiás that day, we left the more developed Southeast for the wild Central West which used to be called Mato Grosso, or Dense Forest. Dense forest it is no longer, but then a good part of Goiás was always a relatively treeless grassland called *cerrado*, an alluring ecosystem which spreads over a fifth of Brazil and would dominate our trip north.

Geographies are startlingly large in the interior of Brazil, as are the states. Small roadside markers tick off the kilometers, such that when you cross state lines on federal highways the numbers jump up to 900 kilometers or more, the distance to traverse. For those who have driven there, it is like crossing one sprawling Texas after another.

No such markings exist for the cerrado, which is the second largest biome in Brazil after the rainforest and consequently gets little respect. Yet it is the richest savanna in the world, stretching from Minas up through Tocantins, just south of Pará, which makes it entirely tropical. The cerrado is an open and relatively dry looking landscape, but appearances deceive, as the ecosystem supports up to ten thousand plant species, nearly half of which are found nowhere else on earth. Such a rich biodiversity, comparable to that of the much publicized rainforest, supports over fourteen thousand different moths, butterflies, ants, wasps, bees, and termites, and up to thirty-five thousand types of beetle; who help feed over eight hundred bird species (making it one of the world's most diverse bird habitats), one hundred and eighty reptiles, one hundred and sixty-one mammals, and so on, up the ladder to more or less one species of man.[14] For an ex-New Yorker, it is trial by total bug immersion.

41

It is hard to explain my affinity for the cerrado, which approximates the dry East African savanna but is more surprising and alluring still. While the ruggedness of sparse vegetation and gnarled tree trunks dotting golden fields gives the misleading impression of adaptation to the winter droughts, it is actually the quality of the soil, that is acid, leached, and lacking in nutrients, yet full of iron and aluminum, which is responsible. Emblematic are the hardy trees, not very tall, whose trunks and branches are eerily contorted by natural fires during the dry season, when linear growth is interrupted to be resumed laterally.[15] The bark itself is deeply grooved, suberose, with a cracked and wrinkled appearance that speaks of the ages. It is the face of ancient Brazil – and a few of the older *peões* working the land.

The rains are heavy much of the year, such that even during the annual dry spell the groundwater remains plentiful just below the deceptively parched topsoil. Indeed, the immense biodiversity of the cerrado is supported by three of the largest water basins in South America, the São Francisco and Tocantins flowing north, and the Prata flowing south. (As usual, a little digging beneath the surface helps.) Thickly grown riverbanks, during wet season or dry, act as living conduits and are called *veredas*, the green forest jam that fills the landscape's cracks. These and water courses in valley folds support dense, perennial canopies that serve as corridors of life, permitting many rainforest species – and a few wandering humans – to venture deep into the cerrado.

During the annual drought most trees lose their leaves and the *mise en scène* adopts a brief winter uniformity, only to burst into flower with the first spring rains of September or October. It is a sturdy landscape whose slow rhythms soothe the most restless of souls and impatient of people – either Paulistas or foreigners.

Our trip was intentionally during the winter months, the tropical temperatures a tad milder, the roads dry and less treacherous than when potholes fill with water and asphalt runs wet with truck oil. It is the time when, far from human interventions such as harvests and other perturbations, the cerrado is at its most serene, the wind in the yellow-flame *ipés* and the falcon-like *caracará* writing unreadable script in the blue dome sky.

Halfway from Araxá to the capital of Goiás lies another hot springs town called Caldas Novas, which bills itself as the state's largest tourist attraction. The name caught my attention from a map spread on my bed at the old Grande Hotel, and with a draw like that I decided to risk another hot springs experience, particularly one with so much popular, even honky-tonk, promise.

To get there we needed to hook up with BR-50, the major north-south route between São Paulo and Brasília (the country's economic and political poles), which, like the rest of them, is a rugged two-laner as the politicians prefer to fly. The best that can be said of the fraying-at-the-edges, ramshackle highway is its 24-hour Brasileirão rest area, where I stopped for a bite at its pay-by-the-kilo buffet of meats, greens, pastas, beans, and rice. As in most by-kilo restaurants the buffet and open seating area run together, separated by a *simpática*, often young cashier who weighs your loaded plate, subtracts the plate's grams, and pleasantly hands you a slip with the main course's cost, usually absurdly low. The cheap-modern atmosphere is often bright and clean, accentuated here by glass roofing under which even the diners are protected, like a human buffet, from nature's sneezes. At the Big Brazilian I spotted a special effort, announced by signs on the off-white columns, called the "Program for Safe Food (PSF) – Table Top," which boasted of being the first in Minas Gerais. A cartoonish food inspector in all-white clothing with a floppy white chef's hat is depicted looking through a magnifying glass at the walls, the food, the food process – and at you – wherever bacteria lurks.

Now, Brazilians are just about the cleanest race on earth; in the occidental half, for sure. They take two or more showers a day, always wash hands before eating, brush teeth after every meal, and are constantly on the alert for cross-contamination. My ex once reprimanded me for placing a *real* note (one of Brazil's most durable currencies, in circulation since 1994) on a dining table, the implication being that the banknote's festering germs from so many unwashed hands would jump from soiled currency to table and then, pronto, to our food. This fastidiousness for squeaky clean is one of the many Indian gifts to Brazilian culture, as it was the nakedly noble savage who first taught the rugged and redolent Portuguese the virtues of bathing.[16]

Needless to say, things were thoroughly scrubbed at the Big Brazilian, perhaps too much so, as my last taste of Mineiro slave fare lacked one too many germs to be particularly flavorful.

We were taking some risks, arriving in touristy Caldas Novas during July's mid-winter break, when nearly every Brazilian family with means will take a goodly portion of their mandatory one month vacation and travel with children in need of sensorial stimulation. So rather than being turned away from hotel after hotel, we drove through the dumpy chock-a-block spread that circles nearly every interior town and went straight to the central square's Tourist Information kiosk – an oasis in the town's festive, holiday tumult.

Having left Atlas to guard the car, I was at first attended by a listless boy-man with blond surfer locks who – thankfully – gave up preemptively, and handed my difficult case over to Elaine, a brunette of only slightly greater seniority. When I repeated to Elaine that I wished to find a room not only for myself but for my dog, she looked crestfallen.

"How big a dog?"

"Oh, medium-sized," I lied, as I have only seen about a dozen larger.

"What breed, did you say?"

"Labrador. Which is a very intelligent breed, and works as seeing-eye dogs for blind people."

She seemed skeptical, but agreed to call a couple of hotels listed in my Quatro Rodas directory. When I told her that he sleeps on his own bed on the floor, doesn't make any mess whatsoever, rarely barks, and is overall much better trained than I am, she smiled.

Luckily she wasn't discouraged by early rejections and started to rise to the challenge, elevating her praise of Atlas's most favorable attributes – though she had yet to meet him – with every call.

"He's one of those super-trained dogs who goes everywhere!" was one.

"He's so intelligent, you won't believe it!" was another.

There are no greater friends or allies than Brazilians who warm to your cause, for no impediment, neither rain nor mud nor storm, is too daunting to overcome when they're in the mood and groove with you.

My favorite selling point, the *pièce de résistance* (and a complete fabrication, besides), she saved for last: "I believe he's won numerous awards!"

Even though this was my first evening in Goiás and Elaine the first real *Goiana* I had ever met, by this point I was ready to throw caution and experience to the winds and propose marriage on the spot, convinced that Elaine and I, as an indelible team, could surmount all obstacles for all time to come.

Victory came during the fifth call, right after the brightly-delivered assurance, "It's just for one night!" She had an immensely satisfied look on her face, as she pulled out the town map and indicated where to go.

Elaine, no doubt, will go on to win many customer-satisfaction awards, but the least we could do was to return on foot, after checking in, to give Atlas the opportunity to thank her in dog-person. When I pushed open the kiosk's sliding glass door, I found her attending a small family, a father and two sons. After all the build up, she actually appeared frightened of Atlas – many Brazilians are bitten by mutts as children and never get over it – and, though emerging from behind her desk, kept her distance.

The pleasant, beer-bellied man and his young sons, seated on the near side, didn't seem to mind being interrupted and, in a good-natured way that would be hard to imagine in many northern countries, were happy to meet Atlas and listen to our story. As Atlas conquers all hearts, other than the petrified, father and sons were in no time relay-patting him.

Intrigued by Atlas's implacably agreeable behavior, the father asked, "What would he do if you slapped him hard on the side?"

"I don't know. Why not give it a try?" I offered, which got a nervous chuckle from everyone except Atlas. As the question took the prize that day, I went on to explain that several good hard pats on the rib cage are fairly riskless, which I proceeded to demonstrate.

Reassured, he now wondered, "And what if a stranger took his leash and tried to lead him away, would he follow?"

Theft of purebred dogs is a problem, especially in the interior, where a pedigree pup can cost several months' salary.

"If I was there and told him it was OK, I think so. But if someone was trying to steal him, I hope he'd resist," I added, glancing purposefully to Atlas, who, slumped to the ground on all fours, only unfurled and furled his tongue with a yawn.

By this time the elder son was asking about my nationality and Atlas, warming up to the crowd, started to clean the youngest's bare leg – of spilled ice cream, perhaps. As licking is often a sign of amorous intent, I decided to leave before Atlas, basking in the warm glow of so much praise, got over-familiar with the younger boy and made Elaine regret her eulogies.

After such a friendly introduction Caldas Novas could do no wrong for me, even though the town's streets and buildings and sidewalks, to the last one, were strewn with gazillions of cheap charms, trinkets, plastic do-dads, and clothing items that unfailingly attract Brazilian tourists rampaging through the emerging economy. You can tell Goiás is a charging, up-and-coming state by the multitudinous volume of cutesy stuff on offer. Such was the thicket, a veritable obstacle course of hanging bazaar material dominated by wildly colored inflatables of alligators, bloated fish, and rings, that the sidewalks were all but unnavigable, with severe risk to head and body. Usually forced into the street, the one time Atlas and I braved a sidewalk where goods hung expectantly like over-ripe fruit, I dislodged the wire frame of a female torso adorned with a bikini top and bottom, which slithered into my arms and luckily not to the ground. The shop girl could not have been nicer about it, saying "It is I who should ask for your pardon!" as though it was all her fault for having placed it in my way.

When, after more ducking, I stumbled by a jewelry shop that also engraves, I recalled that Atlas's metal tag still lacked the I.D. part and returned shortly thereafter for the task. It was pushing day's end, which may explain the somewhat lackadaisical attitude of the store's occupants, two white women and a black engraver, who were passing the while in the time honored fashion of talking as much about as little as possible.

The handing over of I.D. tag with desired text was but a wrinkle in the placid pond of the afternoon. Hearing my accent, they became curious and asked for my country, but hardly changed posture or tone of voice, such exertions being superfluous.

"So do you miss peanut butter?" the owner's friend asked.

"Sure," I replied. "Why, do you like it?"

"I did when I was a kid, I couldn't get enough. My English teacher, an American woman, used to bring back jars from family visits to the States and would offer it to us on crackers after lessons."

"Really? I bring back a jar for the daughter of some friends, almost every trip. So was your teacher living here for long?"

"She still is. On a farm outside of town."

"Do you see her?"

"No. Life changes. But she's still there."

"Are there many foreigners in Caldas Novas?"

"I don't think so. She's the only one I know of."

The afternoon stillness closed over us for a few moments, the natural entropy of the tropics increasing as available energy diminished. I asked about a local restaurant called Papas, which they both recommended, after which the conversation lulled once again and I stepped out for a quick boost of sweetened coffee next door. When the tags were done – with smaller lettering than I had requested, the message afloat in the flat, metallic contumacy – I tried another opening:

"What a big help, as Atlas likes to communicate, and expresses himself well in a number of ways, but he still has a hard time telling you his name or telephone number."

"Like most foreigners," the friend replied, which made the owner laugh.

"Well, yes, but he was born in Costa Rica and speaks Spanish – and usually Spanish-speakers can understand and speak a bit of Portuguese, don't they?"

"Never!" she laughed.

"That's unfair. But tell me, which are your favorite dishes at Papas?"

"It depends. What kind of food do you like?"

"I like everything."

"Well, in that case," she replied with arched eyebrows, "start with the regional chicken dish made with *pequi* and, if you don't like it, throw it away and order the fish dish."

Which I almost did.

Even though Caldas Novas claims to be sitting on the world's largest thermal springs, and nineteen out of twenty license plates were from out of town, I couldn't really see what the fuss is all about. I took a dip in my hotel's spring-fed pool (averaging 35 to 47 degrees centigrade) and enjoyed the same goosey and frizzy sensation that in 1828 miraculously cured Governor Fernando Delgado de Castilho of rheumatism, thereupon priming the tourist gusher. "These waters," the town brochure informs, "when drunk for several days, act as internal cleansers of the digestive organs and are indicated for infections and allergies." Not to mention other benefits such as: "metabolic stimulation of the endocrine glands; diuretic increase and excretion of uric acid; an increasingly sedative effect on the nervous system... lowering of arterial pressure, especially with arteriosclerosis... improvement of gastric and duodenal digestion; increase in sexual activity." Even though so many boons, including nervous system sedatives, were a bit over the top for me, at least I knew where to return for my golden years – just like that lone English teacher, perhaps.

If the state's major tourist attraction was just a little too tacky, the economy of robust pink alligators too up and coming, the state of Goiás itself was fast growing on me. I felt as though I had found an older and simpler Brazil, untouched and undisturbed by oceans and what they bring. Unsurprisingly its history is much like Minas's, only delayed, with the first recorded Bandeirante arriving in 1682 on the hustings for gold and able-bodied natives. The Goyaz Indians nicknamed him *Anhangüera*, or Old Devil, for at their first meeting he set aflame a plate of cachaça (which they mistook for water) and threatened to burn all their rivers if they didn't take him to their gold mines. Rewarded for his blackmail, he returned to São Paulo three years later with both gold and slaves, but it was only when his son organized another *bandeira,* or "banner," in 1722 that the Goianian gold rush sparkled.[17]

We alighted the next day in Goiás Velho, a charming colonial town built quickly during the gold bonanza and then all but forgotten. It used to be the state capital, and so as to not hurt anyone's feelings the state government, including the sitting governor, return on July 25th every year to lord over all for three days – which sounds more like the last blast of winter break than real work. The Federal Landmarks Commission, called *Iphan* from its abbreviation in Portuguese, has tried to spruce the town up, including burying all telephone and electrical lines in the historic center, which has won it the U.N.'s Cultural Patrimony of Humanity designation, whose precise benefits are hard to discern other than, one can hope, deterring the locals from thoroughly ransacking the place.

I immediately liked the town for no other reason than that the first two inns we visited had no problem whatsoever welcoming Atlas. We stayed at the second, Pousada do Ipê, which was closer to the center and next to a good eatery, Flor do Ipê, in the ipê-dominated part of town. One of the Buddha-like women hunched over a small table offered to explain the buffet-style lunch, for Goiás has a distinctive cuisine of its own, a mix of native influence with that of the Mineiro and Paulista gold-bugs. The most intriguing was a rice dish adorned with the typical cerrado fruit pequi, which – the national colors – is green outside, yellow inside, and full of spines. This, actually, is the aromatic pit, often used for local flavoring; the orange-sized fruit of the mature pequi tree contains four of them. The kindly Mineira manager instructed me how to approach the treacherous *fruta*, saying I should eat it as one does an olive. As I am not an olive devotee, I went for the quick route and while in search of the pit almost bit through my first pequi, nearly giving her heart palpitations. After demanding to see the violated fruit – which I spat out as decorously as possible – the Mineira explained one should only scrape the outer layer with one's front teeth. As it has a bitter taste which cooking doesn't easily dispel, my early verdict was: much ado for nothing. But then the pequi's musty taste grew on me.

The historical town is a small, complex delicacy itself, the colonial Portuguese houses cheek to jowl, their white stucco facades brightened by door and window casings splashed with blues, grays, or golden yellows. Atlas and I walked around in a leisurely manner, played ball on the sloping central green, and sat in the main square where the local kids, after the usual hesitations and mis-classifications, took to leading Atlas by the leash around the small park. One girl, barefoot and elfish in a thin wisp of a dress with tussled blond locks, insisted on taking Atlas for several turns, as if she were a tropeira and he a work mule, even though her head barely reached his and her diminutive volume equaled, at most, a third of the black beast's. By our second day we were considered harmless enough for an old man, sitting under a statue of *Nossa Senhora* by the Red River, to call us over and say how glad he was to see my gentle companion playing with the town's children.

Even the restaurants had little quibble with Atlas's lying down by my feet under the table, adding to a shared sense of discovery as I ate an *empadão goiano*, a kind of Shepherd's pie stuffed with chicken, pork, sausage, white farm cheese, olives, and a local version of heart of palm, called *guariroba*, that is – the Goianian motif – more bitter than the norm.

It was back at Flor do Ipê that I noticed a small ceramic statue in the garden, the figure hooded, with a pointy top and two eye holes, and holding a torch: a dead ringer for the Klu Klux Klan. When asked, the waiter explained that the figure comes from the post-Easter *cavalhada* festival (of the Divine Holy Spirit), when everybody gets dressed up as latter-day Crusaders for three days to re-enact the expulsion of Muslims from the Iberian Peninsula. A local shop girl, when I noticed a proliferation of tiny clay Klansmen in her store, elaborated that his name is Faricoco – who was introduced by the Third Order of Carmo in Ouro Preto back in 1796 and represents the Roman soldiers who pursued Christ until his persecution. A flexible fellow, this Faricoco, for he also evolved into a Death figure who announces the Easter processions while fending off the playful assaults of street urchins.[18]

All of which made me wonder if a visit to the treacherous backlands of Brazil, despite all the dire warnings, would be made worthwhile by such discoveries, cultural, culinary, or otherwise. The interior is thicker with tradition and history than you would think, depending on how – like the cerrado or the pequi – you scratch it.

~ 6 ~

JUST WHEN THINGS were beginning to look up, our first encounter with the infamous Belém-Brasília offered a brief but terrible look into the future.

Road conditions are a big topic in Goiás, understandably so. It was July, peak family travel time, and everything I read in the papers or saw on local television emphasized the danger of federal highways versus state roads only slightly less so. Closer accountability helps, as Goiás has contracted out road maintenance to a dedicated company called Agetop, which, even if its name doesn't inspire confidence in the blacktop's freshness, appeared to take its job seriously. Not only were the backroads in less-than-disastrous shape, they were also plastered with small didactic signs to heighten awareness of the cerrado's importance, including:

> The cerrado is the source of life / Avoid fires
> Don't throw trash on highway / Nature thanks you
> Live well with Nature
> To preserve nature is to respect life
> To kill wild animals is a crime

One benefit of poor and unpredictable roads is fewer road-kills – so I can report with relief that I had yet to collide with one wild critter or, inadvertently, commit a crime.

Always respectful of local wisdom, I mapped a route to our next destination, Pirenópolis, with the minimal possible distance on federal roads, only forty-seven kilometers. But what a forty-seven kilometers it was near the outset of BR-153, the dreaded Belém-Brasília, all of it marked in "precarious condition." The potholes were so large, they were craters, the craters so gargantuan and treacherous and unexpected (I counted a dozen before losing count) that anyone in his or her right mind had to slow to a crawl. But there's the catch: not everyone in Brazil is in their right mind. Indeed, in a nation that idolizes Formula One champions such as Aryton Senna, whose violent death, instead of dissuading, spawned thousands of wannabes; in a nation that often seems the crazy step-nephew of mad-cap Italy, where blind passing on mountain curves is child's play; in such a place "right-minded" presumes a rationality that is, well, rationed. So it should hardly surprise that every other motorist appeared the caricature of the white-knuckled, crazy-eyed, grimace-faced mental case about to cash in on an insurance policy to the hereafter. Not to mention the numerous, recently derailed drivers who had descended from their vehicles, on the dirt sides of the free-for-all-way, in order to change tires – mindful that a second flat in a row leaves you stranded.

Yet what really startled me was something else. I had thought that the long-haul truck drivers would be the most deranged, hurling themselves into the breach of battle with only their own earthly cargo and heavenly soul at risk, batting back the road's worst with three to four axles and numerous sets of shock-troop tires. But, no, the truck drivers turned out to be Sunday school sissies in comparison to the certifiably lunatic bus drivers, who not only threw themselves into the fray with reckless abandon but dragged along dozens of wan-faced passengers into communal near-death experiences. The first time a crazed bus came barreling down on Atlas and me, all too quickly filling the rear-view mirror, I felt a lurch of relief that Atlas had been upgraded to the back seat, leaving only our supplies to be crushed in the event of a rear collision. I resisted the panicked urge to speed up over the moonscape (though I did briefly feel weightless), and was amazed when the bus sped by us on the right side, half on partial asphalt, half in dirt. When he did the same to the car in front of us, there were more obstacles and less dirt, so he drove the hapless car into the on-coming lane just as a truck came into full-frontal view. This was only the first of numerous *pas de deux* ballet set pieces interrupted by incoming projectiles, including one onrushing bus gone berserk which drove the cowering car in front of us completely off the road. We, in turn, wacked hard a number of asphalt precipices, but Fofão – the name of my Fiat station wagon which, appropriately, is a term of endearment, something like "Big Cutie" – carried on.

When the forty-seven kilometers were over I seemed to be in one piece, if mildly trembling, and calculated that during the hour and a quarter ordeal we had averaged only thirty-five kilometers per hour, well below the Four Wheels' "precarious" pacing. It didn't take a calculator to figure out that if this pace kept up along the vast stretches of Red Rage Road at the other, Amazonian, end of the Belém-Brasília, it could take twelve hours of daylight to go only four hundred kilometers – and we still wouldn't reach the next real town.

After such a pilgrimage through BR-153 purgatory, the ascent back to the relative sanity of state roads came as a godsend. On the final stretch to Pirenópolis, we passed several "Live Bait" signs and small ponds offering "Catch & Pay" to lazy anglers. Cattle was king, as confirmed by the numerous whitish or brownish blurs dotting distant hillsides, by the "animal auction barns," and by the number of businesses, including gas stations, with the popular Zebu breed in their names. ("Zebu Gas," however, seems an unfortunate moniker these methane-sensitive days.) The narrow road curved neatly between white-washed curbs, while the Goianian veredas down in valley folds, to my eyes, had more palm trees rustling through the cerrado. A large nosed toucan flapped with effort across the country road, whose only casualties were flattened husks of sugar cane fallen from flat-bed trucks.

My spirits back up, I tuned to a local radio station in time to hear a report on the subject of kissing. Radio stations that don't play adolescent pop drivel all day long, much of it American, are a rarity in the backlands, so when you stumble on an exception you pay attention. A recent scientific study had revealed that kissing doubles the heartbeat from an unperturbed seventy per minute to over a hundred and fifty flutterings. It logically follows that the average ten second French kiss consumes an extra twelve calories, after which it was only natural to provide several "kiss recipes" – or their calorie-consuming equivalents – such as the heartening news that a chocolate treat called *brigadeiro* is atoned for with 4.5 kisses, one pleasure leading to another: the story of Brazil.

I can't avoid hypothesizing that the country's notorious sensuality, with more couples per capita wet-kissing than on the streets of Paris, is one of the secrets of her renowned pacifism over the years, a feminization of the macho impulses so prevalent in Spanish America. (Yet given so many on- and off-road warriors, was this mooted pacifism really the case?) Also on the radio were teaser storylines for the nightly soap operas – whose huge audiences not only extend to many males, but to over a hundred countries – with names such as "The Color of Sin" (about a feisty mulatta from the northern state of Maranhão), "Madame Destiny" (which mainlines Brazil's obsession with mysticism), and *Cabocla*, literally "copper-colored," a popular term for mestizo. Among the several plot developments promised that very night – and giving them away detracts not one iota from the suspense – was "Paula traps Tom to keep him from leaving," and "Barbara, hysterical, is certain Paco has returned from hell in order to drag her there."

Other than that day's gaping window into the nation's shocking lack of road-esteem, I was finding Goiás to be a striving, earnest, and civilizing sort of place. Besides the wildly proliferating Hug Nature decrees, I saw one sign advising, "Motorists: Respect our athletes in training," near the modern capital of Goiânia, the first admonition to share the road with bicyclists or joggers I had seen anywhere in Brazil. If only similar signs on the Belém-Brasília admonished the bus-behemoths to avoid road-killing the slower orders – assuming bus drivers bother to lift their eyes from the next prey long enough to read them.

Due, maybe, to the fatalistic roads or to the shimmering quality of light in the high, semi-dry savanna of central Brazil, we were quickly entering a mystic nation within a nation. The first premonitions were in Pirenópolis, another historic gold-boom town like Goiás Velho, only more spiritual. Brasília, the country's highest income per capita city with a pronounced mystical edge of its own, is only a two hour drive away, which may explain Pirenópolis's outbreak of hippies selling Middle Earth dwarves, elf figurines, and marijuana paraphernalia from every corner, presumably to the enchanted, have-it-all children of Brasília's well-off. These are probably the same youth who, as Dona Sonia would say, are tired of being "slaves of the commercial creed" – and incidentally have enough spare cash to make the *de rigueur*, anti-consumerism statement. New Agers can be the most welcoming of people, such as the long-haired local who greeted Atlas and me with a booming hello and gave Atlas some rough hugs and playful pats while explaining that he once had a Labrador just like him – before he was stolen. But as I grew up in freaky Cambridge, Mass., during the Sixties, the commercialism of the well-worn counterculture gives me a frayed sense of déjà-vu, especially here where it appears more borrowed than Brazilian. One wonders if Brazil's last round of military dictatorships, for two decades starting in the mid-Sixties, inhibited the ability to let it all hang out, which now manifests itself in a more crystallized form, postponed but intensified, as if recycling wasted time.

Brazil is certainly a society in ever-transition, from a crony-capitalism fueled by patronage, whose hierarchical and self-aggrandizing tendencies survived almost intact from colony to Empire, from Old Republic to dictatorship, and are only now slowly being undermined by the nation's first tentative years of participatory democracy. This evolution, as halting and drawn-out as it is, is echoed in the much delayed creation story of Brasília, which, fast approaching its fiftieth anniversary, had resided in the nation's collective fantasies for over two centuries before realization.

The metropolis itself, which Atlas and I tried to tour in one day, is a massive concrete elephant of a planned city built on a deserted high plain, and that, against all odds, sprang from the heads of Oscar

Niemeyer and Lúcio Costa, and the heart of President Jucelino Kubitschek, as if fully formed and immutable. Carved from the body of Goiás and inaugurated in 1960, it is one of the most audacious feats of societal planning in history, calibrated to tip the country's critical mass away from the coasts – where, as Friar Vicente's famous saying from 1627 has it, the Brazilians prefer "to cling like crabs"[19] – and into the forbidding interior. No passable roads existed in the region at the time, so massive bulldozers had to be air-lifted in to clear the future metropolitan area of trees. (Few have returned.) It was also founded on the theory that where politicians and money go, people will follow, which of course is exactly what happened – though in a much more haphazard manner than the planners planned. The thousands upon thousands of laborers who fled a harsh Northeastern drought in the 1950's and then built Brasília out of the thin air of the high central plains, instead of disappearing back into the savannas and drought-parched wastelands from where they came, stayed on. But as there was no place for them in the upper middle class utopia that looked so enticing on paper, they transformed their construction quarters into squatters' camps that eventually overfilled into shanty town *favelas* and then "satellite cities." Brasília is another Cultural Patrimony of Humanity site, a Le Corbusier-inspired dream gone awry that enshrines its endearing and expensive optimism, a kind of over-enthusiasm that surfs the continuous boom and bust cycles brought in from the coast. But then I am inclined to think that centrally planned cities are authoritarian in nature, against the human – and especially the Brazilian – grain.

Having said that, I confess that Brazilians are wizards with concrete, which they brilliantly make swoop and dance in gravity-defying ways that trump expectation. Walking among the massive governmental structures of the Monumental Axis, you can't resist being awed by the sheer enormity and ambition of so many sleek concrete mammoths. One feels inconsequential and puny – and then realizes that might be the point. Other than Atlas and I, nobody was out walking under the blaring sun, not even worker ants busy around the bureaucratic nests of various ministries, much less on the dry and dusty promenades that lack any shade trees whatsoever and are cut off from each other by multi-lane causeways carrying their heavy, rushing burden of cars. Pedestrians – dare I say people? – are not really welcome at the monumental heart of Brasília. (As confirmed by a contemporary journalist not so long ago, "With an estimated population of 1.8 million, Brasília has no sidewalks or street names.")[20]

Surrounded by so much solid munificence I had a puckish thought: why not spread only a fraction of Brasília's orgy of concrete over the federal roadway system and be done with it? But then gestures as grand as Brasília are never meant to be practical, and we need to gaze at stars even when stuck in potholes.

The ossified extravagance of the new capital was, naturally, inflation-financed through a gusher of printed money, and followed in the wake of Kubitschek's wildly popular breaking with the punch-bowl-stealers of the International Monetary Fund. Kubitschek's incitement to the nation to "advance fifty years in five" had an unmistakable command and control ring to it, yet caught the roller coaster spirit of the times, a die-hard optimism inflamed by successive Brazilian wins of soccer's World Cup. In the years to follow the nation-wide festivities only intensified, while inflation and an economic crisis accelerated. (As one wag quipped: "Fifty years of inflation in five!")[21] Government officials were enticed with doubled salaries to move from Rio to Brasília, which one contemporary journalist likens to "a theme park given over to politics and wheeler-dealing."[22] There the next two governments – like Brasília, built on sands of hope – floundered on the global seismic shifts between the free and un-free, until the approaching civilian showdown was cut short by a military coup for the fifth time in Brazilian history.[23] But this time it was for real, the military dictatorship lasting for over twenty sullen, sinful years.

The gaily pink pousada where we stayed in Pirenópolis, named the Matutina Meiapontense after the region's first newspaper, turned out to be less welcoming than at first blush. Graciously unperturbed by

Atlas, the young receptionist warned that the only room available was a small one, which it was, no larger than a medium-sized walk-in closet. When I noticed from a sign over the girl's shoulder that check-out was at a leisurely three p.m. and asked if anyone might be leaving that day, a momentarily animated Andrea admitted one couple planned to check out that afternoon. She suggested we come back after lunch, or around four o'clock, to find out.

By our return, though, Andrea had changed her tune, saying that the couple had decided to stay on. "And someone else wanted to rent the single," she added, "but I kept it for you."

I expressed our gratitude, as I had taken the opportunity to confirm that no other place in town was willing to accept a total of six legs: four furry, two less so. The room, snugly fitting a single bed, included a damp bathroom and only one cramped window over the bed, made of the opaque brushed glass found in lavatories. Between this and the bare ceiling bulb the room was shrouded in a permanent twilight, which may explain why one of the panes had a gaping hole, big enough to let in an arm and a hand that, with little effort, could unlatch the door from the inside. When I asked Andrea for a table lamp, she replied they had none. When I asked Andrea if they could fix the window, she was dubious. And when I asked Andrea if the hole could at least be covered with cardboard, she said she would speak to the handyman, but her tone did not inspire confidence. As things could only improve after such blasts of negativism and inertia, we took it.

The concept of Brasília as a shining city on the hills of the *planalto*, or "high plain," had been kicking around Brazil, like a very old soccer ball, for ages. Conception is dated somewhere between 1789 and 1823, but what really got things going, at the end of the 19th century, was when a Salesian priest named John Bosco (respectfully called Dom João Bosco in Brazil), while living in Turin, Italy, dreamed of a new civilization in central Brazil. He predicted it would emerge between the 15th and 20th parallels (which, indeed, now encompasses the Federal District...), with a new capital built between the 15th and 16th parallels (bingo: Brasília!), on the edge of an artificial lake (double bingo!) – not bad as prophesies go. His fabled dream was so widely publicized that the 1891 Constitution of the Old Republic set aside 5,500 square miles on the Central Plateau for the creation of a new capital.[24] Not long after, in 1913, former President Teddy Roosevelt would visit the edge of the planalto and comment that "any sound northern race could live here; and in such a land, with such a climate, there would be much joy of living."[25] (From the sound of it, T.R. either caught a sudden cold snap or the local bug of fawning flattery.)

Yet the roots of such visionary tropicalism were even deeper than that, synthesizing the major veins of New World fantasies as early as 1813, when a local journalist Hipódito da Costa placed the new capital in the "country of the central interior and at the headwaters of great rivers," where there would be constructed

> a new city; which would begin to open roads to every seaport, remove natural obstacles from the navigable rivers, and thus lay the foundations of the most extensive, well-linked and protected Empire that is possible on the Earth's surface.... This central point is found at the headwaters of the famous São Francisco River. In its vicinity are the fountainheads of copious rivers, that flow to the North, to the South, to the Northeast and to the Southeast, vast prairie land for the raising of cattle, rock in abundance for any sort of building, lumber for every necessity, and the richest mines of the quality metals; in one word, a situation which can be compared to the description of Heaven on Earth.[26]

In such a serendipitous manner, the rich mines at the headwaters, Brasília itself, and even the Belém-Brasília highway are all fundamental aspects of earthly paradise – the dreams of far-sighted journalists, priests, and politicians made tantalizingly near.

The accoutrements of our broom closet room in the pink pousada were not so inspiring. The only furnishings, besides the bed, were a luggage rack and a fan, which came in handy as even a quick shower dampened the entire space, misting the polished concrete floor. The bathroom itself was so diminutive that the toilet sat perilously close to one wall, so as to not receive the direct spray of the shower head which soaked everything regardless. While the pink-on-white color scheme had been bravely continued indoors, even the warning splash of electric pink over the bathroom's low lintel couldn't deter me from rattling my cranium several times, as unwelcome as a wayward wheel in an upside-down pothole.

I was already in a dubious mood when the room's only outlet sent a surge of electricity through my laptop's power line, causing the female end to give me a good shock and jolting me with what might have occurred had the computer, instead of I, gotten plugged. This and all the injustices of life drove me into a full, righteous retreat to the inn's living area, where I chose what looked to be the safest outlet on the premises, the one powering the public T.V., in order to test my technology – which evidently had not overly fried. Sensing, or better yet, almost tasting revenge, I realized with a thrill that I had a cat bird's view of the reception area from my ragged sofa perch. This, understandably, threw Andrea into sporadic fits of cautiousness, particularly when a large family from Brasília arrived asking for accommodations and, instead of saying they were full, she inquired, "For how many?"

That was pretty crafty, I had to admit, for then she could safely reply, "No, we don't have room." I was beginning to wonder if Andrea could be lit by more wattage than on first, dim impression, but then her stratagem failed when a room-needy couple arrived, leading her to speak in whispers, which comically, as if in church, caused the couple to lower their voices as well. Thanks to some kind of secular intervention a room was found.

Perhaps it was the broken window by my pillow which made me sleep poorly that night, or the free-range mosquitoes, or the cars entering and leaving the courtyard parking lot at all hours due to the Rave festival (one of those waves of the future that crashes all night long) just outside of town. Such as it is, traveling the hinterlands of Brazil with your dog. In the morning I took groggy pleasure in borrowing the cheap soap from the employees' washroom next door, and using it as my own. So there!

The hold of Dom Bosco's dream over the country's collective imagination turned out to be durable. It may explain why innumerable cults have bubbled to the surface around Brasília and Pirenópolis, like so many hot springs. (Brasília, specifically, has the highest concentration of sects in the nation.)[27] There is Tia Neiva's Valley of the Dawn, whose central town is dominated by an enormous Star of David forming a lake pierced by an arrow. Then there is the Temple of Goodwill, which incorporates seven pyramids with one large cone topped by one teeteringly large raw crystal. Beyond Electric City, which was founded by an ex-airline pilot named Yokanam with the aim of unifying all (of this world's) religions, there's a well worn spot, near kilometer sixty-nine of BR-251, famous for extraterrestrial landings.[28] The Federal District used to publish a brochure called "Mystic Brasília" (from the Tourism Department and with an introduction by the then-governor), treating with equal respect all sorts of groups pushing ufology, parapsychology, alternative medicine, and even the theory (seconded, no doubt, by the Temple of Goodwill) that, due to the high incidence of pyramid shapes in the new capital, Brasília is actually an Egyptian city destined to become the capital of the world in the third millennium – that is, starting about now.[29]

Uncowed by the competition, mystic Pirenópolis may have been trying to tell me something when I discovered the town's center is dominated not by a watery Star of David, but by a large burned-out church that had been demolished by an avenging fire only two years before. The charred carcass was wrapped in shrouds behind the colorful placards of a large advertising campaign for the renovation's sponsors, promoting Petrobras, the national petroleum company whose main sideline appears to be cultural investments to prevent being truly privatized; BNDES, the national public developmental bank; Caixa, a semi-public bank; and CELG, the state electricity company and lone regional representative.

If your impression is that state companies and state employees have their hands in just about everything, you're not far off, as it took a local visit to Iphan, the Federal Landmarks Commission, to trace the blaze's origins.

When I walked in with Atlas, the gray-wisped blond behind the main desk gave us a big hello. "How charming his handkerchief looks!" she gushed, referring to Atlas's one sartorial touch, a slate blue bandana tied around the neck.

I thanked Catarina and, in turn, complimented her on the spruced up and colonial feel to town.

"You've got to do *something* while in this office!" she replied brightly.

The fire, it turns out, occurred not long after an exhaustive renovation, supervised by Iphan, that had cost untold millions – which means, incredibly, that the town had enjoyed a pristine refurbished church for just a few penitent years. While the exact cause of the blaze remains a conundrum, it reportedly began in the sacristy where the Father not only was in the habit of keeping his robes, but running a small candle factory as well, and where – to deepen the enigma or the ineptitude or both – several large gas canisters were stored.

When I commented to Catarina how fortunate the Father and Church have been to find sponsors for the church's re-building, she corrected me.

No, it was Iphan that had organized the sponsors and once again raised the money, which had subsequently been turned over to the same Father, "like doing all the work and then handing the keys over to others," she sniffed.

It was that old Edenic creation story all over again – but here with bureaucrats in the starring roles as Movers and Makers, setting us up for the next fall.

~ 7 ~

I HAVE A THEORY that many of Brazil's best kept secrets – such as Worm Farm Inn – are at the end of a long dirt road. This is due to a related observation that most Brazilians, and especially the well-off, are loath to subject their fancy and overpriced cars to many earth-splaying baths. So it was a good omen that São Jorge, in northern Goiás, is over thirty kilometers of washboard dirt roads from Alto Paraíso, tucked under the southern boundary of the Chapada dos Veadeiros National Park.

Alas, during a winter break weekend in July this didn't dissuade enough nature-nurturers, as it took nearly ten stops over two hours for Atlas and me to find a place that would take us in. Visiting the park was much easier as a diligent guide, originally from Minas, stopped by our owner-constructed Pousada São Jorge during breakfast to ask if anyone wanted to visit Black River Falls that day. She appeared both competent and friendly, so I left Atlas to guard belongings in our small room, where the windows and door didn't latch securely, and made out for town at the arranged hour.

Like all local guides Mari charges ten reals per person, three for the park entrance fee, seven for her, no matter how many takers on a given day, so it behooves her to fill up to the maximum of ten. In the end we topped up with a couple of stragglers down at the park entrance, but only after leaving town an hour late due to a group of three young *Carioca* (from Rio) school teachers who finished up breakfast, made a few phone calls, and forgot hats or suntan lotion with nary a thought that they could be delaying the rest of us. Brazilians are good-natured about these sorts of things and who, after all, would expect Cariocas to be on time? We still had most of the day ahead of us.

At the park entrance, between Mari's explanations and a few fading wall exhibits, we learned that the then-named National Park of Tocantins was founded in 1961 with an optimistic six hundred thousand hectares (by none other than President Kubitschek, on a roll after Brasília), which soon fell to a tenth of that size due to encroachments by farmers and ranchers.[30] Such is the usual path in Brazil, where the rule of law – and plenty of attractive, finely-tuned laws there are – makes way for the reality on the ground. (Indeed, Brazil extends nearly two thousand miles beyond the old Tordesillas line, almost to the Andes, for the same reason.) And yet that this could happen in the Brazilian national park with the best control and infrastructure of any I have visited is perplexing.

It may have been due to our proximity to Brasília, only two hundred kilometers south, but just as we felt primed for a romp through nature we came upon the only legal disclaimer I have seen at any of the country's parks:

> IBAMA [the then-name for the National Park Service] does not take responsibility for accidents resulting from digressions in visitors' conduct or from the non-observation of this unit's security norms.

What these security norms were, other than the park's opening and closing hours or advisories against jumping off cliffs, we couldn't figure out while entering Veadeiros' southwestern tip on a path so narrow we had to walk single-file. Within minutes, Mari slipped off her sneakers to go barefoot and had us stopping at every other plant to explain its medicinal benefits. It was slow going, the scrubby growth of a low, secondary forest not quite up to expectation. (Most Brazilian parks were created well after the forest's first harvesting.) As for evidence of wildlife we saw none, other that the stool of a maned wolf, which, according to Mari, after defecating enters into paroxysms of pleasure by rolling on the ground. This she claimed while pointing out a sample scat that was, curiously enough, balanced atop a severed stump as though delicately rear-deposited out of the way of passing tourists. If only the neighboring farmers and ranchers had been so considerate.

Well before any tourists found their way up the Black River, the Goyaz Indians had been crisscrossing the high cerrado for some time when the Bandeirantes and gold prospectors drove them away in the 17th century. Not finding much of value, the raiding parties moved on and the region suffered various attempts at settlement, including one in 1780 when Egyptian immigrants introduced wheat cultivation[31] – neither of which took well. Only prior to WWI did the *garimpeiros*, the "river panners," arrive en masse due to the high concentrations of quartz and rock crystals, a boom that went bust when synthetic substitutes were developed during WWII. After the park's official boundaries were steadily reduced in the 1960's, the remaining stump was renamed Chapada dos Veadeiros, in honor of the deer hunters who roamed freely throughout.[32] Several of the older guides whose paths we crossed were former deer hunters, or *veadeiros*, themselves: an example of the Brazilian talent for co-opting either the dispossessed or former adversaries in the fullness of time.

After the miners and the hunters came the hippies in search of mega-crystals, as the park contains the largest of the region's remaining quartz reserves. The main town of High Paradise – established before any pun could have been intended – was so named even before houses in the form of pyramids, and others with cupolas on top, became common (inspired by those Egyptian immigrants or while building the New Cairo?). Not far from the Vertentes, the country's watershed, the Veadeiros is "Brazil's water-box," which Mari attributes to deep, subterranean quartz walls that block the passage of water, forming a high, underground reservoir. In a sense we were standing on or near a triple continental divide, from where water leeches and eventually flows north to the mouth of the Amazon (via the Tocantins River), south all the way to Buenos Aires along the Paraná and then Prata Rivers, and eastwards to the São Francisco. For this to be the long-lost Eden, all that is missing is the fourth allegorical, ever-running river – heading west and somehow crashing through the Andes.

The abundance of light-absorbing crystals and life-giving water can only add up to one thing, Mari assured us: that we were standing on the post-Armageddon survivors' belt of the NEW WORLD. In a strangely joyous voice she pointed out that Machu Picchu in Peru and three *chapadas*, or "tablelands," in Brazil (Veadeiros, Diamantina in Bahia, and Guimarães in Mato Grosso) are all found near the 14th parallel. Logically, this is where the new civilization will be born, in a minor tweaking of Dom Bosco's slightly more southern vision. There is something about semi-arid and rocky landscapes – preferably but not necessarily strewn with light-bending crystals – that encourages the imagination to refract with revelations of the apocalypse. Here it has something to do with the lowlands flooding, leading to much pain, suffering, and death, after which the survivors will shed materialistic impulses as easily as leaves do the rain, leading to a re-birth of all that is good and noble in the human race – a *deus ex utopia*, more or less. Emphasizing that the process is just beginning, and will accelerate eight years hence, Mari assured us that the coming years would be crucial, a turning point when the new consciousness will begin to flower – from the rocky aridity of our present condition. All of which made us feel, inclusively and warmly, in the proud ranks of Mari's advance team.

Mari was born on a farm between the mineral water stations of São Laurenço and Caxambu in southern Minas, and grew up to be a nurse. Conventional medicine proved too hidebound for her, so she left to become an alternative therapist, eventually moving, or drawn, to Chapada dos Guimarães where she began work as a park guide while absorbing the 14th parallel's vision of a new age. She admitted that money – still a necessity in these post-Pleistocene and pre-Utopian times – was difficult to come by in northern Pantanal, which led her to move to Alto Paraíso four years before, and from there to São Jorge a year back. As she is a crack guide and works tirelessly every day of the week, her maximum of seventy reals a day theoretically totals a thousand dollars a month, a sizable salary for rural Brazil.

At each and every waterfall visited over two days, Mari would adopt a lotus position facing the falls and meditate for a while, for as long as her guidely duties allowed. She had an endearing habit, when leaving such nature nooks, of throwing her stringy arms into the air and yelling her thanks up to Mother Nature with a good-natured "*Obrigada, Mamãe!*" And when the energy was right she would unite her ten-strong flock in an arm-clasping circle, instructing us to breath deeply in unison three times in a row, releasing the air slowly each time with a long, collective Ommmmmm. Owing no doubt to the air's purity, by the third chant I began to feel the presence of the 14th parallel via a bright red spot floating between my eyebrows, the yogi's third eye made manifest.

Mari is a vegetarian of a certain cut and her body is both thin and tough from daily hiking. There is a loopy swerve to her frame, to her knees, and to how her carriage sits on her torso, that gives the indelible impression of a lean, yet approachable, extra–terrestrial – an alien, like me. She greatly preferred going barefoot, whisking off her white sneakers when the terrain allowed it, her knobby, flattened feet adding to the impression of other-worldliness. Her light brunette hair was unruly, rarely restrained with a head band, and didn't appear to be subjected to frequent washing. Mari mentioned that the Rio Preto's clean, hard water is good for hair, and didn't seem to want to diminish the effect – a throwback to those first river-washed Indians encountered by the Portuguese.

As we climbed into the southernmost tip, where the lackadaisical trails only penetrate one twentieth of the park's length, the cramped scenery finally opened up to what Mari called *campo limpo*, or the naturally "clean fields" of the highland cerrado untouched by man. We tend to look at every open space, these doom-laden days, and to mistake it for a clearing, a by-product of our natural malfeasance – which is often, but not always, the case. The welcome openness made it easier to see a variety of hawks and jays, the latter probably the curl- and plush-crested, as well as several distinctive tree species, including the interestingly named *canela-de-ema*, or "emu's shin," the *buriti* palm whose dreadlock-like hanging fruits are used to make wine, cooking oil, and various sweets, and the *capitão-do-campo*, a sturdy tree which prefers to stand sentry on well-drained hilltops, thriving in the cerrado's poor soil.

As I and one of the teachers from Rio were the only males in a group that included four Cariocas, I commented, "It looks as though we are dominated by Cariocas – but mostly by women."

"You men are here to help rescue us women in case of trouble," offered Nilsa, a fetching blond judge, also from Rio.

"But I think it's more likely that you women will rescue us..."

"That's right," Samara, from southern Brazil, chimed in. "Men talk a brave line, but it is usually the women who do all the hard work!"

For Nilsa, thirty-three and green-eyed, hard work meant stretching out in as many languorous poses as possible and then asking for someone's help to take her picture. Her family had driven three straight days from the coast, spending the first night in Caldas Novas and reaching Veadeiros by the third. With the heat rising she stripped down to a bikini top, exposing the healthy bulge of her half-covered breasts which rose and fell with the rolling terrain. I have never seen someone pose so seductively for tourist snap-shots, a kind of a south-of-the-Equator Marilyn, but if you're going to compete with a national park for your future beau's attention, you might as well do so with gusto.

Cariocas are certainly a lusty-for-life lot, as shown by skinny Marina, a German teacher, who yelped loudly with pleasure while taking a cold shower under one of the Corredeiras falls. She and her fellow instructors had boarded an overnight bus in Rio and, eighteen hours later, de-camped in Brasília – which is not how the politicos did it back in 1960 or since. The next day, at the unimaginatively named Canyon I, I encouraged Marina to jump off the highest possible rock ledge down into the half-filled sluice of a canyon, which she did with another good holler. They say it is seven meters up but I wouldn't place it at more than five, your heightened emotions elongating every one. It felt like a leap of faith, throwing yourself over the edge, for while the dark fluidity of the canyon-clapped water promised a good, perhaps sufficient, depth, it was impossible to verify visually, obscured by its own darkness. I could get used to cliff-jumping with someone like Marina, I thought.

The most eccentric Carioca was named Gil, who teaches history to teens at a private school and had difficulty keeping quiet, even though we reminded him now and then that we were also interested in listening to nature. Emboldened in the evening by beer, he would transform instantaneously into the Singing Professor, due to his propensity to break into song at any pretext. More often than not, it was an old advertising jingle even though he disparaged the capitalist system and bemoaned the fact that his school was driven – debased, really – by the profit motive.

On the second day our merry band's composition changed marginally, when joined by a couple from São Paulo and a Texan from Lubbock, who was doing an internship at the Environmental Ministry in Brasília as a pro-bono break from Law School. John was only the second foreigner (and second American) I would meet between Minas and Belém, the first having been an American woman, married to a *Brasiliense* (from Brasília), introducing her mother-in-law to Pirenópolis. Mother-in-laws are the butts of endless Brazilian jokes, as their notoriety for interfering only underlines the Mary-Mother-of-God devotion most Brazilians, particularly the males, have for their mamães. Going with the groove, Mari showed us a bulbous ground cactus whose terrestrial flatness in no way inhibits the growth of threatening spines, and dead-panned that it is nicknamed the "mother-in-law seat." In such a way even the most implacable and serious problems in Brazil – whether in-law or out – can be reduced to a smile.

It came as no surprise after an unhurried start to both hiking days, when we only managed to roll into the park two full hours after opening, that there was a mad rush to leave before the afternoon closing. Already sly to Mari's ways, I surmised that if the head of our long single-file line reached the exit gate by five o'clock sharp, then it wouldn't matter how much later the relaxed tail slouched by – as the trail is narrow, the rush hour worm long. According to my watch the head did just that, clocking in at one minute before five p.m. the first day, and several minutes earlier on the second, with the stragglers, including Gil, usually talking faster than walking. This is Brazil, after all, where punctuality outside of business centers is the exception, but we didn't want Mari to get into trouble on our account. (Closing hours is one area where Brazilians, like most, appear consistently on time.)

Although we had brought midday snacks for the all-day hikes, I was perplexed when everyone referred to the evening's buffet meal in town afterwards as "lunch," but then I have just about given up trying to understand the logic behind native lingo and culture. (How can I understand theirs when I have a hard time fathoming my own?) Beforehand, both nights, I returned to the pousada to feed and let Atlas out for a pee, and was proud to see that he had behaved impeccably both long indoor days. I have an uncle who claims pets from separated homes are more obedient than most, but I think such a causal relation in Atlas's case is suspect: he just started out eager to please, from his early days in the window display of a Tico shopping mall.

I brought him along both evenings to socialize with my hiking friends, which he did gladly, checking out the myriad bare legs under the long, caterpillar-like table. On the second evening, the cold beer going to my head, I encouraged the gang to break into song, which, as everyone knows, Brazilians (and not only Cariocas) do at the slightest provocation, especially with liquor loosening the vocal chords. Gil had likely mentioned the merits of a certain ditty, which I asked them to sing for the uneducated foreigner that I am, and as if in collective ecstasy they willingly obliged with a touching unison, for every last one knew the lyrics by heart. (I suspect the average Brazilian knows *all* the lyrics to well over one hundred popular classics, without blinking.) But how to bring Atlas into the festivities? Like the well-bred wolf descendent that he is, Atlas has always enjoyed a good howl, which I encourage him to do to get in touch with his roots. This happens frequently enough – such is our enthusiasm for the ritual – that all I have to do is stretch my neck upwards and pucker my lips outwards, without making a sound myself, in order for Atlas to let rip some impressive howls, which he now did several times in a row, stopping the Warbling Professor and his wandering minstrels in their musical tracks. Fortunately no one was wise to the ploy, and maybe it was Marina who wondered if Atlas was a bit skittish from being cooped up all day – a wonderfully guileless concern for the lower orders already corrupted by human contact. I tried mightily to suppress a laugh, and was only partly successful, but such are the corporeal risks of sing-along-interruptus that Atlas and I never attempted the trick again.

A group of us rendezvoused later in the town's center where, farsightedly, there are no street lamps, allowing the night sky to twinkle overhead like a wide powdering of phosphorescent sugar. When we found a quiet bar with an outdoor table, Gil proceeded to order rounds of *pinga* (or cachaça) with the subject, as it had often those several days, returning to music, the most inoffensive topic in Brazil after the weather. That evening's quandary touched on the merits and demerits of Tropicalism, as expounded by the likes of the famed singer and composer Caetano Veloso. Fortified by pinga shots and a captive audience, the Singing Professor proceeded to sing a good part of his ad jingle repertoire, which being from the Seventies and Eighties left Texan John, Atlas, and me in the dark. From there the conversation drifted towards cultural imperialism of the American sort – that awning cataract found at the end of most every booze-sluiced and enlightened discourse.

"Hollywood just dominates culturally," Gil complained, probing the injustice with his tongue. "In any small to medium sized town you just won't find Brazilian films, only American blockbusters."

While this mostly jibes with my experience in the interior of Minas Gerais, I wondered if it didn't have something to do with local taste: once your average movie-goer gets used to Hollywood fare and quality, local productions – often more clunky, ramshackle, or, worse, pretentious – have a hard time competing.

"But that's just it," Gil continued, rising to the cause. "Not only do audiences get used to Hollywood films, but there's the manipulative arrangement whereby local theaters have to show a whole string of mediocre American films to screen a blockbuster."

"You're right about the practice," I replied, as block booking is quite common, "but do you think it could last for long if it wasn't commercially viable, if people weren't getting to watch what they wanted to watch?"

"Ahh, but do you think Hollywood fare is really what people want to watch?" he countered. "And that their preferences aren't being manipulated?"

And so on. As Brazil is a country of immigrants as well, I tried to make the argument more approachable by personalizing the Hollywood bugbear. "You know, the history of Hollywood is pretty interesting. How Jewish migrants started with a new technology and pioneered new methods to amuse people. It seems Jewish migrants were better than anyone else at divining current moods, how people wanted to be entertained and distracted, as that same sensitivity – to what was going on – was really a survival instinct for them. How all of that has evolved over the years, it is true, is an open question. They say that, by Hollywood standards at least, there are only six or seven types of stories, which makes everything pretty formulaic. But Hollywood continues to do what it has always done best: finding new ways to entertain people."

"You're assuming there's free choice in the matter," Gil retorted. "I don't think so. I think people are manipulated into wanting to see such trash. That marketing is everywhere!"

He was beginning to sound like Dona Sonia, convinced that people can't be trusted to make their own, or the *right*, choices.

"But don't you think you're underestimating the intelligence of your countrymen? Are they really so easily misled?"

In the end many such conversations reduce to the false tautology of Poor Us due to Rich Them, with the old zero-sum blinders that someone else's gain has to be your loss. So I tried to counter the gathering gloom with one more attempt to boost confidence in the country's potential. After all, Brazilian music, dance, and beachwear alone qualify the nation as among the most creative. "You know I worked in marketing for over a decade and had to look at advertising from all over. One time a company vice-president asked me where I thought the most creative advertising in the world is found, and I didn't hesitate in replying, 'In London, New York, and São Paulo.'"

At the mention of São Paulo, I thought I saw a flicker of pride in their faces which turned out to be only that – a flicker. How can it be that so many of Brazil's talents remain hidden to, or downplayed by, its own people? It is as though the low road-esteem extends, like a highway without end, to other areas.

Mari, on the other hand, appeared free of such cultural angst, padding barefoot through Brazil's natural and resplendent everyday wealth. During a pause in one hike she told me how she had become a "sister" in the Rainbow Confederation, an organization of nature-lovers formed "only three years After Woodstock." The Brazilian affiliate had started up within three years, or by 6 A.W., and had recently been honored with the first meeting of the international Confederation on her soil, in Diamantina, a colonial diamond-mining town in northern Minas. Mari, unable to afford the prior global gatherings in Costa Rica and Australia, had loved the Diamantina camp-together, recalling with particular fondness how many women had attended in long, cotton hippie dresses, "just like old times!"

When asked how to become a member, Mari replied you simply go to the meetings. (Again – that nice inclusive Brazilian hug.)

On second thought, she mentioned most members live close to nature, as she does, "but that city people" – by which she not unkindly meant me – "are welcome too, of course."

I liked Mari a lot, and at our last seven o'clock lunch I shared a small guide to the Mineiro Cerrado with her, to help identify some of the birds and mammals common to the savannas of Goiás. I called her "my dear Mineira" and she gave me a warm and, for her, demonstrative caress on the back. She also wrote down her phone number, as I promised to return when the park opens a new trail, a truly day-long hike across the park's mid-section, so she can show the way.

It may be from all of those park entrance fees (a novelty at most national parks), but Veadeiros has recently quadrupled in size, back to nearly half of the original proportions laid down by that dreamer, President Kubitschek, eight years before Woodstock. I was encouraged to see an Ibama jeep along the bumpy dirt road back to High Paradise, scanning the park boundaries for brush fires, for it showed they might actually have the resources to patrol and protect a much larger area.

Friends, recently returned from Veadeiros, tell me there are still no definitive plans for the new trail, but I doubt if Mari, at the cusp of a new civilization, has given up hope. In the meantime, I can still see her meditating on the river-smoothed rocks, or gathering her small flock into a mantra circle, or throwing up her sinewy arms skywards in thanks for the day, the sun, and the hard, clean water.

~ 8 ~

A S WE APPROACHED Natividade, Tocantins' oldest and most enigmatic town dating back to 1734, a strange translucent whiteness hovered overhead as if a wide, diffuse light gathering above. It was late afternoon, after a nearly eight hour drive from São Jorge, so perhaps the shifting light overfilled my pupils. Blinking, I wondered if it could be a large plume of wood-burning smoke, but then, as we passed the rustic way stations of a parallel road signed the Pilgrim's Path going into town, the light dissipated – or, just as logically, we had entered it.

Although Natividade is the only historically preserved colonial backwater in the state, it is so unassuming, so far off the track that the comprehensive Four Wheels directory doesn't include it in its thousand listings. That is a pity, for – to the secular minded – it boasts one of Brazil's best examples of primitive art, or – to the more spiritual – one of the most impressive expressions of cataclysmic faith, in the humble home and garden of Dona Romana.

Tocantins is a new state with an old, by-passed heart. A separatist movement from Goiás got underway in the early 18th century, driven not only by the ungovernable largeness of a state longer, at over sixteen hundred kilometers, than California, but by racial differences, with the south dominated by mostly white southern Brazilians and the north by a rowdy mix of the country's three major bloodlines, of Indian, European, and African ancestry. As might be expected, Brazil's geographic center, in a town called Gurupí about 150 kilometers west of Natividade, is found here.

Named after its largest river, Tocantins is the nation's youngest state, only two decades old, and you can't miss the fresh, hopeful feel as you arrive. With one of the only state welcome signs of my entire trip, it declared itself as "The State of the Free, of Initiative and of Justice." The highway signs were more pedagogical than in Goiás, where enviro-trendy messages dominated. Here they were utilitarian, including such basic and touching reminders as:

> Avoid damage to signs
> Coming or going, dim headlights
> Always pass on left
> You're not the only one / respect other traffic
> When in doubt don't pass
> Don't spill oil on roadway
> Everyone deserves to live / so stay alive
> &
> Believe in signage

which nicely underpinned the rest. Not to be entirely outdone, the fewer environmental messages were models of didactic brevity:

> Hunting & killing of predators is a crime!
> The cerrado is the source of life / avoid fires
> Say no to pollution
> Don't run over wild animals
> Without nature there's no life
> Avoid fires on our cerrados
> To protect nature is to protect our life

Our own self-preservation technique was to avoid the Belém-Brasília for as far north as possible, with the added benefit of the slower the backroad, the better. Yet state highways, usually in more passable condition, are generally without services such as gas stations and hotels, which can only be found with luck in the small towns separated by a hundred plus kilometers of East African savanna, dotted with umbrella-like acacia trees. Natividade, or Nativity, was one such isolated and decrepit town on a minor state road, several hundred kilometers east of the Belém-Brasília, and likely still mourning that geographical fact. While I didn't see tumbleweeds skipping down main street, the stunned, lethargic atmosphere reminded me of American ghost towns.

Fortunately the one Brazil-moderne hotel in the region – that is, aseptically clean and without a shred of character – decided to take in Atlas and me, which was kindhearted as the only other accommodations we saw were pensions whose crumbling walls showed the tell-tale black mold marks of water infiltration, that starts at floor level and slowly creeps upwards. Hotel Serra Geral looked luxurious by comparison, including a heat-retarding atrium design whereby the outward walls, under the eaves of the veranda (originally a Portuguese invention), contained latticed ventilation windows, the rooms' only glass panes looking inwards to the shaded patch of grass. By now we were already on a parallel north of Salvador, Bahia, and had exchanged the refreshing coolness of the Brazilian winter for a summery sun and buttery heat, here year-round. I felt in my element, the heat a catalyst for discovery.

We walked around the quiet center that breeze-puffed evening, poking around the ruined and roofless slaves' church, Our Lady of Rosary of the Blacks, abandoned five decades back, and noting the Moorish-inspired trellised windows and the fake, decorative columns of some colonial facades. Grandmothers loitered on doorsteps, children skittered down sidewalks, and nothing-to-do policemen commented on Atlas's build. The sparsely decorated municipal museum lauded the town's heyday, for six years from 1804, as the seat for the colonies' Northern Government, and exhibited a few tantalizing pictures of a rock and sculpture garden belonging to a certain Dona Romana.

The town's eerie light lingered and then was gone, which left a visit to Dona Romana's, just north of town, for the following day. As there were no signs, an early morning jogger pointed the way down a narrow dirt drive – a promising beginning. Words can barely do justice to the expansively small world that opened before my eyes: of scores of two-dimensional concrete statues, ranging from a meter to three high, many with outstretched arms; of myriad stone gates and towers interspersed among short lava-rock fences, corrals, and bas-relief animals; much of it mysteriously adorned by wire configurations, effects, and grounding connections, as far as the eye can see. I circled around an outer ring lost in wonderment, intrigued by what on earth could have motivated all this, before hazarding to enter the two-turnstile arched portal where a small boy instructed me to proceed through the left-hand side. (One has to enter and exit the premises, I later learned, in a clockwise manner.) On his way out, he told me, yes, Dona Romana is in.

The house was open to the outdoors, which facilitated finding the dining area and adjoining kitchen, whose wood-burning stove was attended by several Bahian-looking women, white blouses shining over dark skin. (The rotund state of Bahia lies directly east.) I was told Dona Romana would come to table shortly, affording me more time to look around. Most rooms were bereft of furniture, except for the main room's long dining table with benches and a number of low-slung, thin mattress beds in the children's dormitory. In both the entrance hall and a room to the side, I found strategically placed wall sockets for hanging sleep hammocks, presumably for teens and adults. Other than home-made posters with all-cap admonitions that read Fear God, Confidence in God, Jesus Eternal King, King of Glory, and, more succinctly, Forgiveness and Hope, the walls were decorated with an Apostle with a long key, the black Our Lady of Aparecida (the patron saint of Brazil) surrounded by five cherubic angels in puffy clouds, and a white Avenging Archangel with drawn sword standing over a prostrate satanic figure with mulatto shading and kid-sized horns.

When Dona Romana emerged from a nearby room, she invited me to join her for a coffee, allowing us to pass through introductory pleasantries in a leisurely fashion. In her sixties, likely, Dona Romana has an ample welcome smile and kindly dark pebble eyes under coils of hair pulled back tightly and frosted with white. She appeared at ease with guests, as though a common occurrence, so when offered a tour of the garden I gladly accepted.

Following her outdoors and back into the moist, tangy air, I asked, "So what inspired you to create such a beautiful garden?" Nearby, the last wisps of morning mist curled around a stone prophet's feet.

"This here?" she replied nonchalantly, as if of no great

consequence. "When these objects of stone started, and only just a few were ready, I already found it hard work. So I did my prayers and gave myself to God. I offered that I didn't want this work with stones. But then a voice said to me that I had been born to do this foundation work. That this here was the spiritual foundation for the stability of the earth's main axis. That God had already ordered Man to do this when the world tilted. But then Man was lazy and didn't do it. So that now, when the earth rises up, if this wasn't done then all life on earth would be lost."

"Oh – really?" I asked, trying to disguise my surprise.

"She would rise and fall into pieces – ending everything. So I thought the responsibility too large by half, but then out came the stones," she motioned to the statues with a sweep of her arm, "like that! But I don't take credit for the beauty you can see here, no. That's not a problem. One knows that human hands aren't responsible for divine beauty, but are only instruments for its expression. So that is how they came out."

She ended her introduction, which had the cadences and familiarity of a oft-sung hymn, and looked for my reaction.

"What's the idea of the world's tilt you mentioned?"

"But the earth," she replied, looking puzzled for a moment, "the earth has been tilted for millions of years. You know what 'to tilt' means?"

"Yes, I think so."

"So now it is going to rise." Pause.

"And how is that?" I pursued.

"This asteroid that is approaching," she said, as if self-evident, "will make her rise up."

"Oh!"

"It's going to fall on her, you see? Now, according to Him, after it falls only a moment will pass before she rises up. But given that it's one of His little moments, nobody knows for how long – you know what I mean? But it is with this shock that she will rise."

"And where will it hit, do you know?"

"My goodness, I just don't know."

"Which part of the earth?"

"All I know is that it will be over there," she gestured beyond her cement flock. "But where exactly," she added with a chuckle, "I don't know."

"How do the stones function, then? While the rest of the earth rises, everything here will stay in place, is that it?"

"I don't know. I just don't know. This He didn't tell me."

"But it is to protect life, you mentioned."

"It's to protect the main axis, to make it firm – and to protect life, yes. Look at it as a ball," she explained with her cement-smoothed hands, "and she's full. Something hits it here and the surface of the ball rises up." It was a good, visual explanation; fit for a soccer-mad country and clear enough for kids.

"And here will it rise as well?" I pressed.

"Everything will rise. Everything will change, it will be a general catastrophe over the entire earth," she proclaimed, widening the whites of her eyes.

As it was still early, the hoisting sun cast a slatternly light on the garden's stone army, whose shadows marched slowly across the earth's still surface.

"But there's something I don't understand yet. What does this garden do, then?"

"I don't know. Don't know. It only pertains to God. Only God knows."

Puzzled, I tried a new tact. "And the inspiration for the designs? Inside I saw some nice drawings, apparently done by children. But here, outside, the designs are yours?"

"That's not, no, that's not it," she replied good-naturedly. "What's here doesn't pass through paper, which won't accept it. What arrives as stone, only the stone accepts. If it arrives as wire, only the wire accepts the work. If it comes as cement, only the cement accepts it. If it arrives for the sketch book, it only comes out in the sketch book. So everything just arrives as it is! And everything has its place."

"Dona Romana, are you still creating things?"

I had switched to using the honorific *Dona*, which occasioned a shift to kindly familiarity on her part. "No, my son. Nowadays I can't support much of anything anymore. I'm a very tired creature, my column just can't keep up. My column's in bad shape. I went to the doctor, took one medicine, then another, but it doesn't resolve anything. Not a thing." A pained look compressed her forehead's wrinkles, one over another.

"But then the garden also looks completed, isn't it?"

"No more stone pieces are arriving, it's true. After starting in January of '90, they stopped in January of '97," she replied, shifting her weight. "But then I was sent to collect cement, food, clothes, footwear, books, and water. Anything I could store, I had to store. From then on I went collecting, collecting, collecting. The house was a mess and stacked to the roof with so many things. The house was of old adobe and it was too full. So He told me to make that storage barn over there. So I started to put one up, got together the wood, put up the beams, but what else could I do? There wasn't enough money, you see? Just wasn't. So then he – the governor – came by here, saw the posts standing up, and asked me what it was for. And I told him. Then he asked to see the things I had saved up. So I showed him. And he took up the project and ordered it to be done."

"The storage barn?"

"Uh-huh. He arranged for the storage barn, he arranged for the bathroom – ours was only a latrine with a little thatched-straw fence. He sent them to make the real one out front, so that when it fills up here with too many people, there's a toilet for everyone!"

"What a generous man," I offered, curious about such an old style of building and plumbing patronage.

"He's terrific! Just terrific! Ones like him are so difficult to find. But then, when only four days were left for his workers to finish the barn – it was in January – the house suddenly collapsed!"

"You don't say, really?" I exclaimed, while we both laughed at the coincidence – or was it? After all, anything of importance in Dona

Romana's life happens in January.

"The house just tumbled down. The structure was made of an inflexible material, so when it gave a twist here in one part," she motioned with her expressive hands, "it just tore apart, from corner to corner."

"Imagine that!" I exclaimed, getting caught up in the story. "While the governor's workers were still here!"

"Then I picked up my things and moved into the barn, to the part already done. Okay. So while I gave witness, there arrives the governor's secretary to tell me that his boss already knows my house has fallen down in one piece, but that I shouldn't worry as he would give me a new house. I said 'No! He already gave so much. The house I will build up slowly, bit by bit.'"

"What year was that, Dona Romana?"

"It was in two thousand and...two. So, after all of this, his secretary said 'No, he sent me to tell the Senhora that he's going to give the Senhora a house.' So while I gave witness, the workers arrived and it was time to work again."

"What a tale! And during these seven years of working here in the garden, how did you make money to support it all?"

She looked at me with a kindly pity. "No, I never had money. The way it is here is this: I work making *garrafadas* for people's health – since '77."

"Garrafada is a medicinal drink, is that right?"

"Yes, a person brings a bit of pinga, I pour in a little water and give a blessing, look at his condition, and then give him the garrafada for his continued health."

"I see."

"Then come others who don't want a garrafada, but they bring candles for me to do a spiritual cleansing, or a prayer for their homes."

"And then leave a couple of reals?"

She looked at me compassionately. "No, no, we don't charge anything."

"And food? How do you survive?"

"My son," she explained patiently, "God lacks nothing, don't you see? Someone brings a small something, another brings a juice, someone brings rice or gives a piece of meat or a portion of beans. It's enough that we are never wanting. And my home is always full this way. There's not one that is a child of mine, not even a relative of mine, no. All this and the house is full the entire time, you see? The entire time. One pair leaves, three people arrive. Five leave, four arrive. As with every piece that arrived during those seven years, things just filled up more and more."

What a generous, entrepreneurial, and risk-taking faith, here in the old Dense Forest region of Brazil. Something about vast, empty interiors seems to motivate extraordinary human efforts.

"So my home works this way – with nothing lacking, no. I'm not afraid of making money, but I am also not afraid of work. Today, somewhat, because my column can't support it. Much pain in the column!" Dona Romana exclaimed, rolling her pebble eyes upwards.

"And do the sculptures signify something?" I asked, changing the subject after a respectful pause. "Can you explain some of them to me?"

"Sure, they are like this. I think those which attract more attention are the antennas, such as this one here, which is called a XS Gala Galastera antenna, responsible for all of the electricity for the other pieces."

"O-kay," I replied slowly, "I can see the wires."

"But there are many antennas. Among them there are those which are called master antennas, receiving antennas, distribution antennas, filtering antennas, well antennas, basin antennas, spring antennas. Then there are male antennas and female antennas, you see?"

"But why so many antennas?"

"I don't know. Just don't know."

"To receive messages, that sort of thing?" I offered.

"I just don't know. But could be – or something about stabilizing the foundation of the earth's main axis. Then there are the spiritual intermediary antennas and the capturing antennas; which makes me think they are meant to capture energy for the main axis, like a great big lightning rod – but I don't know, I just don't know."

There was something inspiring about Dona Romana's humility, so many "I don't knows" from the master builder/gardener herself. At the same time it was frustrating to someone raised with clear, ready, and instantaneous answers to nearly everything – or so I thought. Among the dozens of statues were interspersed a droopy cement shack or two, looking like oversized sand drip castles. So, true to form, I asked, "And this little house here, does it have a specific purpose?"

"No, but I do know that everything has a purpose, and that we can only prepare ourselves. That everything here will work when the earth rises up."

"That's good news, I guess."

Dona Romana, taking pity on me and unprepared to give up, explained one last time: "It works this way, right now it's without life, it's sleeping, only later will it wake up. Right now it needs me, to be guiding, to say, 'Okay, let's do this, let's do that.' But after the earth rises up, and everything here wakes up, it won't need anyone anymore. It's the people who're going to need all of this foundation. But then I just don't know how we'll take part."

"If I can ask, does the Dona have relatives to take care of this place after your departure?"

Looking up, she said, "When you receive a spiritual mission, my son, your relatives let go of you. They don't accept it, it's very difficult. Have you ever seen the case of a person who's on a spiritual mission, where the relatives help? It's very difficult."

"I see what you mean," I replied, as the long-odds of books don't seem very different.

"The relatives run away. They consider you crazy, you see? Such that most of my life since I started this, my relatives have considered it crazy, the townspeople thought it all crazy, that it's *macumba* and all of that ugly stuff. But now that I receive visits from so many people, some have modified their views and show a bit more respect."

"But who, then, will take care of things after your departure?" I persisted.

"The earth will rise up before then."

"Okay – so no need to worry."

"No need."

Dona Romana had been carrying a bulky set of keys all the while, including a large iron one the length of a hand, which she now used to open the door to the governor's barn. The interior was surprisingly cool and dark before she opened several louvered shutters. After the windows, she unlocked the barn's storage rooms – the inner sanctums – where thick white-washed concrete shelves supported the weight of hundreds of full plastic bottles, along with row upon row of sacks of staples, cement, clothes, bedding, and mattresses: the ultimate in doomsday survival storage.

"Here it's this way, my son. Everything that can be stored, I am gathering and gathering. People bring a bed, a mattress, everything you can imagine, everything!"

Dona Romana took a 2-liter bottle, that had been filled with water and left outside the barn door, and laid it down in a small, open space among the others. The sheer quantity of the collection made me speechless, the liquids absorbing and magnifying the diffuse light.

Outside the storage rooms hung a series of images, one of which particularly caught my attention.

"And this picture here, who painted it?"

"That's by the children from here. Each one invents something new."

The panel showed a simple airplane pulling a banner addressing a plaintive hope. "'Take me away, Brazil'," I read out loud. "But the children are talented. Where did they learn to paint?"

"I don't' know," replied Dona Romana, as modest as ever, "the Spirit moves them."

In the barn's largest space, and centered around a tall supporting post, stood a waist-high circular corral, with each sector carefully divided and laid out, the objects, many representing animals, neatly pointing in wedge-formation to the center, to the shed's axis. The scene reminded me of an exclusive Noah's Ark, for the fence posts were topped with leaning spears, tilting outwards.

"Here's the area for animals," Dona Romana wanted to explain, my attention drifting back outdoors to the strengthening sunshine, as it burned off the morning dew and dried the itchy feet of so many stone prophets. From there my imagination took flight with the banner-towing, single-prop airplane: to the sleepy town of crumbled churches and moldy walls, along the Pilgrim's Path leading out of town, and then along the dusty roads snaking through the cerrado's rough grass to the far corners of the newly formed state of Tocantins. What drives the human spirit, I had to wonder, to such heroic lengths in the face of so much – for lack of a better word – futility? Impending catastrophe is one answer, though not a very persuasive one. I would have liked to ask, but Dona Romana's voice pulled me back inside, to this musty, twilight niche of salvation in the shadows of a Brazilian chiaroscuro.

"Here's the area for cars," her voice droned on. "These planes, these cars, it's difficult for us to make them. It is very difficult. Only here," she paused to say with a sudden laugh, "difficult is not to say impossible!"

"That's right," I replied, finally understanding, "it isn't."

For only then, in the open space of her laugh, did I realize the source of Natividade's diffuse cloud of light that had mystified me since first approaching this small, obscure town near the geographic center of Brazil – it could only be one more manifestation of Dona Romana's divine inspiration, the triumph of faith over hope.

~ 9 ~

ARAGUAIA NATIONAL PARK: a national park, comprising the northern third of Bananal Island, that is no longer under federal or state control. Bananal Island: the largest fluvial island in the world named after supposedly extensive banana groves, few of which are found today and whose one-time prevalence is doubted. John the Texan asked me if I planned to visit the park and, if so, how, since he hadn't found any useful information in Brasília. As Bananal Island lies roughly a hundred kilometers west of the Belém-Brasília, I was already considering a visit despite the lack of apparent roads to get you there; now this curious lack of logistics or directions in the nation's capital only further piqued my interest. But were Atlas, Fofão, my decidedly two-wheel drive station wagon, and I really prepared for a potentially all-terrain detour?

The immense island was originally called Santana after the Catholic saint of the day by the first white interloper, José Pinto Fonesca, who came in 1773 to enslave as many Carajá Indians as possible and ended up, after crisscrossing the land and repeatedly encountering the same rivers, surmising that he might be on an island. A year later the Viscount of Lapa established a garrison to ensure safe passage on the Araguaia River, but it was soon abandoned.[33] Steamboats, after being transported in pieces over thirteen hundred kilometers from Cuiabá near the Bolivian border, navigated the river for a decade or two in the early 20th century. Eventually these fleeting riverine attempts to link the western hinterland to Brazil's southern and northern beachheads gave way to roads, which in turn faired poorly in areas flooded much of the year. Only in 1959 did the expansive President Kubitschek decree the island, with its transitions from Pantanal-like wetlands to cerrado to Amazon rainforest, an environmental reserve, and after Brasília's inauguration built a full-sized hotel near São Felix, just southwest of the island, which he frequented. But the Indians were unimpressed by Presidential fiat and, as aggrieved parties are wont to do in Brazil, burned the offending, frivolous structure to the ground.[34]

Atlas and I would have nearly as much difficulty reaching Bananal Island as our predecessors, but enter we did, with Atlas enjoying his first visit to the, technically, off-bounds territory of a national park. This makes it sound easier than it was, as finding the key to such a sodden puzzle proved elusive. Long and narrow, the island is swallowed as if whole by the giant anaconda of the Araguaia River which delineates Tocantins' western border with Mato Grosso state, and whose eastern branch, the one we would need to cross, is named Javaés. Few roads try to tickle the anaconda's belly, none of them paved. Bananal is larger than the state of Sergipe and is so waterlogged it contains an entire two hundred and fifty kilometer long river within its curvaceous bulge. Yet on my Quatro Rodas map I could only find two dirt roads that dead-end across from the island on the Javaés River, one reaching Cangaçu to the north and the other, further south, leading to the aptly named Barreira da Cruz, or Cross's Barrier.

The region has a darker side as well – as jungles often do. Not only was Bananal used for a time as a penal colony, but the Araguaia region of the Amazon Basin saw the most successful rural guerrilla uprising of the Sixties, when Marxists gained the sympathy of the impoverished locals. The ruling junta in Brasília at first sent a poorly trained force which was easily routed by the guerrillas, led by a black man named Osvaldo Orlando da Costa. Only with the arrival of an elite corps of ten thousand counterinsurgency troops were the guerrillas defeated, after two years of repeated assaults, with Costa's body paraded in front of the locals, much as the Portuguese Crown had done with Tiradentes' head in 1792.[35] Several months after my trip – in one of those coincidences of time/space travel – the Brazilian government tried to make public the armed forces's files on the Araguaia guerrillas, in the hope of finding the final massacre site and recovering any bodily remains, as decreed by a Federal tribunal. In another bridge over time, a recent president of the governing Workers Party – who eventually resigned in disgrace – was a former Araguaia guerrilla himself. So if ambitious politicians could survive and prosper, for a time, despite the difficult local conditions, why couldn't we?

The overhead sun during the drive from Natividade was so hot and direct that I turned down the windshield's visors against the glare. We were arriving in the middle of the Central West's four month dry season, the tall roadside grass already browning. It is a more hardscrabble region than most, where squatter shanties of cut bamboo and black polyurethane plastic string along the roadside's red soil like Morse code writ large. We passed several watermelon trucks, the high shimmer of their bright orange canopies hinting at a translucent wetness within.

So which wildcat road to take? One guide book, Lonely Planet, sang the praises of the "ecolodge" at the Cangaçu Research Center, extolling the virtue of its mission to preserve two thousand square kilometers of "virgin rainforest," the variety of its touring options (including boat visits to the park), the spaciousness of the accommodations on stilts, and even the quality of the food which "– as long as Rosana, the manager/chef with a degree in nutrition, is on hand – is undoubtedly the best you will taste in Brazil." All in all "one of Brazil's most beautiful and comfortable ecolodges,"[36] which sounded plenty good enough for me, if over the top. The only catch was that you had to make a reservation through Tocantins' capital, Palmas, which I was loath to do as the chance of an organized tour accepting Atlas was nil.

So even though the dirt track to Cangaçu, at over a hundred and twenty kilometers, was twice as long as the one to Cross's Barrier, the culinary payoff seemed worth the investment. Besides which, Barreira da Cruz was described as only a large fazenda, from where river crossings need to be negotiated with the local ranchers, with the closest accommodations sixty kilometers back inland.

I should add that information in this part of the world, which was explored and mapped well after Central Africa, is habitually suspect. Brazilian reference books place Araguaia Park's founding at various years from 1959 to 1973 to 1983 – with two of the dates provided by the same author.[37] The number of the island's inhabitants (granted, more of a moving target) is even more elastic, ranging from several hundred to seventeen hundred to over three thousand remaining Indians, of the Karajá (now spelled with a "k") and Javaés tribes.[38] My small potpourri of guidebooks agreed on one dispiriting point, however, which was that any visit to the park requires prior authorization from Ibama's offices in Brasília or Goiânia, while any visit to one of the island's Indian villages must be cleared through Funai, the National Indian Foundation, in Brasília. Not overly cowed by bureaucracy, I decided to plunge on regardless.

After restocking supplies, plus a full automotive pit stop along a surprisingly calm forty kilometers on the Belém-Brasília, we turned off at Pug-Mill in direction of Pium, where the patchy asphalt ends and the dirt fun begins. In Pium, the last town before our jungle destination, I asked a man on the side of the road if he thought Cangaçu was open, which he did, and how the road was, to which he replied that he had heard they were fixing parts of it. This made sense as many roads get spruced up during the dry season. Only afterwards did I realize that a potentially hard-up local now knew that a lone gringo with his docile dog was heading towards Cangaçu without prior experience or reservation, information which could be shared with others.

It was early afternoon and the gravel road started out washboard graded. While the map suggested a left turn after only eight kilometers, I neglected to keep track on the odometer, distracted by the condition of a road where one good surprise could be our last. We passed a dusty left turn promising a Fazenda Aguas Claras seventy kilometers down that way, but pushed on, believing that Cangaçu would merit its own sign. Increasingly concerned – in part because the wrong dirt road would curve fifty kilometers back to the Belém-Brasília – I opted to backtrack to the Clear Waters Ranch road, where we fortunately encountered a crew of road workers within minutes. They confirmed, despite the misleading map, that we had been going the right way after all. Relief. Yet we had just lost another half hour of afternoon light, which would make it more difficult to reach our destination and, if turned away, return before nightfall.

We passed a few ranch entrance gates and several dirt-caked pickups that barreled by at high speeds with massive plumes of dust in tow. While I could get Fofão up to 100 kilometers per hour on the better stretches, I had to slow drastically for sudden wash-outs or high cattle crossings which were worse than speed bumps. I noticed that my cell phone had long ago lost any signal. Atlas, alert to my tenseness, sat attentively in the middle of the back seat with tongue in, snout and eyes forward, scanning the unrolling road.

"We've got ourselves into a bit of an adventure, haven't we my Atlas boy?" I asked rhetorically, as we flew over the dirt roadscape, all eyeballs ahead.

Shuffling through maps laid out on the passenger seat, I discovered one showing a dirt turnoff half way in that spanned forty or so kilometers to a parallel asphalt road – which might diminish the chance of nighttime potluck driving. When we reached the actual turnoff, I gladly noted a public phone among a few shacks and then, even better, that the by-pass road had been recently paved. The interior of Brazil is developing too quickly for the rest of us, including map-makers, to keep up.

With roughly fifty kilometers to go, I felt confident we could reach the ecolodge and, if need be, backtrack to the turnoff in daylight, as our progress averaged some seventy kilometers per hour. But then the road worsened – without one sign mentioning the existence of a place called Cangaçu. First, the reddish dirt road started to soften up with whiter patches of sand. Then it narrowed, showing fewer and fewer signs of ranch, or any other, traffic. One depression contained over fifty meters of bone-dry sand, where the deep beach-like ruts indicated that I would need to speed over it and hope for the best. We scraped the undercarriage almost the entire way, luckily without the anticipated *clang!* of a hidden boulder hitting the car's underbelly. By now we were on a single lane road, as the austere dryness of the winter cerrado gave way to a gallery forest heralding the approaching river.

Suddenly a rainforest denseness closed over the road, shielding muddy patches from the sun. Then came a rickety wood-slat bridge with a gaping square-meter hole awning over a dark, bottomless creek. Two middle-aged fishermen – the first carless mammals since Pium and environs – told me their van had traversed the same crossing without mishap, but I could see that most compact cars would have too narrow an axle-span to make it. When I lined up Fofão's tires the two men kindly sighted the crossing, indicating that I could proceed, despite the risk that a bridge blocked by a nose-dived car could greatly extend their fishing trip. We inched over uneventfully. At a fork in the rolling hard dirt road, I turned left onto the more beaten track, and within a hundred meters came upon the wide, slow procession of the Javaés River, glimmering in the low, westerly sunlight. Across the river lay a jumble of rainforest green, our first glimpse of the elusive Araguaia Park.

The pocket camping area was filled by one largish van and a number of tents surrounding a small campfire area, where a handful of vacationing anglers were savoring the day's end with beer. To the side, a large falling down sign warned, "Predatory Hunting or Fishing is a Crime." A fellow with somewhat flat Indian features, possibly their guide, confirmed that the other fork leads to the Cangaçu Research Center. If he looked dubiously at our city-slicker wheels, I didn't notice it, before our first carefree motoring into the Amazon rainforest.

A half-Indian guide would be historically appropriate, for the story of Indian and European interaction in Brazil is unlike any other of the Americas. (Only Paraguay's comes close.) What differs is the extent of miscegenation, cultural and otherwise, that occurred from the get-go, and the subsequent impact of Indian mores on the developing nation, an influence which remains widespread, if mostly hidden, today. In

Mexico the Aztec lines can still be seen on many a mestizo's face, whereas in Brazil the mixing of bloods is so thorough that, outside of the great northwest quadrant of the Amazon, the lineage has become flooded by history, so prevalent and submerged as to become murky and indistinct. As early as 1922, the famous poet and "Pope of Modernism," Mário de Andrade, called on Brazilians to recognize their "Tupi Indian soul."[39]

There is a common saying (with racist undertones) that someone "has a foot in the kitchen," meaning a trace of black blood, and it is Brazil's fluid gradations from black to white, the compelling mix of color opposites, that captures the world's attention. Yet the more profound and older conflux, the miscegenation so widespread as to have become almost unremarkable, is that of white and red corpuscles. The more acute observation, potentially so prevalent as to be banal, would be "to have a foot in the jungle" – sometimes easier said than done.

Unlike the Aztecs and the Andes' Incas, the aboriginal Brazilians did not create great city-building societies, nor did they have standing armies. The older tribes left few tangible records, other than rupestrine paintings in caves, earth platforms called *aterros*, and elaborate ceramic pottery discovered on Marajó Island at the mouth of the Amazon River.[40] More recently, the outlines of numerous and extensive towns are being excavated throughout the Amazon jungle, suggesting a hitherto unsuspected degree of settlement within the "pristine" rainforest.[41] Estimates of the Indians' prevalence prior to the Portuguese invasion suggest one hundred different languages spoken by a half to two million people.[42] The Tupi-Guarani language group, as delineated by the discoverer Cabral, dominated in an expressive way the entire resplendent coast. Such an unusual geographic spread has given rise to theories that the Tupi-Guarani, some time before the Europeans' landfall, had themselves conquered the coastal territories from other indigenous peoples, a pre-colonization which greatly facilitated the Portugueses' task, requiring that they learn only one language and one culture in order to conquer nearly all.

The power of language is hard to overestimate, this unique human ability to request, manipulate, and command, that allows learning and traditions to be shared and rapidly spread – like fire over rivers of cachaça. The first smelting of cultures, appropriately, began almost immediately with the Tupi-Guarani language, which the Portuguese acquired by marooning prisoners between sailing expeditions with the option of either learning the tribal language or languishing. The Portuguese were the first to transcribe Tupi, elucidating its grammar and rules, and so began the long synthesis. Such was the success of this elucidation, such was the importance of communicating with the keepers of the jungle's secrets and with the young colony's Indian slaves, that Tupi-Guarani became Brazil's dominant language and remained so through the beginning of the 18th century – for over two centuries! – when Portuguese finally edged it out as the lingua franca.[43] It helped that the Tupi language, as João de Laet described in his 1640 history of the New World, was easy, copious, and very agreeable[44] – not unlike the women, he might have implied. Many documents attest to the frustrations of one Church emissary after another who complained, as did the Bishop of Pernambuco in 1697, of the need to bring an interpreter as "they don't even speak the language." By means of explanation, and perhaps more telling than intended, he continued:

> They [the Brazilians] don't even differentiate themselves from the most barbarous Tapuia other than saying that they are Christian, notwithstanding the fact that as soon as they are married they are assisted by seven Indian Concubines, and from there one can infer how proceeds the rest.[45]

Such were the difficulties in civilizing the rollicking Torrid Zone of the New World, for indeed the rest proceeded and continues to proceed to this day.

It is tempting to treat the clash of cultures as a grand farce that ended, more or less, happily, but such were the sparks – humorous, at times, from a safe distance – of a grand conflagration. Today it is believed that, including Bananal Island's hundreds, under four hundred thousand Amazon Indians remain[46] (though deep in the rainforest new tribes are still being "discovered," with perhaps dozens still to be contacted).[47] They live on reserves whose twelve percent of national territory represents a land mass equivalent to the states of Minas Gerais, São Paulo, and Paraná combined, or the size of nearly two Frances, with a population density as low as the Sahara Desert's.[48]

And the vanished million or two? Many were killed, fatally diseased, or in fleeing died an unnatural death; while the blood of untold ancestors folded into the mighty currents of the Brazilian confluence, sweeping all before it.

For more recent wayfarers who, like ourselves, tempt uncertain fates, would the roiling Javaés River have a similar impact?

The right fork, as promised by the half-breed, started out well enough but soon deteriorated into a narrow jungle corridor with deep muddy ruts left by the rainy season's hangover. The tracks were mostly dry and drivable, but at times were no more than tire-wide ridges above the muck; if a front or rear wheel slipped off – and there was evidence that a jeep had repeatedly done just that – we'd be stuck. By the time I realized how precarious the situation was, there was no way to turn around. Back on the long dirt road, I had shut the windows and turned on the air conditioner to prevent the hot, billowing dust from quickly covering Atlas and me. Here, when I opened the windows, the jungle's thick mesh of bird screeches and insect droning cascaded in.

As we hopped and swerved over more ruts and treacherous mud-moats, driven by the imperative of forward momentum, the rainforest continued to close in. I could hear it all too well from the prolonged scratching noises along Fofão's sides, which rasped loudly in my ears, along with the scraping of not-so-small saplings along the undercarriage. It was either go forward or retreat, but backing up had long ceased to be a viable option. After three tense kilometers, I decided to turn around at the first opportunity, no matter how precarious, and give up rather than sink Fofão into the bog of her first jaunt into the Amazon rainforest. Just as the road surface started to flatten out and offer enough space for a many-point turnaround, I noticed that the way ahead looked marginally drier and decided to press on. Sure enough, within half a kilometer the forest opened up to reveal a series of thatched-roof wooden buildings on stilts with eye-level walkways and a few communication towers, basking in the late afternoon sun on the ample banks of the Javaés River. So this must be Cangaçu.

When the driveway curved inland I stopped the car but didn't turn off the motor, which was still wheezing and laboring mightily, concerned if it would start again. Getting out of Fofão I looked around for a moment but could not see any sign of human life: no cars, no smoke, no people. Against hope I clapped my hands in the traditional Brazilian equivalent of knocking on the door and called out, "*Alô! Alô!*" No response.

I clapped again and suddenly two short, stocky men emerged from the woods out back. There was something about them – or perhaps I was just keyed up from the jungle drive – which made me thankful that the windows were low enough, if required, for Atlas to leap out to defend me. Atlas, sensing my anxiety, started to bark.

As the pair approached I could see that one of them was just a boy, most likely the man's son, even though they were the same height and build, and shared a similar shuffling gait. They stopped a good distance away.

Though it was difficult to make out their expressions, I could imagine the inscrutability of the scene before them: a scratched station wagon where only jeeps and pickups had ventured before, in which roared a black devil of a dog, and before which stood a crazed gringo acting even more strangely than most foreigners do – all at the end of a long, humid, formerly unruffled day.

"Hi, good afternoon – Atlas be quiet – can you tell me if the lodge is open?" I yelled a little too hopefully.

The father and son looked at each other for a moment, after which the father replied that the lodge was not open and, not too surprisingly, that reservations can only be made through – where else? – Palmas.

(The one accurate bit of information, it's a pity, had to be this one.)

When asked whether a group might be arriving by chance that day or the next, the caretaker replied no, none that he knew of – and still kept his distance, his features as mute as his son's.

So that was that. With her engine's fan still blowing hard, I turned Fofão around in a small grassy area and started back. I considered camping out with the fishermen, but the space had looked cramped; besides which, I didn't like the pinched and predatory look on their faces. Even though it had been three hours since we last saw asphalt or a town, I decided to head back, returning slowly over the muddy tracks with more loud scrapes and scratches, the sounds of the jungle magnified by the stillness of day's end.

We reached the asphalt turnoff just after sunset, and it felt good to have a reassuringly smooth, hard surface underneath. The road was so newly constructed, however, that the bridges were roughly improvised wooden spans constructed of planks that were loose and often jarred out of place, presumably by passing construction trucks. While picking our way slowly across, on the lookout for raised nails, I fretted that all we needed now was a flat tire or two in the middle of the Brazilian boonies without cell phone signal or sign of human habitation in the gathering tropical night.

After joining up with the dead-end yet paved road that leads from the Araguaia River well north of Bananal to the Belém-Brasília, I was startled when a warning light in the dashboard's control panel started to flash. Paging through the car's manual, I gathered that the light was trying to tell me something about the brake pads, which was odd, as they had recently been checked during a pre-trip tune-up. Then I caught several whiffs of burning rubber, which caused me to reduce speed and welcome the infrequent sight of oncoming cars hurtling past, fleeing west from the thickening darkness.

Apparently a wave of state-pride had swept the land after separation from Goiás, as evidenced by the large number of towns with the appendage "from Tocantins" added to their name. Such was the case when we passed Divinópolis do Tocantins and eventually came to a late rest in Paraíso do Tocantins, where the Serrano's Park Hotel mercifully protested little about taking in one exhausted man and his faithful dog, worn ragged after well over nine hours of semi-dry navigation. Perhaps a big, protective dog is not so uncommon in these parts after all.

Like a bulked-up medieval castle, the hotel regally overlooks the Belém-Brasília, about which the Quatro Rodas listing for Paradise of Tocantins warns, "avoid the highway at night, when it is customary for assaults to occur." We had returned if not to paradise, then to a rough and yearning civilization – for now.

~ 10 ~

MANY REAL EXPLORERS besides the marauding Bandeirantes have tested their mettle in Brazil's unforgiving interior, and not all lived to tell about it. Richard Burton, of White Nile and Mecca-in-drag fame, rode muleback across Minas Gerais in the 19th century – and was none the worse for it. Teddy Roosevelt went on an Amazonian hunting and collecting expedition accompanied by the Indian specialist Cândido Rondon in 1913, which resulted in a broken leg and a debilitating fever that precipitated his early death several years later – but at least he had a Brazilian river and Indian reserve named after him for his efforts. Closer to my objective, the English explorer Colonel Fawcett – in search of the Lost City of Z – had the misfortune of traipsing around the Araguaia region early last century only to disappear and become permanently lost himself. He left a note instructing that no rescue party be sent should he not return, which has been so thoroughly ignored that, so far, almost a hundred men have died contravening his last wishes.[49]

Atlas and I did not plan to join them as our own search, on a more mundane level, was for something far larger and presumably easier to find. So even if foolhardy, we decided to redouble our efforts to set foot in the Araguaia National Park the next day. You might wonder what compelled us to want to visit a, until recently, rain-inundated bog of an island – home to guerilla redoubts, incendiary Indians, and, it turns out, fleeing bureaucrats – and there is no straight answer other than to say that whenever a national park came within striking distance we struck. And struck again if necessary. Call it a hobby, but I have visited dozens of national parks throughout the Americas – those windows into the New World's first innocence – and cannot easily be deterred from adding one more to the list.

The last option approaching Bananal Island from the more developed east was to breach Cross's Barrier. The map indicated a paved road until Lagoa da Confusão, followed by sixty-two kilometers of dirt and gravel to the river. So before turning off the Belém-Brasília, which looked almost benign in daylight, we made a pit stop to re-fuel, check tires and liquids, and thoroughly hose down the wheels of accumulated dust in the hope of avoiding the flashing red warning light. But when Fofão heated up again, the light blinked back on – proving once more the eternal mystery, to the mechanically-challenged, of what makes cars tick.

It was an easy two hour drive to the village of Confusion Lake, which, appropriately, sits on the edge of a five kilometer long lake bursting, after the rains, from its banks, with many a palm tree submerged in half a meter of water. The confusion part, apparently, stems from the tendency of the lake's central rocky outcrop to move.

Alika, the bleach blond receptionist at the Lagoa da Ilha club and hotel, didn't mind about Atlas and confirmed that, yes, day-long visits to Bananal Island and an Indian village could be arranged through the manager. So we stayed – delighted that the obstacles, after all, weren't insurmountable. To celebrate, I took Atlas down to the lake's edge to throw his worn tennis ball out into the glassy waters. Some boys joined us through a hole in the fence from the nearby camping ground, including Aginaldo who asked me with wonderment if I lived alone and exclaimed "Hail Mary!" at the slightest provocation, usually when Atlas performed a trick.

The graying, paunchy, and affable manager, Neziu, couldn't have been more welcoming. He told me he has one son at a technical college in Massachusetts and another who supervises construction projects outside Philadelphia. Furthermore, he delighted in listing all of his favorite and long-gone movie actors, whose names, such as Errol Flynn, Cary Grant, Gary Cooper, Yul Brunner, and the recently deceased Marlon Brando, rolled off his lips with an accented ease that made them nearly indecipherable. (Before I left, he proudly showed me a Captain America VHS tape and an architectural sketch of the large aquatic park that will heroically transform Lagoa da Ilha one day.) He confirmed that he could find me a guide "for fifty reals and who doesn't drink," and that my station wagon should be able to make the trip. With the Brazilian knack for demolishing barriers, social or otherwise, he took to calling me "Beng-jamin Frank-leen" every time we bumped into each other.

Alika, during one of the many lulls of a languorous afternoon, took the opportunity to show me her small album of photographs on the pretext that it contained some undoctored shots of the lake's elusive rock. Interspersed – surprise, surprise – were seductive poses of her standing in lingerie in, of all places, the bathroom (mostly in front of the toilet), perhaps the only private place at home where a friend could discreetly capture Alika's dollishly lithe form – but then again, where else is semi-nakedness more natural than in the lavatory? When Atlas and I returned from a local fish dinner, she was no longer on duty, yet I couldn't help recall, as I settled into my mosquito net-shrouded bed, how she had proclaimed "Oh!" with false modesty every time we came upon one of her girlie photos, unsure of how it had gotten there.

So how had our small cast of characters, broadly speaking, gotten here?

The story of rampaging Bandeirantes channeled by Indian guides is really the primordial story of the building of the Brazilian nation. It is fair to say that the Portuguese didn't colonize or settle Brazil, the Brazilians did. As the German historian Georg Friederici elaborated from the vantage point of 1936:

> The discovers, explorers, and conquerors of the interior of Brazil were not the Portuguese, but the Brazilians of pure white blood along with, particularly, mixed-bloods and half breeds. And also, jointly with them, the indigenous primitives of the land. All of the vast interior of Brazil was revealed to Europe, not by Europeans, but by Americans.[50]

That is likely putting it a bit too collegially, as the Tupi-Guarani, among others, did not go hand in hand off into the wilderness with the Bandeirantes on a joint crusade to open the green heart of South America, they were forced to.

Yet what startles is the revelation that Brazilians were so thoroughly mixed and mixing by the end of the 17th century, the Bandeiras leaving São Paulo could already contain such a motley warring party. (The custom of leading a raiding party with a Bandeira, or "banner" – and hence the root of Bandeirante itself – was an Indian one, adopted by the Paulistas.) It would be as though Lewis and Clark, one hundred and fifty years before their vaunted expedition to the Pacific, had not only brought Sacagawea along, but a whole rainbow coalition of crew members, while carrying a drop or two of Indian blood themselves.

The Portuguese had a tall order on their hands trying to pacify, settle, and hold onto a colony nearly one hundred times the size of the motherland, and all but adopted a policy of miscegenation, of randy Portuguese men mating with willing or not so willing Indian women, in order to populate the colony as quickly as possible.[51] The first explorers and colonizers were all men; crossing the wide oceans with family only became common with much later waves of Italian, Portuguese, German, Japanese, and Spanish immigrants in the second half of the 19th century, when slavery was abolished and export crops from the Southeast, such as coffee, overtook the Northeastern lodestar of sugar.[52]

Whether it was the drive to dominate or the economic pressure to work with the human "materials" on hand, the Portuguese were much more relaxed about intermixing with Indian, as opposed to African, slaves, though the latter phenomenon became both prevalent in the course of time and more famous – perhaps due to its pioneering audacity.

In other words, while the Javaés Indians' ancestry was both self-defined and clear, there was really no way of telling if Mari of São Jorge or Alika and Neziu of Confusion Lake did or did not have Indian blood, other than asking them directly, and even then they might not know.

Neziu knocked on my door before the appointed hour to tell me the guide had arrived. Already dressed, I came out to share a coffee with Jackson, who had worked for Ibama for a number of years. A young man with close-cropped black hair and open, lean features, Jackson was not thrilled about taking Atlas along, but when I assured him that Senior Neziu had said it would be alright, he relented with a shrug which implied, "Those crazy foreigners will do the darndest things!"

When I asked if there would be a safe place to park – which I imagined would be on the near side of the Javaés River – Jackson replied yes. He added that I should leave my wallet in the car, making me wonder momentarily what we were getting into.

The dirt road was better than the day before's, which allowed me to drive and listen to Jackson's story at the same time. During his seven years with the national park service he had worked for three regional managers, each one more corrupt than the prior. The last, a pretty thirty-six year old from the southern state of Paraná, had been the worst, going so far as to falsify a receipt with Jackson's signature on it. Suspecting mischief, Ibama hired an internal lawyer who then turned the case over to the state authorities, who in turn handed it over to the Federal Police. Jackson was obligated to testify three times that he had never received such a quantity of money for the services indicated. Based on Jackson's, and others', testimonies, the young manager was indicted, but fled prior to her arrest and has not been found since. Jackson felt obliged to add that not all Ibama managers or offices are corrupt. The Palmas office, where he worked for a time, is too busy to wallow in much graft, whereas the Araguaia Park Headquarters, a rough seven hour drive from Confusion Lake along our same route, had too much money sloshing around with too little to do.

Our early drive was a pleasant one, the sky the color of a large inverted robin's egg. As we passed dozens upon dozens of cultivated fields, I could see why a recent Palmas newspaper had reported on the doubling of farm equipment sales. They were soybeans, Jackson confirmed, part of the surge which has made Brazil the largest soybean exporter in the world, supplanting the U.S. We also passed rice paddies and a few lonely watermelon patches. Produce-laden trucks, like comets, passed us with long, debris-filled tails.

Two surprises were in store. The first was that, other than on paper, the park no longer exists, as the Javaés Indians have confiscated it. I had read something along these lines in one of my foreign guidebooks, but given that the news was four years old I thought the situation might have improved. It hadn't. The most dependable information places the establishment of the Indian Reserve in 1971, twelve years after Kubitschek's creation of the environmental one, covering the entire island and, as usual, administered by Funai. A decade later the national park, run by Ibama, had been carved out of the northern third of Bananal. Yet within a generation the Javaés were claiming that Ibama had stolen "their money" and, when Ibama's regional manager broke off negotiations, decided to re-claim "their island." This was done by putting fire to most of the park, including burning down the headquarters with its three million reals of equipment – not unlike the torching of President Kubitschek's hotel at São Felix. Jackson recalled how Indians had set fires in front of park employees and then challenged them to "stop this." Since then not one park employee has set foot on the island. (The risks are real: since the 1970's, 120 Funai employees have been killed by Indians.)[53]

I should note that Brazil has more than five percent of its extensive territory under some sort of environmental protection.[54] Besides the federal, state, and private environmental reserves, which include forest, extractive, and sustainable development reserves, as well as the myriad state parks, there are forty-two national parks at varying stages of development or disrepair. Some, like Veadeiros, are relatively well organized and protected, while others, such at the Amazon National Park at the Pará and Amazon state line, are so inaccessible, remote, and unmarked they only exist in theory. In a country with myriad demands on limited resources, only half of the national parks are officially open to the public, and a majority have no infrastructure whatsoever.

Still, given how limited the funding is – that is not leached by corruption – it was a pity to see the process in reverse, with so many resources destroyed. If Araguaia had once been technically "open," it no doubt moved to a "closed" park after the Javaés's confiscation.

The second surprise was that not only Atlas, but Fofão as well, would visit the former park that day. I had assumed we would have to leave the car in Cruz da Barreira and take a canoe across, as not one guide book had mentioned a passable road on Bananal, with one flatly stating "there are no roads on the island."[55] Yet at Cruz da Barreira we found a rickety river barge, whose amiable pilot needs to be tracked down to attend to the infrequent crossings.

Descending the barge ramp, I duly noted a string of threatening signs, including one from Funai warning that entry without permission was a breach of the law and subject to fines. One Brazilian reference book specified the crime as trespass.[56] I didn't even bother to ask Jackson if he had the necessary permit.

Though only mid-morning, we could feel the gathering heat while crossing the windless, largely sediment-free expanse of the Javaés to the long, ragged line of greenery on the far side. The unimproved dirt road which greeted us was no more than two tire tracks through the dry cerrado, which often deteriorated into sandy ruts that required more bumpy gassing of the engine, with more scraping, to get through. Here it was a fine, talcum-powder dust which soon transformed my black Fiat ("let it be done" in Latin) into a powdered pale-face.

At the first small habitation Jackson suggested we slow down and honk, as we would need to find a native guide to proceed. There, with luck, we found Paulinho at the hut's outdoor kitchen area, marinating a deep pan of venison. We would have to negotiate a fee, Jackson explained, but as Paulinho was not yet ready to conduct business, when offered a bead and feather necklace for ten reals I promptly purchased it.

No sooner were we back in the car and ready to press on to the *aldeia* (originally the word for Jesuit missions where Indians were converted), then we were confronted by a jeep coming in the other direction with the letters FUNAI painted on its hood and sides, blocking our way forward.

"Great," I thought to myself, "ten minutes on a dusty road to nowhere and already busted!"

Yet Jackson betrayed little sign of anxiety and, upon closer inspection, I could see the jeep was filled with Indians. The last time a Funai employee had driven onto the island, apparently, he had been promptly relieved of his vehicle. We got out and chatted up the jeep-full, whose driver was the local *cacique* or tribal leader, a man with a stony countenance that, now and then, cracked open with a smile. Wagner, it turned out, was running for local councilman – as most of Bananal Island is part of the township of Confusion Lake, in what could be called the Confusion District – with four Indians and five whites contending for three positions. When Jackson ascertained that Wagner was on his way into town to, among other things, pick up his electoral stickers, he made a grand display of peeling a sticker with an Indian competitor's name off of the windshield and dropping it into the dust, causing smiles all around.

When we bumped and scraped into Boto Velho, a small Javaés aldeia without electricity or telephones, we parked Fofão under the shade of a large cashew tree and, leaving Atlas in the car, got out to arrange things with Paulinho. (How he made it back to the aldeia before us I'm not sure – probably by canoe.) We found him in the first of a line of orderly, packed dirt floor huts, surrounded by parents, children, and one grandmother, all of whom I made a point of formally greeting. Following a few more pleasantries, I was offered a small, beautifully carved jaguar, but declined as the price of a hundred reals seemed high. It was cool inside, even though the smoke of an insect-repelling fire warmly darkened the domestic tableaux.

After we settled on the reasonable price of twenty reals for his services, Paulinho showed us down to the riverbank and canoe while keeping an eye out for any wild dogs who might consider Atlas an intruder. When a mean-looking threesome lopped in our direction, he threw a stone to ward them off. Jackson had already explained that I am particularly attached to my dog and had refused to leave him behind at Confusion Lake – all of which is true. Paulinho didn't seem to mind. Such peculiar behavior could be attributed not only to my whiteness, but to my foreignness as well, a double barrier.

With the outboard motor of the aluminum wide-bodied canoe on the blink, Paulinho had to paddle. Regardless, within a few minutes we were in a maze of bloated, slow-moving waters of tributaries and flooded plains. Within half an hour I had seen more bird species than before in so short a time, including snow-white great egrets, thick-necked tiger-herons, Amazon kingfishers, cormorants (usefully called "big divers" in Portuguese), a few piping-guans, and the graceful roseate spoonbill, a flash of pink skimming the water's skin.

It was Atlas's first time with me on a boat and he appeared more than game to go birding – though a bird dog he is not. Only when we pushed through some mangrove funnels and the branches made eerie, hollow scratching noises against the gunwales did he get spooked, at first leaning his body hard against my back and then jumping over me from the canoe's rear compartment to the wetter, central section by my feet. Paulinho had brought his two mop-top daughters, who didn't speak any Portuguese and, all grins with glistening eyes, were far less perturbable than Atlas.

When we returned to the curving lake in front of Boto Velho, we saw the surfacing flash of several pink dolphins for which the aldeia is named, reflecting an air-beating flock of roseate spoonbills, pink filaments above and below. To cool down, Paulinho took us for a swim off of a high, dry sandbar fingering the lake. When he showed me a half-devoured fish carcass and explained that the piranhas off to that side were hungry, I encouraged Atlas to do his diving and fetching elsewhere. When we saw a small dog paddling across the lake's deceptively calm surface, Paulinho blithely commented that the caimans often delight in such an easily snatched treat.

Upon returning to the village, with Atlas safely back in the car, our guide showed us the town's first bathrooms being installed by the municipal government, the new school house funded by the state, and the small health clinic run by the federal government. Could such a profusion of activity from all layers of government, I wondered, be taken as reward for burning down the national park? Or as a goodwill form of bribery to get it back? Paulinho then pointed out a well-constructed, commodious building which had been intended as guest quarters for visitors and tourists, but when the tribe learned that the big city Paulistano consultant involved in the deal was slated to receive a two hundred thousand real fee for his services, they killed the project and pocketed the rest of the money. The funding had come from a public pay-out to smooth the construction of the new capital's airport, in Palmas, which had risen, Brasília-like, from the high plain at the state's founding in 1989. The unfinished guest quarters was occupied by a needy family and the town's one shortwave radio, its only means of communication with the rest of the world, other than by road or river.

Back in the canoe, I had asked Paulinho if there was any way that Ibama could regain his confidence, such that he could welcome the park service back onto the island.

"Nothing," Paulinho flatly replied. "I don't trust them anymore. All they do is have long meetings, write proposals and papers, and get nothing done"– which, while indelicate, more or less jibed with my own corporate experience in Brazil, where meetingitis rules. (Another American visitor laments "the Brazilian penchant for endless theoretical and ideological discussion.")[57]

"They come here, and they try to lecture us Javaés on how to preserve the environment, something we have been doing for hundreds of years before consultants even existed. And do they ask us what to do? Do they try to learn from us? Never."

Jackson, whose great hope is for the two sides to work together again in mutual respect, retorted, "But they are just trying to help you plan for the future. Maybe they are too arrogant sometimes. But it is in everybody's interests to avoid destroying our natural resources."

"It is not my people who discovered chemical arms and the atomic bomb!" Paulinho started to rant. "And yet we are accused of being destructive?"

Paulinho had a valid point, for the roughly twelve percent of Brazil designated as Indigenous Territories is experiencing an even slower rate of deforestation (a good indicator of destructive practices) than the federally protected environmental reserves are – which makes sense as Indian reserves have motivated people on the ground willing to fight the encroachment of poachers, ranchers, miners, and loggers. This struggle over land often ends in violence, as when twenty-nine prospectors illegally mining diamonds on an Indian reserve in the western state of Rondônia – named after the same Cândido Rondon of Roosevelt's journey – were massacred by *cintas-largas* or "wide belt" Indians earlier that year.[58] (An action which both the head of Funai and the federal Justice Minister justified as self-defense of Indian lands, pointing out that the prospectors had been committing a crime.[59] Which makes one wonder: if the Justice Minister is willing to justify extra-judicial murder, why have a Justice Ministry in the first place?)

Yet it is a stretch to argue that Indigenous Territories are better off from an environmental perspective than national parks, and with two-thirds of Bananal Island already under Indian control, was it really necessary to occupy the rest? Jackson bemoaned the many signs of ecological degradation we encountered, most of them activities prohibited under the old park rules, such as ranching, deer-hunting (that marinating venison), pasture-burning, and primary tree-harvesting. His resigned comment was, "They're going to finish it all." He granted that both Ibama and Funai had been too restrictive, too controlling of both outside contact and local development – including no new construction, practically no tourism, with only a few permitted crops – such that neither, now, has any influence whatsoever.

Implying that most dealings with outsiders were fruitless, Paulinho emphasized that despite his "white clothes" – including his Carnival t-shirt which read "Without a condom, don't even think of it!" – and his ability to write and speak Portuguese, his thinking is entirely different from that of the "whites," the indigenous term for all non-Indians. He said he would never consider leaving, that he was glad that no one has to pay for electricity, gas, or telephones (as they have none), and proudly pointed out that the aldeia's population has grown to over one hundred.

As if to underline these differences, the last place Paulinho showed us was the traditional *Aruanã-heto*, the House of Men, which guards the straw masks and costumes used for communal ceremonies, often related to the moon's phases or to harvests. From under the open thatched roofed structure, Paulinho explained that the *pajé*, or the spiritual leader a step above the cacique, sets the ceremonial calendar. The local pajé, who lives in town, rarely leaves his house and, when he does, has to be carried as his feet are prohibited from touching the ground. The rite-of-passage ceremony for adolescents, during which the men get to dance around naked, may be why no females or boys are allowed to visit the House of Men – ever. If a child does, he or she is supposed to be sacrificed.

The pajé's word is law, according to Paulinho, who emphasized the fact by commenting "federal law doesn't exist here" – not the most reassuring thought. When a neighboring village was found culpable for the death of one of Boto Velho's bulls, the pajé ordered the destruction of the offending village, which was dutifully burned down. Nowadays, Paulinho assured us, the pajé doesn't so often order killings – though if he did, his desires would be duly executed – as work through potions. Back when buying my ten real necklace, I had kidded Jackson that it was for my protection – not such a misplaced desire, it turned out. Brazil is already a fairly lawless place in the eyes of many visitors and inhabitants alike, so here at the western border of Tocantins where an orderly, predictable world seems impossibly far away, every bit of protection helps.

I was heartened to see Atlas when we got back to the car, for my patient and well-behaved dog is also a symbol of man's careful, incremental control of the environment, both faithful and dependable. He confides his life in me, and I do what I can to merit his confidence. At times such as these, letting him out for a pee and a bowlful of water was sufficient but not enough. Even a good swim – something he adores – with the piranhas was but a token of my appreciation. His fealty is one of the few things I can always count on.

Tucked under the shade of the large cashew tree could also be found the federally-funded health clinic which, the size of a bedroom, was constructed of wood, now weathered, and topped by a tin roof. We met the nurse and then sat out on the small veranda, Paulinho and I with Atlas underfoot, gazing over the lake rippled by dancing breezes.

We discussed the possibility of "eco-tourism," a catchall phrase for just about any slipshod tourist activity in Brazil, and Paulinho confided that he would like to open a native-food restaurant to cater to overnight tourists. I thought of what it must be like after sunset, in a place without electricity, television, cell phones, or even radio, where the stars are bright and no nearby townlight melts away the profound depth of the universe, nearly visible to the far corners of creation. In a careful way I suggested to Paulinho that without an accord with Ibama, few tourists would have the confidence to book a reservation and stay the night – though I would. And within minutes we were gone.

Jackson was surprisingly quiet on the way back to Lagoa da Confusão. At the crossing, while we waited half an hour for the ferry operator to reappear, he chatted with a plump young woman, whose mother was washing clothes at the river's edge. With the ferry finally stirring on the opposite bank, Jackson gave the woman a long, affectionate hug from behind, but when I asked with a raised eyebrow if he wished to stay, he curtly replied, "No."

It was a weekday, with his wife teaching at an aldeia two hundred kilometers further south on Bananal, only to return to Lagoa for the weekend – but this didn't seem to explain it. I pointed out his pensiveness, and asked Jackson if he was sad to see the unraveling of his seven years of work building and protecting the Araguaia National Park.

"Yes," he replied, but only in a hollow way as if the subject now wearied him.

Perhaps our conversation with Paulinho had taken the air out of his let's-all-work-together attitude, for Jackson only partially re-animated when insisting that just two hundred thousand of the airport's 1.6 million real payoff had been destined for the Indians, not more.

When asked if outside groups had been bad-mouthing Ibama, such as local ranchers or farmers, chafing at the various constraints of the environmentally protected area surrounding the park, Jackson replied no, they had been neutral. Instead it was Funai, he lamented, which had always emphasized Ibama corruption, Ibama incompetence – and now Ibama was out. He admitted it would take a long time to get back in.

Shortly before I dropped him off for work at the town's small health department, and while we were cautiously navigating the last kilometer of dirt road that passing trucks had turned into a solid tunnel of dust, a small white car careened out of the cloud of traffic and almost broadsided us, despite the fact that we had our headlights on and were far from his side of the road. After the electric silence of the near-collision passed, I asked Jackson if he recognized the car, which he did, and if he knew the driver, whom he did as well, an old man who "should have his license revoked."

~ 11 ~

S O WHEN SHOULD a non-fiction writer's license be revoked? When he mistreats, twists, or distorts his subjects, perhaps? At another level, what about a government's license to govern – and responsibility to its own citizens? Do people always get the government they deserve, or do other factors come into play?

Here, on the wild western frontier of the United States of Brazil (an early name for the republic), questions of civilization and citizenship are ineluctably mixed. Without the promise of an agreeable civilization, why bother with citizenship? The Javaés Indians seem to discard both. If only the liberty to opt out or in, to decide where to belong, could be so easy for the rest of us.

These are oddly Lockean thoughts to have on the western edge of a new state as unformed as fresh riverbank clay. But to think of myself as a pioneer would be misleading, for I am far from the first Anglo to wonder about such things while in search, like Colonel Fawcett, for the Lost City of Z. While it's true that the trans-Atlantic migration flow, in a Eurocentric way, receives most of our limited historical interest, there is of course the sizable, if more recent, exchange among the Americas of the New World – in more than one way.

One of the earliest examples of intra-Americas exchange dates back to early 17th century when the first Jews to settle in North America, in New Amsterdam no less, arrived from Brazil, trying to keep one step ahead of the Inquisition. Portuguese Jews who had chosen conversion over death were called New Christians on the Iberian peninsula, and the Inquisition of the 1590's followed them all the way to Brazil to ensure they were not backsliding in the permissively New World. Tiring of persecution, they fled north to a nascent America.[60]

Among the few cases of organized emigration from – not to – the Big Dipper of the United States, most occurred after the American Civil War when Southerners not ready to give up a slave-based livelihood moved to the Bahamas or, in greatest numbers, to Brazil, where Emperor João Pedro II provided inducements for as many as twenty thousand Confederates to re-settle. (These included exemptions from military draft, guarantees of religious freedom, and land for only 22 cents an acre.)[61] A small town in the interior of São Paulo state, named Americana, was founded among others in a sea of stiffly waving cotton fields.

Such histories, however, fade away like messages written in sand before more contemporary floods. Understandably, the more recent migrations northward elicit more interest these days, and Brazilians have been no less eager to taste the northern fruits despite the longer trek to harvest them.

Take the case of Christian, the owner of Confusion Lake's main car wash. While three days of effort to breach Bananal Island had not defeated Atlas or me, they nearly defeated Fofão, who looked and sounded like an allergic, wheezing mess. So what better remedy than to visit the local car wash for a pleasantly superficial solution to her ailments?

Brazilian car washes are quite manual affairs, given that outside metropolitan hubs automatic scrub-downs are unheard of. Even then I should have realized we were in for special treatment when the sign read "Car Wash" without translation, and the owner insisted on practicing his English with me – a rare event in inward-looking and largely language-shy Brazil.

"Yesss. So full car wash it is? Undersides and on top? Inside and outside? That's really good. OK!"

Christian, a man with bright, upward-slanting features, had already attained after seven years of dedicated labor in the U.S. what has become, due to so many local impediments, the Brazilian dream: with enough savings from the North That Works, he had returned with enough capital to open his own business in Brazil, the Land of Family Opportunity. (For where else, outside of Italy, are so many businesses, due to the flimsiness of most societal ties, family-run?)

After settling on the price of twenty reals, I was startled to learn that it would take ninety minutes or more, as car washes back in Minas can take as long as two hours but usually cost a tenth of that, such is the slow dance of low productivity. One could logically expect a higher price to buy more or quicker hands, but after clearing out Fofão's rear compartment of trip miscellany, I reasoned why not dodge the hot afternoon sun while learning about a rare success story of social advancement? So I put out a bowl of water for Atlas and sat across from Christian in the shade of the covered lot, while a pair of workers laid into my scratched, dirt- and dust-caked car.

Christian's parable began with the key hurdle, a visa to the insanely prosperous part of the New World. His occupation as a distributor for Petrobras had helped him to secure a tourist visa to the U.S. as well as a two year leave of absence from work – as though seeking northerly advancement is something that local companies can help you plan for.

Drawn like so many others to the bright, twinkling star of Disney, he flew into Orlando where, with a week on his hands, he felt obliged to visit the amusement park that countless Brazilians have told me epitomizes the "country where everything works." As his English was "zeroed out," it took courage to practice a sunny "Hello, how are you?" on the first park employee he bumped into, who replied, "*Muito bem, e você?*" in fluent Portuguese, for she was Brazilian. This early encounter may have led Christian to realize that Florida is crawling with his compatriots, yet that was not the way he put it. Instead, while at the Orlando Airport, he overheard a small group of Brazilians claim that Atlanta was where good jobs were as common as weeds; whereupon he approached them, saying that he, too, was on his way to Atlanta. Such is the serendipity, eased by a few white lies, of life. They asked him if he had a place to stay, and then offered to share their contact information. When he arrived at the apartment on Atlanta's outskirts, he squeezed in among the ten Brazilians already bunking up there.

Such was his good luck that within his first month he met an American who, saying he prefers hiring any Latino other than Mexicans, took him on as a driver for his construction business. To test Christian's internal compass, he sent him out in a pickup truck with a mobile phone and called him up at intervals with new instructions, places to go. Christian enjoyed recalling with a kind of ipso facto pride how poor his English started out and joked that the only word he needed to be able to say was "OK," after he had written down the directions to such-and-such a place from a given page of the road atlas.

He was hired and soon delivering construction siding all over Atlanta. Then one day his boss called him into the office. Christian, afraid he was about to be fired, was taken aback when the manager handed him the keys to a new pickup and said he would have three Puerto Ricans working for him. But instead of delivering siding, he would now have to put the stuff up himself. Despite his lack of experience he was paid seven hundred dollars a house, two houses per six day week, very good money indeed. As he got more efficient and took on more houses, he started earning three thousand a week and feeling rich beyond belief. Things were looking up and up until another Brazilian felt the gust of his windfall and undercut him, guaranteeing that he could do the same work for a flat fee of a thousand dollars per week, without commissions. From this betrayal Christian concluded that Brazilians overseas could not be trusted, as all they want is enough money to set themselves up back home. "Business is business," his boss told him, and he was out of work.

The afternoon progressed quickly while Fofão descended through deeper and deeper levels of clean, to a degree unmatched, as far as I know, in her lifetime. When I realized that Christian was sharing his life's, and his family's, redemption story, the turning point in all their fortunes, his wife stepped out of their on-premises home with their two year-old daughter. He had met Luciana, originally from Goiás, at a

Brazilian barbeque at a Catholic Church in Atlanta even though both of them are evangelicals, or Protestant.

By this point my station wagon's inside door panels were receiving a voluminous coating of cleansing foam, a technology I had never seen before. "The dust is so intrusive here," Christian explained, "that it's the only way to get it out. Vacuuming just doesn't do it."

Christian, unsurprisingly, is a crack cleaner, though like most migratory challenges it didn't come automatically or easily. The period after being laid off was his most difficult in the States. He took on a number of low-paying jobs, including Pizza Hut delivery, while looking up various hiring agencies in the Yellow Pages. At one promising cleaning agency, the Mexican woman switched from English to Spanish, which Christian had learned in school. "It was, like, this is so much easier! I can actually communicate with my boss!"

Though the Mexicana, whom he called one of his journey's "saving graces," came through for him only after several months of growing debt, in the end this would be the job that secured his future. By now Luciana and he were a cleaning duo, and were given a large apartment complex where they were paid seventy dollars per flat, up to ten a day. When a satisfied client asked if he could clean more apartments on the side, Christian replied, "Don't worry. I manage my own time." And in a short while they were cleaning dozens of new apartments in other housing complexes during off-hours.

The turning point of Christian's tale came when the owner of the cleaning agency offered him an administrative job and a green card. His intent all along, unlike that of his money-grubbing compatriots, had been to receive just such an opportunity after gaining his employer's confidence, and now that it came, with the offer of working papers for him and his wife, he wept with joy. Yet the financial sacrifice of reverting to his first American paycheck of seven hundred dollars a week was too painful, so they turned down the offer and had to leave the company, to work full-time with the second agency.

After six more years of back-bending work, they returned to Brazil (for the first visit in as many years) to set up the car wash. Luciana confessed that she cried for weeks after repatriating, while Christian boasted that for the longest time he completed his sentences in English. This occasioned much ribbing from his employees, who seemed to delight in the tale, energized and inspired by such living proof that the national dream can come true – largely outside of the country, that is.

One of the most damning things that can be said about Brazilian governments and leaders – and about Latin American elites in general – is their inexplicable dereliction in not creating more opportunity at home, to capitalize on the abundant talent, drive, and good cheer of their own countrymen. Too often they are smugly satisfied with the anemic growth of the status quo even though it drives millions of their best citizens out of the county. That is the human potential-stifling tragedy of the current situation, with only marginal improvements demanded or received.

In a land were opportunities are far from open to all, the passivity of the underprivileged truly amazes. As the poet Elizabeth Bishop, who lived seventeen years in Brazil, once wrote: "Other people undergoing the same trials would surely stage a revolution every month or so."[62]

So why haven't they?

By now the sunlight was cutting horizontally through the billowing dust that runs, like silent dogs, after passing cars. Despite the deep shade Atlas was panting, ready for the breeze-catching benefits of movement. After Fofão received a light polishing, to modestly reduce evidence of the wounds to her armor from the Battle of Bananal, she looked her cleanest and most pristine in ages, a faint twinkle in the constellation of over-washed Brazilian cars. "American quality!" Christian exclaimed, to which I replied, "No, better."

For I couldn't help compare my own story with Christian's, and notice that my seven years in Brazil had been a good deal less visibly productive than his up north. My marriage had fallen apart, I had no children, and my high-risk, low-return creative foray – something I and others find difficult calling a career – was bearing little if any fruit, other than a few modest assignments here and there in Brazil.

When we pulled away from the most extraordinary Car Wash in Christendom, the image that stuck with me and wouldn't fade away for days was that of their pretty little daughter, playing intently in the grass and concrete lot surrounding their home and place of work. She had been born on American soil with all the attendant privileges associated with that geographical fact, including the right, someday, to those elusive working papers which her parents had turned down. They had named her Victoria, not after any queen or regal lily pad, but due to its Portuguese and Latinate meaning of victory, pure and simple.

~ 12 ~

VICTORY, FOR ATLAS AND ME, would be measured in different terms. Both of us foreigners, we were just trying to get by from day to day, avoiding pitfalls, and, if reasonably alert, learning a thing or two along the way. One often sets geographic goals for overland travel, of distances traversed or places to reach, when the true objectives are more inward than out and remain obscure for longer.

The outward challenges, at least, were becoming clearer. With our options dwindling, for the foreseeable future the only paved road north would be the dreaded Belém-Brasília, which happens to run along the old Tordesillas Treaty line. In other words, if the Pope's compromise had held over the centuries, they would be speaking Spanish to the west of the highway – including everyone on Bananal Island and, naturally, *Lago del Confusión* – and Portuguese to the east. Instead, the itinerant and hardy Bandeirantes, those manifold facts on the ground, had pushed the borders of Brazil as far west as the Andes, nearly tripling its continental spread to the Amazon's headwaters in Peru, or over three thousand kilometers further inland from the arbitrary demarcation line.

There continues to this day a certain arbitrariness to the Belém-Brasília itself. Constructed in the 1970's by the military governments of the time, it was part of a master plan, called the Program of National Integration, to populate the stubbornly wild Amazon region by re-settling half a million families from the poor, drought-stricken Northeast and, as a bonus, to keep all foreign aggressors at bay. Catchy slogans at the time included "Land without people for people without land" or, more succinctly, "Occupy it or lose it," and the military overlords even tried to force Caetano Veloso to pen a song in its praises, but he chose exile instead.[63] Due, in part, to the satellite imaging with which the U.S. Government helped their Brazilian counterparts to map the area in the 1950's, there are oft-resurrected rumors that the next place those crazy Yanks will invade is the Brazilian rainforest. (Over three quarters of Brazilians, until recently, were sufficiently paranoid to believe the country will be invaded for its natural resources.[64] But, then again, the neighborhood is a rough one.) Many international efforts to preserve the Amazon are seen in the same light, as a conspiracy to pave the way for foreign domination. So why shouldn't the Brazilians pave it themselves? (The climate of the times was captured by an American journalist, saying, "The Belém-Brasília was three years in the making. From the air it looked like a red thread running dead straight through the Green Hell of the rain forest.")[65]

At the time asphalting a route between Brasília and Belém had scant economic justification, with commercial volume at a minimum, but as a symbolic gesture it was grand. Not only did it physically extend the nation-building project of Brasília further north, with many of Brasília's laid-off construction workers laboring their way up the new road (a convenient way to empty the new capital's satellite favelas), but it symbolically ended the geographic isolation of Brazil's northern coast, which had been accessible from the rest of Brazil principally by hop-scotch plane or, even more circuitously, by boat.

Due to the dearth of towns or outposts between Palmas and Belém, I had to plan the coming days carefully. To lower the risk of getting stranded at nightfall by perforated tires or a broken axle, we left early in the morning, at first light. There remained only two more stops of medium import which could be counted on, if need be, for repairs or supplies. The first, named Araguaína, was five hundred kilometers away in northern Tocantins, while the second, Imperatriz, was a further day's trip and located in western Maranhão. Beyond Imperatriz it would take, in theory, one last long day pushing across the virtually uninhabited length of that bandit state called Pará, to its capital by the sea, the Belém of my dreams.

*   *   *

Our first full day of undiluted Belém-Brasília driving, to Araguaína, went uneventfully enough. There were fewer barreling trucks and madcap buses than feared, over a bumpy asphalt road that contained only several dozen deep potholes, nothing in comparison with those first, terrifying kilometers in northern Goiás. So much dust had permeated Fofão, even after Confusion Lake's deep clean, that the CD player started to play erratically, and soon enough the brake pad light flickered back on, signaling that not all was well with Fofão. Yet we had already passed the exit for Palmas, which, as an added disincentive for doing the sensible thing, lay one hundred kilometers out of the way to the east. Onwards!

Araguaína, like one-track railroad towns in the western U.S., strings along the dusty Belém-Brasília before fanning out, tentatively, to its parched sides. It is hard to see why anyone would establish a town on this precise patch of scrub land, other than as a pit stop.

The roadside Hotel Olyntho, at eighty-seven reals a night, was the most expensive since Minas, but it was a big open place, with shaded parking, a tall lobby, and a swimmable pool. Despite being the town's one business-oriented hotel, the hot water ran rusty, the Swedish sauna was busted, and the room's lighting so poor I could only read and write in the bathroom – where I pulled in a chair. During the drive's latter half the CD player had stopped skipping and spitting out CDs, which made me marvel how mechanical things can right themselves in the patience of time. But then a faulty wall outlet at the Olyntho shorted my power cable with a *poof!* and a flash, putting an end to such comforting thoughts.

In spite of all this, Hotel Olyntho could do no wrong for me. For starters the charming receptionist, a bright local brunette named Diana, worked diligently to allow not just one but two aliens into the establishment. Then the entire hotel staff piled outside in shifts to marvel at Atlas catching and retrieving balls. Diana could not have been friendlier, praising my erratic Portuguese, asking me how long I had been in the country, and even allowing me to take the lobby's local newspaper back to my room.

"Can I ask a favor of you?" I added at one point.

To which she replied, "Not just one, but several."

Diana recommended the town's main restaurant, the Praia Doce, where the seating was mostly outdoors and the waiters all found an excuse to pass by in order to inspect and comment on Atlas, who lay quietly by my feet. Here they were the adults who innocently asked, "Pitchy bull? Rottweiler?"

At one point a lowrider car with pulsating, booming sound rolled by, setting off a symphony of car alarms on both sides of the street. That is except for Fofão's, as she, like Atlas, is not an easily excitable beast.

When we left the next morning, I complimented Diana on her irrepressibly positive outlook. She had worked the night before, yet was up early due to a double shift and already cheerfully administering to guests' needs.

"Are you going to visit the Northeast after Belém?" she asked me.

"Yes, I hope so."

"I've never been to the Northeast, and would just love to go. Will you take me with you?"

"Of course," I replied without hesitating, "come along with Atlas and me. There's plenty of room."

"Oh, I was just joking," she blushed. "But I've hardly ever left Araguaína, and am just dying to."

When I asked her about assaults along the Belém-Brasília, she replied they were down of late – but, then again, she rarely leaves town, so who knows?

As we checked out she made a point of saying goodbye to Atlas, which is a sure way to win my loyalty and gratitude. After packing the car and paying the bill, I told her, "We'll come back after visiting the Northeast and tell you what it's like, alright?"

"Just make sure you come back," she replied with that enchanting Brazilian smile.

* * *

On our second day along the Belém-Brasília, one of the most-feared events occurred, fortunately, in one of the best of all possible places.

The road steadily deteriorated throughout the drive until it surpassed even the worst that Goiás had offered. And that was just the beginning of it. After we left Tocantins with real regret – for it was one of the finest discoveries of the trip, an up-and-coming state where the people are as marvelously open and warm as the cerrado landscape – the road went from bad to ridiculous as soon as we entered the western rump of Maranhão. Much worse than a poorly maintained dirt road is an asphalt track which has regressed, spottily, to a prior evolutionary state. All of a sudden entire swathes of gravel and dirt stretched across our path, sand moguls erupting from the earth as if from a bumpy beach track subject to tidal floods. Potholes were so prevalent that, for lack of space, they shamelessly hid behind the redundant speed bumps, whose down slopes became surprisingly deep culverts that eased in your tires before rudely slapping your undercarriage on the way out. When we approached yet another black diamond mogul-strewn trail, shimmering like a mirage in the mid-distance heat, I spotted some workers laboring on the shattered road ahead and felt relieved that some government official somewhere was actually keeping an eye on things, so they wouldn't spin hopelessly out of control on the Belém-Brasília. But, alas, they were only boys with makeshift hoes and shovels, shifting the sand from one place to another in order to extort a toll as you crawl past. (What boys do during the day is left to men at night.)

Whether it was due to sun, heat, neglect, or all three, even the warning speed rumbles, those concrete ripples meant to vibrate warnings to de-accelerate, had crumbled into flaky ghosts of their former selves, creating sharp-edged ditches capable of slashing sidewalls.

As we lurchingly, painfully approached the town of Imperatriz, or Empress, I was grateful to see the return of distance-to-destination signs, those medium-sized signposts of civilization that lull you into believing forward progress is possible. The first indicated only forty-eight kilometers to Imperatriz, below which the aspirational, mirage destination of Belém was pegged at a wistful six hundred and eighty-four kilometers away. Doing some behind-the-wheel arithmetic, I was surprised by a distance well above the six hundred kilometers suggested by my maps. Just as I was thinking "So what are, among friends, a few dozen more treacherous, virus-poxed kilometers while on vacation?," a second, equally faded sign leaned towards us as we passed. This one, incredibly, while feasibly reducing the distance to Imperatriz to thirty kilometers, jacked up the kilometers to Belém to a mind-boggling seven hundred and sixty-four with the know-it-all precision of an engineer.

Journeys are flexible affairs, varying jaunts along the time/space continuum, whose perceived length depends on the condition of your measuring mechanism, that over-taxed muscle called the brain. But this was too much even for my credulity to encompass. It was as though, in the space of a few minutes, the mighty Amazon had surged well above normal and swept Belém one hundred kilometers out to sea.

When we docked at Empress, tying our boat securely to some posts so that when the city moved, so could we, our first stop appropriately was at the Posseidon, the only abode mentioned in Quatro Rodas's normally exhaustive listings. As it was a high-rise, of a handful of stories near the open-grid downtown, I wasn't too hopeful, and in fact the receptionist was all smiles until I mentioned the lamentable detail of Atlas's existence, which immediately dented his professional optimism.

I went through the honor roll of reasons why Atlas should be a welcomed and distinguished guest, and the reception area's Seventies-style of plush, padded materials with gold and black metallic trim lent hope that there could be little to fear from Atlas's worsening the decor, to no avail. When I insisted, pushing the receptionist into an adjoining office to "ask the manager," the reply came back the same. As a last resort I tried to speak to Oz himself, who refused to emerge from behind the dusty curtain.

Earlier a kind passerby had mentioned that a rear tire was low; by the time I emerged, deflated, from the tiny lobby, so was it. At the last pit stop I had noted that the tire's pressure had been a spot lower than the others', and now the dreaded flat, instead of happening along the scorching length of the burning hot sand-way, had occurred helpfully – for us, at least – in the shaded half-circle entrance of Empress's one and only listed hotel.

Flat tires are so common in Brazil there exists an entire category of establishments to attend to them. They are called *borracharias*, whose root, *borracha*, means rubber, appropriately enough in the nation that practically discovered the stuff. Spanish speakers are often surprised by the *faux ami*, thinking that local highways are strung with pit stops for drunkards – not such a bad idea, considering the road conditions. Tire repair shops are often no more than filthy shacks that house pressurized air, various glues, plugs and patches, and, if you're lucky, a vise with a heating element to vulcanize patches onto inner tubes.

The borracharia behind the hotel was closed, the next one five blocks away. There I asked Nevon, the owner, if one of his men could walk back to help me put on the spare. A short, hardy fellow accompanied me in his flip-flops, and I was relieved that we could understand each others' Portuguese – probably because his street grammar was as basic as my own. At the hotel entrance I noticed that an elaborately festooned dragon lady, whom I presumed to be the Great Oz, was trying to free her spotless black BMW blocked by my stranded, dirt-coated Fiat, which required moving several other cars – a well deserved comeuppance. It was a good thing that Nevon had sent Flip-Flops with me as Fofão, once jacked up on the entry ramp's slight incline, decided to roll off to one side, nearly crushing the tire jack.

At the borracharia Nevon and his wife, who emerged from the quarters behind the small, dingy garage, could not have been more pleasant. They insisted that I let Atlas out, even though I feared he might scare the tire changers, and made a point of offering him water.

A nail, I was told, had caused the flat, which led me to speculate that I must have picked it up coming into Imperatriz, for it is in town where construction crews scatter extra nails around like calling cards.

"But no," Nevon replied after pulling out the metal sliver as long as a finger, "you must have picked it up several days ago."

How did he know? He pointed out that the nail was not only rusty, due to the humidity inside the tire, but its head completely sheared off with wear. Thinking back, I could have only picked up such a whopper of a nail on one of the improvised bridges after our failed visit to Cangaçu, three days before. Three long days before! If so, then the nail had visited Boto Velho and Bananal with us, the nail had traveled over five hundred kilometers to Araguaína, and the nail had only exacted its price at the end of a second day of excruciatingly daft driving, the worst the Belém-Brasília could offer, the moment Fofão had pulled into the only medium-sized camel tent for a day in any direction, in the covered half-circle of the Posseidon. Three long days before! – and only now our wanton past had caught up with us.

I shouldn't make a mogul out of an ant hill, but changing a flat in the equatorial midday sun; worrying about Atlas in his best winter coat of black fur; pulling everything out from the wayback to access the spare (not in very good shape itself); without mentioning the fear of getting stranded, robbed, or kidnaped on one of the most God-forsaken roads in the New World – well, you get the idea. In an attempt to alleviate my gathering paranoias, for the last several days I had taken to balancing my fedora, secured by an intricate system of shock chords, on top of the passenger head rest, in the forlorn hope of dissuading attackers with a second human silhouette. Whether it actually deterred an assault or not, I'll never know. What I can confirm is my embarrassment whenever I forgot to dismantle my faux companion before town or refueling stops.

In a driving country as rough-and-tumble as Brazil, a good *borracheiro* can use a degree in clinical psychology, such are the number of traumatized clientele (with or without imaginary companions, like Jimmy Stewart's full-sized rabbit sidekick in *Harvey*). Nevon deserved an honorary degree at least. He expertly calibrated all the tire pressures and, inspecting the worn inside circumference of the fixed tire, warned that it only had another three thousand kilometers to go. He further confirmed that a balding edge was due to the tire's prior poor balancing, and not from currently being out of whack. I gladly paid the modest doctor's bill of ten reals, and then Nevon's wife called me back so I wouldn't forget Atlas's water bowl.

At the unlisted Alcazar Palace – where it was still a royal pain to gain entry – I slept poorly that night. It was a Saturday evening, which typically is a noisy one in just about every populated corner of Brazil,* and I was worried about the last day's drive, the length of Pará to the elusive and receding destination of Belém. It would be our longest drive to date, mostly through deserted territory. My map indicated a dozen tiny villages, or one roughly every fifty kilometers, with one town-less void three times that length. Fortunately the flat had occurred just before such a thinly settled stretch, yet lack of sleep wouldn't help, as I was going to need all of my wits to avoid more flats or worse during the most challenging drive of the trip, almost all of it designated "precarious."

To complicate things, my Four Wheels map warned that, between the Pará state line and the final turnoff to Belém, the highway "is intensely trafficked by trucks with the road surface both spent and patchily repaired, with many potholes." Accordingly, I had planned the final push for Sunday, figuring that duelling trucks and buses during weekday peaks could make navigating the obstacle course much worse. But now, feeling contrarian, I worried about something else: what if we needed help while traffic was minimal, leaving us to the mercy of the Bad Samaritans? Things appeared bleak, any way you looked at them. While still dark out that morning, I wrote in my journal: "If I drive well today, I should be fine. If I don't, I'll be toast."

We mounted the Belém-Brasília bull by seven a.m., hoping for

---

* So strong is the Brazilian urge to party that in 1726 the Bishop of Olinda had to decree: "do not consent to the holdings of comedies, conferences, performances, nor dances inside any Church, chapel, or its surroundings," according to sociologist Gilberto Freyre in his magisterial work *Casa-Grande & Senzala*, p. 327.

cooler temperatures the first several hours out. Kilometer postings for this, per national maps, "major federal highway" had disappeared in Maranhão, so we were back to relying on signs indicating towns and distances ahead. Yet for the first hour after Imperatriz, I didn't see one sign at all. Could we be lost already? The sun, at least, seemed to confirm a northern bearing.

Fofão, after so many rude encounters with road brawls and rumbles, was making a whole cocktail of strange gurgling and rattling noises, and the brake pad light was continuing to flicker on, drawing my attention to the car's frailties and away from the road ahead. Just make it for one more day, I coaxed her, before an overdue check-up in Belém.

Only when we reached the first town called Açailândia, named after the local palm tree's purple berry-like fruit, was our trajectory confirmed. The road was no worse than the prior day's, with dry gardens of elephant traps followed by short stretches of deceptive, booby-trapped calm. Then more pygmy sand dunes, one tribe after another.

Although we had passed numerous federal highway police stations after mainlining the Belém-Brasília since Palmas, including one after Empress and another just before Açailândia, we had not yet been waved over for the obligatory document – or other – inspection at any of them. So it was with some surprise, soon after passing a Shell gas station on the far side of BerryLand and towards the top of a small rise, that I noticed a string of orange highway cones along the roadway's single dividing line, with a patrol car parked to the side. Only rarely have I encountered improvised checkpoints – as highway police tend to prefer the comfort of their roadside palaces – and knew that when exposed to the elements they have nothing better to do than to work, stopping traffic with alacrity. And that is just what happened, as one officer strode across the road to wave us over. Renato's warning, delivered back in Tiradentes, to avoid contact with the region's corrupt police returned with a flash somewhere between my neo-cortex and limbic brains and made me feel the hair follicles on the back of my neck.

The elder and slightly graying of the two troopers carefully approached the car from behind, which led me to think they probably don't see a Fiat station wagon very often in these parts. Somewhat reassured, he swung by to take a look at the front (confirming if both license plates agreed?), before reaching my window.

"Your documents and those of the car."

"Sure thing, officer."

Car documents are a challenge in Brazil. I'm still not sure if I understand them, but there's the title, which gets re-issued every year once you've paid all fees and taxes in full. There's an obligatory and minimal public insurance fee – which I'm told is next to useless in the event of accident – plus a big fat tax for what I'm not sure (for highway, or political, repairs?), both of which are due at a certain time depending on the last digit of your license plate. (Private auto insurance is another matter altogether.) Then there's the licensing fee itself, which you can't pay if you have any outstanding tickets and seems to fall due around tax-filing time. The problem is that you can pay all three in full and on time and still wait half a year for that year's renewed title to be issued, in which case you need to carry the prior year's documents plus all of the payment confirmations from the banks where you paid them. Now that I've written it down, suddenly it all seems so clear and simple.

So here we were in the month of August and all I had to show were last year's documents plus a flurry of little papers. "The receipts are folded inside, OK?"

"Where are you staying?" he asked, while fingering my papers.

"I was in Imperatriz last night."

"You're going to Belém?"

"Yes, I hope so – I mean, if the road permits."

"You're American?"

"I am. From the United States."

By now the younger patrol officer had sidled up to the car, at a slight remove behind his partner, and repeated "U, S, A," in halting

English.

"So you speak English?" I asked brightly, as a compliment.

"Where were you born?" the younger replied in Portuguese.

"In Boston, north of New York."

"BAW-ston," he repeated, imitating my pronunciation.

The elder one, all business, asked what I do for a living. I discarded replying *writer* or *journalist*, as I've seen the kind of trouble they can get you in other hot places such as Uganda, and offered "photographer" instead, with my single lens reflex camera in a bag under my legs should I need a prop for the part.

"Photographer. Professional photographer," the junior officer repeated, savoring each word.

He wore dark aviator glasses, the near-perfect image of a Californian highway patrol officer, which may be why Atlas took a good look at him and started to bark.

"No!" I told Atlas.

"Calm down, Rex," the younger one said coolly.

"Which brand is he?" the older one asked.

"He's a Labrador."

"Does he bite?"

"Never! But he does protect the car, like a house."

Then came the clincher: "Do you have your dog's documents?"

Under normal circumstances, at this point, I would have collapsed in defeat, spread open the flaps of my wallet, and pleaded for the transformative force of a large donation to the church of his choice, but then I remembered something. Luckily Atlas's mother had prepared us for just such a test, and had taken the precaution of getting his vet to prepare a vaccination report as well as a Testament of Health, both of which I retrieved from a file of maps and important documents (with notarized copies) stored behind my seat.

It may have confused the officers that the vet's address and where my driver's license had been issued were in São Paulo, prompting the question, "You live in São Paulo?"

"No," I replied, "I live in Minas Gerais. In Tiradentes."

"Minas, in Trindade."

"No," I corrected him as politely as possible, even though Tiradentes is the name of a national hero, with a national holiday in his honor, and is displayed clearly on both my title and license plates, "in the town of *Tiradentes*."

The older one had been noisily shuffling my various, irreplaceable papers around, and now handed them over to his younger partner with a pursed-lip look of "everything's in order here."

But, then, as if remembering one last detail, one last opportunity for small time graft, he asked, "So is the LD4" – or some such indecipherable jumble of abbreviations – "already paid?"

The worst pair of highway patrolmen I've encountered was in the state of Rio, where they pretended to have never seen a national driver's license issued from São Paulo, among other games, and when I refused to make their time and effort worthwhile, they responded to a call on their walkie-talkie by screeching away with all of my car and personal documents (including my passport), kicking back some dust along with a promise that they'd return within a few minutes, leaving me without identity or legality – for all intents and purposes, stranded and naked – on the side of the road. Made to wait for half an hour, I realized I had next to no recourse, for how could I complain at the next highway police station that I had been fleeced by their colleagues, when without documents I practically didn't exist? (Or worse: without Fofão's documents I could be taken for a car thief.)

Not caring to repeat the experience here, several precarious weeks further into the lawless backlands, I nonchalantly replied, "Sure thing, the receipts are all there." This led the younger officer to carefully open up the folded bank receipts once again, peering at them through his shades, before carefully folding them once again, one by one, and handing the small collection back to me.

Game over, I relaxed a bit and asked, "So how rough's the highway ahead?"

"There are some bad parts," the elder one replied.

"Where, in Pará?"

"There too. But Maranhão, before the state line, still has some bad stretches. Pay attention."

So I thanked them, and even though it was Sunday wished them a nice rest of the weekend.

"No," the elder one replied with a flourish of politeness, "– thanks to you."

~ 13 ~

PARÁ IS A STATE whose fame well precedes it. Dona Sonia of Jubuticatubus claimed it is full of bandits. Alfred of Araxá warned about the gold, wood, and women there. And with reason too: while deadly land disputes are common throughout Brazil, over a third of them occur in Pará.[66] The most publicized murder since that of rubber-tapper Chico Mendes in 1988 happened months after my trip, when the American Sister Dorothy Stang was assassinated in Anapu, just off the Trans-Amazonia swamp-way in Pará. While defending the rainforest's poorer inhabitants against land grabs by the local ranchers, she had been threatened so often as to plea for protection all the way up to the federal government, to no avail. Her assassin claimed in court he was paid $20 for the job.[67] Yet another place where federal laws don't reach very well.*

Falsified property titles are easy to come by in Brazil. One trick is a document aging process called *grilagem*, or "cricketing," whereby forged land deeds are placed in a box of crickets and, pronto!, insect-aged documents result. The practice is so common that the word grilagem has become synonymous with dodgy land grabs, which according to government estimates extend over twelve percent of national territory, an area larger than Mexico and Central America combined.[68]

The economic incentives are substantial, as a good hardwood tree can be clandestinely cut down for as little as one hundred and twenty-

---

* The killer was tried three times and served only eight out of a twenty-eight year sentence before an early release.

five reals, and, in a transformative process that even Midas would admire, within a year can be worth over eight thousand dollars in Europe. The Amazon region supplies over eighty percent of Brazil's wood and wood-derived exports totaling some four billion dollars, over half of which stems from illegally felled trees.[69]

Which makes you wonder: if those are the forces behind pilfered wood, what kind of tempests rage around women and gold in the bandit state of Pará?

The Trans-Amazonia highway, or BR-230, was built in the 1970's during the same military Program of National Integration. Originally intended to spread over five thousand kilometers from João Pessoa on the Atlantic to Boqueirão de Esperança on the Peruvian border, or further than from Dublin to Baghdad, less than half of it was built and very little ever paved. Over the years the western part, the Trans-Amazonia itself, has more or less reverted to bush, with practically none of the "highway" passable during the rainy season and large stretches of it now closed year-round. We had driven by where the National Integration highway would have traversed northern Tocantins. While the Amazonian part never reached the Belém-Brasília, its eastern terminus is on the same latitude as BerryLand in Maranhão.

Although conventional belief has it that any road construction in the Amazon is necessarily detrimental to the long-term preservation of the rainforest, sustainable development plans and reserves are encouraging more creative thinking on how to reconcile the short-term needs of subsistence living with the long-term benefits of forest preservation. Durable roads such as the Belém-Brasília, which have typically caused deforestation corridors fifty kilometers wide, may in the future be the most effective way to bring supervision, policing, and the law of the land to large swaths of forest that are otherwise vulnerable to speculation and the rule of the gun.[70] While monitoring of deforestation and fires has become more effective from the air with planes and satellites, enforcing laws is next to impossible without an inexpensive means of reaching threatened areas on the ground – while avoiding the sandy land mines of the ongoing, everyday roadwar.

As promised by the highway patrolmen, the last stretch in Maranhão was in fact awful, with even more sand mogul shushing and boys out in force than before, one of them so well outfitted as to be shifting the dirt around with a real hoe. The last town before the border, Itinga de Maranhão, boasted a bureaucratic sign promising two hundred and twenty-five "improved toilets" for the patient population.

The Pará state line came and went without notice, with no welcome sign or kilometer readings to signal the change. Only when we reached the first town did we see a state sign near the Fiscal Inspection Post, which are common at such jurisdictional transitions and direct you to stop if transporting "agriculture" or "animals." Most of these are quite voluntary affairs, but here in Pará, the bastion of illicit trade, on balance I was glad to see inspectors out and about, ready to flag down suspected smugglers and muggers. Even though Atlas had already passed his first documentation test, in order not to push our luck (do pets count as "animals"?) I had him lie down out of sight on the back seat – which became our routine at all subsequent state crossings.

Despite Four Wheels' warnings, the blacktop started out in a less precarious state than I had imagined. One novelty was long ruts in the soft asphalt, melted under the double pressure of heavy trucks and proximate sun, which deepened as you moved forward – once in their clutches, they don't let you out. The lowrider from Araguaína would have immediately bottomed out.

About two hours in – at a blistering average speed of eighty kilometers per hour – we passed a big truck whose Minas license plate placed it from my neighboring town of São João del-Rei, a discovery which made me almost deliriously happy. I can only explain my euphoria as the exaggerated hope that if we broke down on the "deserted" (per Quatro Rodas) and long highway ahead, at least this truck and this driver would take pity on us and stop to help. With over four and a half thousand kilometers behind us, the ten kilometers that separate our towns shrink to a negligibility that practically makes us neighbors, from the same band of brothers. Who knows? I likely know someone who knows him, creating the type of family and social circles that help protect the average Brazilian against all sorts of state and third party degradations. (The importance of an actionable network of contacts is recognized by its own word, *panelinha*, literally a small cooking pot.) So as we began to pass, I honked in a friendly beep-beep manner and, slowing down by his cabin, flashed a thumbs-up sign to the driver, while leaning over the passenger seat duly topped by my hat. He probably wondered why this decrepit and once again filthy station wagon was making such a fuss, but when I pulled ahead and he spotted my Tiradentes license plate, he replied with a few intimate blasts of his horn, the most welcome honks of the trip.

The surprises of Pará had only just begun. After Ulianópolis the small kilometer postings resumed, boosting the appearance of heaven-sent terrestrial care despite the three or four major potholes – so large that it would only take one visit to break an axle and end the trip – along every kilometer of road that otherwise looked deceptively calm. These trip-breakers, as I came to call them, were so impressive that even in direct sunlight I could not see the bottom of some of them. Their lurking prevalence also forced me to slow down for each and every approaching car, in order to maintain freedom of movement in case a trip-breaker yawned ahead. As a succinct road sign put it: "Don't speed, don't kill, don't die" – where to "speed" means anything above a trot.

Signs of commercial activity, from eucalyptus groves to large processing plants whose kilns burn eucalyptus logs into the *carvão* that fuels a billion Brazilian barbeques, were accompanied by visible costs of development. Road kills, for instance, were increasing from the occasional cat, dog, and armadillo to, here, a dead horse. Trucks with stacks of enormous tree trunks began to lumber by. Signs for Paragominas, the largest town en route and only thirteen kilometers off the mother road, lauded it as "The Land of Bauxite," the principal ore of aluminum, making it the first hint of the massive mining operations that march across the state, much of it managed by the Sweet River

Valley Company last seen near Belo Horizonte. In southern Pará, indeed, Vale runs such an enormous mining operation within the Serra das Carajás – which boasts the world's largest deposit of iron ore – that they privately operate a nine hundred kilometer rail line to the Port of São Luís in Maranhão, providing our first railroad crossing in weeks.

Even though Imperatriz sported a highway sign trumpeting, "Welcome to the Gate of the Amazon," we had yet to see a postage stamp of tropical forest, whose absence was felt well into Pará. Technically we were transitioning from cerrado to Amazon rainforest, but it didn't feel that way. The corridor of deforestation after three decades of unhindered effort had cleaned things out impressively along the highway, with pasture lands in the ascendant and what little agriculture we could see looking dry and spent, even along the riverbanks and the valley cusps of vereda life-lines. Each tiny town we passed looked as dry as sun-bleached bones, with gusts of wind billowing dust balls across the sand-swiped asphalt.

Then, after four hours of relentless aridity, everything suddenly turned a lush green between the frontier towns of Ipixuna do Pará and Mãe do Rio, several hundred kilometers short of our destination at the mouth of the mighty Amazon. The pastures turned golf-course bright, rimmed by abundant and bushy vegetation; trees started to gather in smaller groups, then larger and larger; and the dust-balls, in or out of town, blew away. More astonishing still, as soon as the roving clouds of dust dissipated so did the potholes. Quatro Rodas had gotten it wrong, or perhaps had sufficiently shamed the authorities into action, for we would drive a freshly re-paved road the rest of the way to Belém. Miracles exist.

It is difficult to exaggerate my stunned delight upon reading the roadside sign, "Welcome to Belém, the City of Mango Trees," for we had made it at long last, without breakdown or mishap. Months of planning had preceded this moment, along with a growing sense of impending peril, if not catastrophe, yet all of that seemed to fade away in the here and now, as rain washes away dust.

The image itself, of a city full of juicy, yellow-green mangos, was refreshing to the point of intoxication. Who, after all, had ever heard of a major city bursting with ripe mangos? Where a venerable canopy of fruit trees is so prevalent, their shade-giving properties so widespread in a city nearly four centuries old, that I had already been warned to take care where parking my car for the simple reason that in the equatorial Garden of Fruit mature mangos are known to fall with frequency – and can dent or ding your vehicle's thin skin. More treacherous yet, one resident would recount how a falling mango had bombed her on a drive down one of the spacious, tree-lined avenues, cracking her windshield. Such are the hanging fruit risks of a tropical paradise.

Lurking in deeper pockets of shade were even more surprises, including open man-holes. Not since Dar-es-Salaam in Tanzania have I seen so many missing man-hole covers, whose iron can be melted down for lucrative use elsewhere (mostly in China). There was a certain poetic justice to this, of course: that the end point of the famed Belém-Brasília, the object of desire that had floated ahead, like a receding mirage, ever and ever further away, should be the Capital of Potholes itself. Luckily some of the same lessons applied, from highway to city, such as the need for caution when overtaking a rickety rust bucket or diesel-fuming truck down the spacious two or three lane avenues, where tire-traps wait patiently in any suddenly clear passing lanes.

To be fair, since the city center appeared well served by substitute covers, they were the outlying and poorer neighborhoods that offered most of the existential voids. Yet even along the broad boulevard spokes emanating from the center, I found it safer to follow a local car as it careened down the obstacle course. Indeed, it felt like the old child's game of a swiveling board top designed for the maze-like meandering of your marble, which – with a jerk to the left, a jerk to the right – has to avoid the open holes or perish. One can only imagine the risk for motorcycles, whose lack of training wheels complicates. The same native who warned of windshield-bombing mangos once steered a tire through one of the iron rings, before momentum pulled her through. This, come to think of it, was not unlike our experience on the Belém-Brasília, whose own relentless and staccato momentum had carried us all the way, at last, to a safe port in the gathering storm.

Back in Araguaína I had discovered, to my astonishment, that Quatro Rodas includes an index of hotels and inns that accept dogs, and that – *miraculum caninus* – one such place was listed in Belém. In the vast interior of Brazil it was the first such civilized listing since southern Minas Gerais, multiplying Belém's virtues many times over in my estimation – which is saying quite a lot, as my esteem for the city was already considerable. I had already heard about Belém's abundant colonial charms, its dilapidated rubber-boom era structures, its intriguing mix of tropical and equatorial, of sweet and salty *ennui*, its regal place at the tail waters of the humid, damp, and life-stunned Amazon, a major port and gateway to and from the immense jungle of our imagination. So that it could boast, in addition to all of these exotic virtues, a hotel that officially welcomes pets – well, that seemed too good to be true.

The Beira-Rio Hotel, on the banks of the Rio Guamá tributary, is by Brazilian standards nothing short of a pet paradise. Not only were Atlas and I received like royalty by the seasoned receptionist, Viana, who summoned Atlas to the reception balcony in order to welcome him with a pat, but the hotel's displayed price list even included a line for "Animals," with a surcharge of thirty reals. Rather than looking dimly on such pet charges, I was actually thrilled to see the acceptance of animals institutionalized, written in black and white with next to no wiggle room – even though Quatro Rodas had cautioned that the Beira-Rio only accepts "small animals." In fact, the hotel appeared to have more restrictions on children than on pets, as one reception area sign read:

> For Minors Under 18: In accordance with Brazilian Penal Code, article 23, minors under 18 can only be accepted with the following documentation: [followed by a list of documents such as Proof of Parentage].

Though this is meant to discourage child prostitution, one of the enduring vogues in destination-tourism, it didn't for a moment dent my enthusiasm for the place. Quite the contrary: that pets enter more easily than children could only be a sign of deep and discerning taste.

We were put in a room with a river view and wall to wall carpeting only after I convinced Viana that Atlas would rather defame the name of his mother than soil one centimeter of their rugs. I promptly took Atlas for a triumphal parading around the grounds, which, while not large, were ample. Besides the swimming pool – regrettably, homo sapiens only – we encountered a sandy volleyball court to one side, various boarded walkways out to the restaurant, and docks on stilts over the river's edge. While the volleyball pit afforded sufficient space to toss a ball, the multiple bushy sand-areas along the wooden walkways provided many enticing areas for canine relief. Not to mention the front entrance ramp's tuft of jungle or the good sized parking area on one side, with many attractive, and dry-looking, tire rims and plant-beds on offer. Not even an uninvited guest in our bathroom, a small, free-loading cockroach likely fleeing the renovation on the floor above, could dampen our enthusiasm. It had taken us seven hours over almost exactly six hundred kilometers since Imperatriz to reach Belém, and our relief was almost as palpable as the rich, perfumed river lapping underneath the hotel's dockside restaurant.

Every time we passed the reception area, Atlas received a bigger hello than I did, whether it was Viana, Rosaninha, or the night clerk Marco. All of which made us feel, after anticipating the multi-splendored wonders of Belém during three weeks of unpredictable travel and months of preparation, that we had reached the languorous comfort and safety of a home away from home: we had arrived.

~ 14 ~

WHEN I CALLED JOACELI, our first panelinha contact since Minas Gerais, and told her we had just arrived after driving the length of Pará, her immediate question was, "So you weren't assaulted?"

A former French professor, Joaceli is both a friend of a friend from Tiradentes, as well as my friend's brother's mother-in-law, which makes her an excellent cooking pot connection. So I invited her to our riverside restaurant for a bite to eat that evening, to shoot the breeze, and prove we were in one piece, but when she arrived Joaceli had other ideas. She took a look around the hotel, introduced herself to Viana, and in no time was being called "Doutora Joaceli," the honorific gained when it became known that she is a retired professor from the nearby Federal University of Pará. In such a manner Atlas and I became grounded and connected, all but official guests of one of the world's most enchanting and steamy stove-top cities.

With the light slowly draining from the pearl sky in anticipation of the equatorial twilight that descends, like clockwork, at six p.m., Joaceli suggested we head down to Guarajá Bay to see the sunset from Praça Frei Brandão. It is an old square only recently transformed into Belém's showpiece, as the city for centuries turned its back on the river whose banks, one can imagine, were sordid, dirty, disease-sponges, below civilized attention like most ports. Over time, the growing city simply walled off the shifty, perilous river from view.

The counter-transformation began several years back when the riverside military installations were converted to civilian use by the state government, spruced up, and made to value the light – from the luminous river and the extensive lighting which turns the plaza into a colonial fantasy park at night. Near the Equator there is a damp, prehistoric quality to the sunlight, with both an intensity and puckish softening that suggests even the properties of light are unfixable. Add to that the slow march of the wide river at day's end and the palette multiplies: the warm pastels seeping across the horizon as the sun slumps behind the far shore's jungle wall, each evening re-touching a luminous watercolor that never dries.

Surrounding Friar Brandão Plaza is a motley mix of buildings, including the duplicitous Catedral da Sé, with a baroque exterior and a neo-classic interior; the Sacred Art Museum which, though the site of the city's first church, stood abandoned for fifty years before the recent renovation; the Forte do Castelo, a large stone pile that began as the settlement's first humble construction of wood and thatched roof, and passed through various life-stages, including a nursery, before growing up into a fort; and the House of Eleven Windows, a name with a charming Portuguese literalness to it, which belonged to a plantation owner until becoming a hospital in 1768, whose patients fled before the state's recent make-over.

Joaceli mastered in Linguistics prior to becoming a French professor and, behind her tinted glasses, carries an owl-like wisdom to her eyes, underlined by an insouciant grin curling thin lips. While she prides herself as the family's intellectual, her wry comportment and knowing posture reveal a certain tropical lustiness, as if accustomed to heat. When we passed a well-appointed park near her home, she explained how she walks early mornings with arm weights and often practices with her volleyball team, the Golden Crown Club of Pará, a band of ladies whose oldest member is seventy-four and for which Joaceli has played over thirty dedicated years.

Her husband, she sighed, has not taken care of himself quite so well and, after a stroke six years back, gave up smoking but not the twin vices of booze and fatty foods. A former director of a coffee processing plant, he subsequently suffered a cerebral hemorrhage and, though he could still speak, was incapacitated, requiring constant attention. "He had it coming!" Joaceli joked in a good-natured way, which relieved me from much need to sympathize. Yet the confidence made me feel welcome and tucked under the wing, eager to hear more from the likes of Doutora Joaceli.

Belém was founded on December 25th, 1616 as The City of Our Lady of Bethlehem, near the mouth of the Tocantins River, a hundred kilometers up the Amazon's main estuary.[71] Even though the explorer Francisco Castelo Branco's arrival is treated locally as the Second Coming, in reality it was a rush job, for the Portuguese had only the prior year expelled the Dutch from São Luís, eight hundred kilometers down the coast, and were anxious to claim the Amazon as their own[72] – even though none of it lay on their side of the Tordesillas line. The Spaniards, in fact, had the distinction of stumbling upon the Amazon first, during a deadly 1541 expedition from Quito, Peru, when Francisco de Orellana, in a desperate search for supplies, floated all the way to the river's mouth. (The subsequent descent, at all levels, of the "mad Basque" Lope de Aguirre was fictionalized in German filmmaker Werner Herzog's *Aguirre, The Wrath Of God*.) Attacked along the way by various tribes, Orellana claims to have fought one composed mostly of warrior women, whom he named after the Amazons of Greek mythology.[73] Like many a legend, it is too good not to be true, though it is just as likely the Indian men of the times, with long dark hair and no body hair or beards, looked achingly feminine to the hirsute Spaniards. (Many visitors nowadays make a similar mistake when meeting Rio's world-class transvestites.) All the same, Alfredo of Araxá's warning about local women is historically sound.

Castelo Branco named his makeshift fort in the Amazon's delta Feliz Lusitânia, thereby seeding another myth, of the "happy" Portuguese overseas paradise, aided by awed and grateful Indians. Originally a protective fort, Belém regressed within several years into both a slaving port and a trading center for cacao and other valuable backland spices called *drogas do sertão*. When the gold of El Dorado did not materialize, the colonists turned to Indian slaving, inciting attacks from the previously friendly Tupi-Guarani only three years after the first encounter. The Portuguese settlers, predominantly from the Azores, quickly became dependent on the *filhos do mato*, or "sons of the forest," to collect wild vanilla, indigo, cinnamon, sarsaparilla, and cacao for export to Europe. But as the slaving became less abundantly easy, the Portuguese had to strike deeper and deeper into the Amazon for human material, carrying the white man's diseases with them. It was a northern repetition of the Bandeirantes' forays into the south-central interior, and may well have persecuted some of the same Indians who, fleeing down the Tocantins River valley to escape the Bandeiras, eventually succumbed to the river-borne *Belenenses*.

The end of Belém's first boom-and-bust cycle came with the decimation of the local Indian population that, along with similar trends elsewhere, persuaded the Portuguese Crown to issue a decree in 1755 to re-animate growth, giving every white who married an Indian woman "one axe, two scissors, some cloth, clothes, two cows, and two bushels of seed."[74] (This is as close as Brazil got to a Homestead Act, focused more on settling Indian women than the land itself.) The Portuguese name for the half-breeds from these sanctioned unions – an effective, assimilatory form of colonization, if there ever was one – is *mameluco*.

For centuries Brazil remained an agrarian society, with the preponderance of power and wealth in the countryside, the towns and villages no more than appendages of convenience, not even fit as marketplaces. Most fazendas were self-sufficient, and while the large landowners owned houses in coastal cities they were used almost exclusively during religious festivals. Colonial visitors were constantly surprised at how empty the towns were, as the absentee homeowners tended to their casa grandes and plantations back inland.[75]

Joaceli's ancestors followed a similar pattern, delving into the interior where the money was to be made and only gravitating back to cities in the last generation or two. One of her maternal great-grandfathers was an ambitious professor in the southern state of Santa

Catarina when he set his sights on the daughter of the Baron of Barcarena, a sugar plantation owner with hordes of hectares and slaves. When the professor realized that a courtship would be impossible without greater means, he struck out for the Amazon during the rubber boom to make his fortune, which he did, finally able to marry his love after amassing forty *contos de reis*. The married couple returned to commerce in the Amazon, where their *seringais*, or rubber plantations, were so large it took forty-eight hours to circle them by boat. When his wife died before him, the Rubber Baron inscribed on her grave stone:

> It was my glory to adore her
> And my martyrdom to lose her

Their daughter, Joaceli's grandmother, was the only female teacher in the interior town of Afuá on the far side of Marajó Island, where her husband became the local judge and, later, chief of staff for the governor of Pará. He wrote many a love poem to his wife, Joaceli relates, and the town's courthouse and school bear their respective names. While less flamboyant, Joaceli's paternal grandparents also heralded from island towns of the interior, linked to each other by ever-flowing highways of water.

Only when Joaceli's father floated, along with a portion of the family's growing cacao wealth, to grade school in Belém did city life re-enter the family history. It wasn't easy, as Grandfather had to contract a boatman to take his son to boarding school. While equipped with a sail, the canoe often needed paddling when the wind failed. At night they slept on narrow river beaches, where the boatman would bury himself in sand and cover his face with a straw hat to ward off mosquitoes. Yet Joaceli's parents still spent most of their lives in Abaetetuba, fifty kilometers upriver from Belém, where her father became mayor and, being a devout man, built the town's main church.

Indicative of modern times is how Joaceli's eight siblings achieved higher education with a good deal less effort. An elder brother became a doctor and moved to Manaus, fifteen-hundred kilometers upriver. Another brother, an engineer, moved to Porto Velho, near the headwaters of the Amazon's Rio Madeira. Yet another, a painter, studies at the Belas Artes in Rio. Two sisters, like the father, were pharmacists in the interior, and the last two brothers are local businessmen. To culminate the family's rapid urbanization over two generations, Joaceli's one daughter lives in the mega-city of São Paulo. When I told Joaceli that I have visited Manaus twice – never by car, as it is inaccessible by land except from Venezuela – she jealously asked which city I preferred. Fortunately my reply was the correct one.

Belém's history, despite the incentives for miscegenation, was not a harmonious one. Following years of national turbulence, caused by the regency during Dom Pedro II's minority, a dispute among Belém's ruling elite over the appointment of a provincial president opened the way for a popular rebellion among the Indians, the mamelucos, and the *caboclos* (black and Indian blooded), who comprised a large majority. It became known as the Cabanagem War, due to the *cabanos* or poor riverbank dwellers, who took the city after nine days of bloody fighting in 1835. Led by a 21-year-old from Ceará, they declared independence from Brazil until a British naval blockade, along with the reinforcement of several thousand federal troops, put paid to the rebellion, ending in the re-capture and nearly complete destruction of the city. (Recalling the recent adage: in order to save the city, it had to be destroyed first.) During this and the subsequent four year campaign to eradicate the Cabano revolt throughout the interior, as many as thirty thousand people were killed, or over a fifth of the province's population.[76] Brazilians are not quite as pacifist as they make themselves out to be.

One evening Joaceli took me to another sunset spot called Ver-o-Rio – with the river suddenly accessible, sundowns appear quite popular. There we found a recently installed Memorial to Peoples of Indigenous and African Descent. Despite the fact that the Cabanagem rebels, during their brief reign, never tried to abolish slavery – with the Cearense leader in fact putting down an internal slave insurrection[77] – a statue of a "Negro Patriot" explained that he was "one of the leaders of the Cabanagem War (1835-1840) and brave defender of the abolition of slavery." The emphasis on African slavery is intriguing, as it played a relatively minor role locally, but then why not share the feel-good credit for such a good end?

With Indian slavery outlawed by the 1750's – around the time of those incentives to settle land with Indian wives – the only official slaves in Belém eighty years later were blacks, but the local economy, lacking the Northeast's lucrative sugar cane, couldn't support many of them. Only later, during the Amazon rubber boom seeded by Charles Goodyear's improved vulcanization process in the mid-19th century, did large numbers of Northeasterners, among them freed slaves and mulattos fleeing the sertão's cyclical droughts, migrate to the Amazon to become *seringueiros*, or rubber tappers,[78] bringing with them a precious cargo of Afro-Brazilian habits in food, dance, and religion, strong new tributaries to the Amazon's broad cultural sweep.

During the height of the rubber boom that straddled the turn of the century, when Brazil was the world's only exporter of high-quality natural rubber (accounting for forty percent of her exports),[79] massive wealth flooded Belém. The elegant city became known as "Paris of the Tropics" – in more than one way, as the wealthy took to sending their dirty laundry to Paris by boat. Both Belém and Manaus boasted electric streetcars, piped water, telephone service, and electric street lighting when they were luxuries in the rest of the country.[80] The then-governor, Antônio Lemos, wisely invested in city planning and public works, creating "everything that is beautiful in Belém today," Joaceli told me.

The party was short-lived, as most are, after an English botanist smuggled seventy thousand rubber tree seeds packed between dried banana leaves to London and from there to British Malaysia, where they started to yield in sufficient quantity by 1910 to break the Brazilians' natural rubber monopoly.[81] Belém never recovered, and has drifted inexorably into a somnolent decline barely ruffled by lumber, nuts, or nascent tourism.

With some frequency Joaceli enjoys traveling up the Amazon – where one sister, until recently, lived near Santarém – to help her daughter find craftwork to sell in São Paulo. The Amazonian frontier, like the river itself, occupies a large space in the imagination of Belenenses, as became clear one evening when Joaceli explained the Legend of the Boto, the same dolphin species I had encountered off of Bananal Island, which mostly frequents the Amazon, Ganges, and Yangtze.[82]

It is widely believed that the Boto, the largest of the Amazonian dolphins, regularly seduces young river girls, who then bear children whose paternity, officially, is unrecordable. As legend has it, in the first hours of night the Boto transforms itself into a good-looking young man, tall, strong, a good dancer and drinker, who shows up at parties, flirts, converses, and then punctually attends rendezvouses with women under his spell. In other words, the perfect date. His only defect is that before dawn he jumps back into the water and sprouts fins.

Filho de boto is such a common parentage that Joaceli has met families in the interior who proudly introduce all of their children, including the "Boto's son" who is not ostracized in any way. She recalled one father saying, "this one is mine, that one as well, this one's the Boto's." With a burst of laughter Joaceli told me how the boto has saved many a marriage – for what husband, no matter how manly, could be jealous of a pink dolphin? – and that one visitor, a Parisian woman, had bemoaned the lack of Botos back home in France.

During that first evening in Belém, Joaceli took me to a recently spruced up dock area to taste some regional dishes, which I enjoyed so much I returned the next night for seconds. As usual, the peculiarities of local food serve insights into the surrounding culture.

Belém and Pará claim to have Brazil's most distinctive regional cuisine – which may well be an understatement. One of the more representative restaurants is called Lá em Casa, whose owner, Ana Maria, insists that Amazon cooking is the only truly Brazilian cuisine, untouched by European or African influences. One unique sauce, a native specialty for over five hundred years, is called *tucupi*, carefully prepared from the juice of the wild manioc or cassava root, whose lethal cyanic acid requires painstaking boiling. The milky tucupi is then stewed with a kale-like paracress called *jambu*, which has a tingling analgesic effect on the lips and is reportedly an aphrodisiac – along with most other Amazon herbs, it seems. This may explain why I hurried back, after consuming the traditional Pato no Tucupi the first night to try the Pato do Imperador, or Emperor's Duck, on the second. The royal dish was created in honor of the Japanese Emperor Akhihito's visit to Belém, which contains the second largest Japanese-ethnic population in Brazil after São Paulo. The Emperor's Duck, cooked with the local fowl *marreca*, is a somewhat drier dish served over several leaves of Swiss chard, but no less tingling to the lips and taste buds.

Belém and São Paulo, it seems, have a lot in common. Not only did their development follow similar paths, as distribution centers for agriculture and Indian slaves from the interior, but their subsuming of Indian culture and blood under the colonizers' project was far more extensive than elsewhere. Mamelucos and enslaved Indians made up an impressive part of the Bandeiras – since warring as opposed to farming was a more attractive option to most indigenous males – as they did among the raiding parties of Belenenses into the large shag rug of the Amazon. In both cities the pidgin form of the Tupi language remained the dominant colonial tongue for far longer, into the mid-18th century.[83] Both regions served as economic magnets, with rubber in the north and coffee in São Paulo, bringing hordes of European immigrants to their shores, along with the internal migrations of poor Northeasterners that only recently abated in São Paulo.

Jesuits, furthermore, played critical roles in both geographies, until the Order was expelled from Brazil (and Portugal) in 1759 for creating "a state within a state." São Paulo itself was founded mid-16th century by two Jesuits, Fathers Nóbrega and Anchieta, in search of Indians to save instead of enslave, who built a Jesuit school there. The Jesuits' Santo Alexandre Church, part of the refurbished Sacred Art Museum, is Belém's oldest standing place of worship. Aldeias, the original mission villages or reductions, were built by Jesuits to protect Indians from Portuguese slavers. By 1740, as many as fifty thousand Amazon Indians resided in Jesuit and Franciscan aldeias, in greater numbers than the total population of Salvador, the nation's capital and largest city at the time.[84] So intertwined were their fates that both Indian slavery and the Jesuits themselves were banned within one year of each other – to theoretically end the protective segregation.

Yet historical parallels only go so far. The results in today's terms could not be more different: whereas São Paulo is the most industrial and industrious region in Brazil, Pará remains the bandit state, the long-time outpost of jungle riches and lawlessness.

One fine morning Joaceli introduced me to the Ver-o-Peso Market, or "see the weight" as originally shouted by the colonial duty collectors, down by the old port. Over a thousand stands line the waterfront, anchored by the wrought-iron Mercado de Ferro which was imported piecemeal from England in the 19th century. Ver-o-Peso is one of the world's great markets, commercializing a fraction of the Amazon's unimaginable cornucopia.

Among the cashews and Brazil nuts, which come dry, toasted, or ground, can be found the ubiquitous cacao, in the green and yellow colors of the Brazilian flag, whose insides are full of large, wet whitish seeds. Besides jambu, there's *jambo*, the ruby-red fruit of the *jambeiro*. The star-shaped carambola as well as *graviola* fruit are prevalent, along with custard apples and the black currant-like *jabuticaba*, whose grapes grow directly from the trunk.

Joaceli has her preferred stands, and spoke with each owner as though to a dear if distant cousin. We stopped at one of her favorites, offering an assortment of palm fruits. Among them was the *pupunha*, or peach nut, and the assai grape which explodes from the palm's trunk in grape-laden strands like frozen fireworks. From its cherry sized pit is extracted oil for, among other things, a homemade anti-diarrheal remedy. The fruit's pulp is used to make *vinho de açaí*, a juice which is sold for its energizing qualities on every sun-baked street corner.

This wouldn't be the Amazon's most famous market without a

mind-boggling array of herbs and concoctions, in surfeit at our next stop. Here was dried cat's claw, from a vine prevalent in the westernmost state of Acre, whose antioxidant and anti-inflammatory properties are used in some HIV treatments. There was *muira puama*, an aphrodisiacal plant whose efficacy is starting to be felt outside of Brazil. But my favorite were the little pots of "natural Viagra," a concoction made up of muira puama leaves, the *catuaba* seed of a medicinal flowering tree from the Atlantic rainforest, and powdered *guaraná* seeds – along with the cut, dried, and ground penises of both the coati (of the raccoon family) and the river dolphin (whose Boto-virility is beyond question). Guaraná, the famed Amazonian energetic drink, is a carbonated soda as widespread as Cola in Brazil. It was first developed by Indians who used the paste in stick form, by scraping off shavings with the dried tongue of a large fish before mixing them with water and sugar.

Almost done, Joaceli and I stopped by the Mercado de Ferro to pick up some fresh shrimp for lunch. Inside we passed tablefuls of yellow fish called *filhote*, or "puppy," the fresh-water fish *tucunaré* with a false eye on its tail, and the sea-faring *xaréu* whose meat was the reddest, most bovine I've seen.

Terezinha, Joaceli's maid, relieved us of our purchases upon entering her home, which is kept cool by closed shutters and dark wood throughout, including *acapú* furniture and parquet floors of *macacaúba* wood lightened by strips of *pau amarelo*, or yellow wood. After introductions, Joaceli took me on a tour of the garage converted into a small food-processing laboratory. Her daughter's big-city business is called Frutos da Amazônia, and sells a variety of sweets containing *cupuaçu*, *bacuri*, and Brazil nuts, which Joaceli plans to more efficiently garage-process prior to shipping in bulk to São Paulo.

Joaceli's maiden name is Guerreiro, or warrior, and I could see why: as a protector of people, traditions, and culture. (It wouldn't surprise me if her ancestors included an Indian warrior or two.) While preparing lunch, she and Terezinha had such an easy banter, one's memory seconding the other's, that I asked if Terezinha, whose diminutive height seemed to augment her cheerfulness, had been with her for a long time. Sixteen years, Joaceli replied.

"I helped her to buy her house recently. It's not a very big house, and needs some fixing up, but it's Terezinha's first house of her own and she's quite pleased with it," Joaceli commented within earshot of Terezinha. "It is being renovated now, with everyone chipping in. Her son – who's a Mormon and a very good boy – is contributing the sand, I'm paying for the cement and the mason's work, and the son and his church members are donating the labor.

"She deserves it, poor woman, as her husband was murdered last year. Yes, I know – stabbed to death. He was a big man and when a young thief tried to steal his tools, he resisted successfully without injury to himself. But an hour later the thief returned and stabbed him from behind, killing him. Just over a set of tools!"

In short order Terezinha emerged from the kitchen with a dish that has been served in Pará for generations. It is called Assai with Shrimp, the *açai* soup served in the traditional *cuieira* tree gourd – with a touch of sugar and a few floating ice cubes – and sprinkled with granulated cassava meal to add texture. The fresh water shrimp, after being steamed and cooled, is served separately. Prior to each spoonful of the refreshingly cool and tarty assai, you take a shrimp, peel it, and pop it in your mouth. It is a slow, steady meal, both delicious and sociable, a perfect antidote to the simmering, equatorial high noon.

It had taken over five thousands kilometers of haphazard and unsettling travel to become so grounded, yet I felt honored: from boiling pot to panelinha.

~ 15 ~

YOU'LL BE WONDERING what happened to Atlas in all of this, and with good reason. The unavoidable truth is that in big cities – with Belém at well over one million inhabitants – even the most sophisticated and well traveled of dogs is not everywhere welcome. The newly renovated dock complex didn't allow dogs with or without leashes, and I didn't even try to take Atlas to the misleadingly named "There, at Home" restaurant. Come to think of it, I just didn't see many dogs in Belém, purebred or not. The day I took Atlas into town for a walk around Praça da República, we passed only one other dog walking his master. Some military police called out a few questions as we sniffed by, but then Atlas and his good-sized chest always incite the interest of body-building types.

So Atlas stayed back at the Beira-Rio most of the time, keeping fort. I'd like to think after so many curves and bumps along the Belém-Brasília that he was getting his land legs back, but this was demonstrably not the case. The maids were afraid to service the room with such an active beast behind the door, which was just as well as they might have unwittingly let him out to terrorize the guests, so I always informed them when we were going out for a stroll or would be dining together downstairs at Chez Beira-Rio. After walking the grounds and playing catch by the volleyball field several times, we explored down the road one day, even though this caused one of the hotel's security men to hurry after us at a discreet distance. Perhaps Atlas's chest was not so developed as to deter all-comers.

It was high time to take Atlas on another adventure, something on the order of Bananal Island, and it didn't take long to settle on just such an opportunity, another isle no less. Belém sits across from Ilha de Marajó, the largest delta island in the world, bigger than Switzerland. What towns it has hug the Pará River (the Amazon's main outlet) like crabs to the coast, while its few kilometers of roads are only passable outside the rainy season which runs late, from February to May.

As I doubted an organized tour would take Atlas aboard, I asked Viana at the front desk about car ferries and the like. But Viana, bless his heart, is truly a dog's best friend and persuaded me that an excursion, booked through the hotel, would work just fine: I could leave Fofão in the hotel's parking lot and the tour van would take us to the passenger ferry. He phoned one such outfit and, speaking to the head of sales, persuaded her to take us on. Now Atlas could return almost within striking distance of his Central American birthplace.

The hotel, typically, went out of its way to have breakfast ready for me at five-thirty the morning of our departure. But then the van didn't arrive. So we waited. As the night clerk Marco is a good deal less alert than Viana, and immediately ran out of options, I pulled out the sales rep's number which I had copied as a precaution. Dona Mara assured us we hadn't woken her, and sure enough within fifteen minutes the driver careened into the entrance half-circle in a metallic turquoise minivan in which, after loading up, off we sped.

As the ferry was scheduled to leave within ten minutes, Augusto – short, affable, and determined – ignored most red lights on the way to the port and, while flooring it, chatted easily in the stunned city silence of dawn. Atlas and I would have enjoyed the ride thoroughly if Augusto hadn't asked about Atlas's documents, as the port might require them. I replied, yes, I had them – back in my car at the hotel parking lot.

Since Augusto had phoned ahead to the captain, there appeared to be little risk of our missing the boat. Yet when we arrived the ferry boat was full, the dock-side empty, the gangway ready to be withdrawn. When Atlas and I got out, with one bag for me and one for him, the problem didn't turn out to be documents, it turned out to be Atlas. The captain, standing athwart the gangway, didn't want to take Atlas aboard without a cage. And so several of the crew, plus Augusto, promptly fanned out in search of a good-sized box to put Atlas in. But none were to be found at this early hour and nor were any dock workers about, the warehouses still locked.

I tried to explain to the captain that Atlas is a rather tame dog, who wouldn't harm a soul, that his breed is so smart they serve as seeing-eye dogs, etc., and that he is, modesty apart, flawlessly trained. And to prove it, amid the turmoil of the ready-to-leave boat, the bustling crew, with most of the passengers watching and wondering what was holding up their departure, I told Atlas to sit.

I should also mention that some early morning port-mutts, over to one side or another, had already started barking at the presence of a black-coated interloper with beady eyes and bright pink tongue; which normally would distract even the best intentioned dog given that the port-hounds were obviously taunting him, making fun of his leash and the company he keeps.

So with all eyes on him and much commentary from the ferry's double-decker peanut gallery, Atlas waved his tail once and – sat.

This produced no immediate effect on the cast of characters, though it quite possibly opened a few chinks into the dungeon of the captain's thinking. Augusto was on his cell phone by now, perhaps to Dona Mara, and then conferring with the captain, while I stood and Atlas sat, waiting. Whether or not a monetary promise was made, I don't know; in any case Atlas and I were ushered onto the lower deck and made to take a seat near the engine, in steerage, but we didn't mind.

The captain, pleasantly enough, came by to shake my hand in welcome and warn me that a cage would be necessary for our return. After we settled in and the boat pushed off, a graying and agreeable old man, who lives in Belém and has a weekend home on Marajó, came by to say that he could see that Atlas is not an aggressive dog from all of his tail wagging on the dock. And yet every other passenger on the way to the head, upon seeing the tip of Atlas's nose or paw or tail visible from under my seat, gave us a wide berth or returned mid-ship, in order to retake the far aisle to the stern.

The crossing itself started out calmly, as most do, but the ocean swells from a hundred kilometers away soon had us rolling in the spray. Three hours later, after successfully traversing and descending the Amazon's mighty Pará River, we landed on Marajó Island where, distracted by the novelties of getting there, I could not have been more in the dark on what awaited us.

Marajó is very much a sedimentary island, built up over millions of years by tons and tons of Amazonian flotsam, detritus, backwash, and dirt. When the sea is high, the waters surrounding the island are tinted green; when the river swells, they turn a light brown – as they were now. When the two forces are equivalent, the *pororoca* is born, a tidal bore phenomenon whose waves, several meters high, march upstream, attracting a surfing competition every March during the full moon. The name Marajó, full of hope, means "sea barrier" in Tupi.[85]

It is also one of the longest inhabited corners of Brazil, where pre-historic Indian tribes thrived for millennia before summarily disappearing. While some of the earliest known pottery in the Americas, called Tapajônica, is found further up the Amazon, near Santarém, the most sophisticated ceramics come from Marajó, where the ancient indigenous culture reached its apogee. Here, to escape the habitual floods, the Marajoara built earth platform *aterros* and buried their dead in elaborate funereal urns – to protect them, presumably, from a soggy afterlife. Their most productive phase spanned from roughly 400 to 1350 A.D., when hundreds of aterros were raised around Lake Arari in northern Marajó. After the Marajoara mysteriously petered out, their successors the Aruãs were first encountered by 17th century raiding parties from Happy Lusitânia and, after being found guilty of trading with the arch-enemy Dutch, were driven off the island and made to flee further up the Amazon, where all traces of them washed away.[86]

What remains, much of it still buried, is mostly pottery, including vases, urns, plates, and other household objects, with stark geometric designs in relief. The designs include symbolic frogs, birds, eyes, crosses, axes, and the human form. Many of the vases themselves have lovingly anthropomorphic shapes of rotund bodies and splayed, beady-eyed heads, whose complex workings indicate an elaborate ceremonial life. One of the more interesting household objects I saw was the *tanga*, a rounded clay shield in the shape of a triangular patch that is worn over the woman's crotch. It is no coincidence that the name is the same as the provocatively small bikinis worn on Brazilian beaches, where the Tupi tradition of near-nakedness lives on.

Atlas and I were met in Camará by Joãozinho in a slightly more ample midivan, which filled sufficiently to push Atlas and his forty kilos onto my lap in the front seat, from where he could survey our new surroundings with ease. When, on our approach to Salvaterra, we came upon our first inky-black water buffalo ambling into town, Atlas barked, causing Joãozinho to smile. He told us that the first water buffalo arrived on Marajó by shipwreck, when a French galleon on its way from India to French Guiana foundered, with some of the cargo swimming ashore. Well suited to water-logged environments, there are now four varieties of buffalo on the island, with as many as six hundred thousand shipwreck descendants – greatly outnumbering human residents, as sheep do in Wales. Water buffalo lack sweat glands and need to wallow in water to hydrate their thick skins. As such, they are capable of floating around for days while living off a rich diet of aquatic muck. When not taking long, luxurious baths they do much of the heavy lifting on the island, such as pulling carts, and are the principal form of transportation during seasons wet or dry, ridden by policemen, cowboys, and children alike. Not only does the local fire engine take advantage of their locomotive powers, so do the military police, whose buffalomobile was one of the finest and most colorful carts I've seen, suitable for a homecoming parade.

I asked Joãozinho if they can be as aggressive as their African cousins, but no, he explained, here they are mostly domesticated, with some even serving as pets. And when the children tire of their pets, the pets are eaten, for buffalo steaks "have twelve percent less fat, ten percent more protein, and fifty-five percent fewer calories than beef." When I chided Joãozinho that the numbers don't seem to add up as protein is caloric as well, he assured me the statistics are official. "Well, if that's the case," I replied, "then I'm going to eat more." Whatever its dietary content, I tried a local delicacy called Cowboy's Fry at the hotel one evening and, though smothered in a gooey, bland cheese called *catupiry* worshiped by most Brazilians, the buffalo cut was quite tasty.

The eastern half of Marajó, which peaks at only twenty meters high, works tirelessly to stay above the Amazonian floods. Most towns, subsequently, line the east coast, where ranching is the principal activity, followed by pineapple and palm fruit cultivation. The slightly drier soil doesn't ensure easy transportation; we passed a turnoff to Cachoeira de Arari whose seventy kilometer dirt road, during the rainy season, requires a truck with a half a ton of rocks and twenty people to get through, each way.[87] The forests that cover the island's western half are thick and often submerged. Local custom has it that one needs to ask the forest's permission before entering which, if overly sodden, it denies.

The last leg of our midivan's itinerary was a short ferry crossing over Rio Paracauari to Soure, the island's oldest settlement. Here, as we entered the rough, *mangueira*-lined streets, I saw a group of children practicing a local version of cricket, called *raquete*, played with a wood bat and tall, empty oil cans – evidence of the seafaring influence of the British. Homes vary from squat mud adobe houses covered by densely thatched palm fronds, to railcar wood-slatted homes with slanting tin roofs, to exposed brick or stuccoed buildings graced by Mediterranean tiles. Closer to downtown, I was surprised to see a pale blue building in tropical Art Deco style, complete with stucco eyebrows over the windows, ornamental ocean liner balustrades on flat roofs, and decorative portholes. Joãozinho proudly explained that Soure's grid plan was designed by the same urban designer, Aarão Reis, responsible for Belo Horizonte's. As we drove down an empty central avenue lined by tall mango trees draped in Spanish moss, Joãozinho proudly called it Soure's "Fifth Avenue." Heaving a sigh of relief, I called out, "At last I feel at home!"

It pains me to relate that I almost killed Atlas that afternoon. (Something about the isolation of islands brings out the insistent and obsessive in me.) Having reached our hotel by late morning, I decided to explore the small town of Soure before lunch and brought Atlas along for the walk. I took the precaution of putting on his rubber-bottomed booties – having read that the dreaded bicho de pé is prevalent on Marajó – and while Atlas got used to them, the natives did not, as his exotic footwear occasioned many looks, comments, and much amusement. "Look at those crazy foreigners!" I could almost hear them say.

We were crazy, alright, but for other reasons. It was midday and it was hot, with little shade over the two kilometers into town, on an island that partly straddles the Equator.

Atlas was game, as always, but when his tongue expanded exponentially in an effort to cool down his impressively coated body, I realized how quickly he must be dehydrating as we approached town. Water we found, with the help of a boy on a bike, but Atlas was panting too hard to drink much. The sane thing to do during equatorial high noon is to take a *sonequinha*, a good snooze, and nearly everyone in Soure was doing just that, with most shops closed. We eventually found an old corner store open, which was a godsend, as it was shaded inside with a breeze passing through, and the polished worn tile floor felt relatively cool. The initially scared shop girls took a liking to Atlas and, when asked if they had an outdoor faucet, kindly filled a small plastic tub in the back yard. Atlas was still breathing so hard that drops off of his tongue immediately formed pools of saliva by his feet, but the girls didn't seem to mind. Yet when I noticed that Atlas, even after drinking at leisure and laying on the cool floor for five and more minutes, still had his tail tucked between his hind legs, my heart plummeted. Whether an imposition or not we were staying put – which we did for a good long while.

The return, however, would be worse due to lack of trees in the second half. We started out well, considering, and hugged many a facade and house front to catch a sliver of shade where trees were lacking. Atlas worsened more quickly than on the way in, and once again began panting noisily. I was considering flagging down a car and explaining it was a medical emergency when the clouds closed overhead. Such was my concern about Atlas that I hadn't noticed the rain clouds rolling in. When it started to drizzle we were saved, for in reality there were next to no cars in town and no midday buffalo carts in sight, even if we had needed one.

We tackled the last kilometer slowly, as in a light rain it was still hot and humid, with Atlas making frequent, instinctual pee stops, lifting his leg and aiming with nothing coming out. By the end he was panting harder than I have seen before, with a froth of white saliva ringing his mouth – truly a mad dog with his culpable American. When we finally reached the hotel lobby, Atlas heaved himself onto the tile floor and quickly created a fresh saliva puddle while I retrieved the key. The last fifty meters to the room seemed the slowest, and needed much encouragement as Atlas's head swayed close to the wood planks while he stumbled along. In the bathroom I made him lie down on the ceramic tiles under the sink, the coolest place in the room, placed a bowlful of water in front of him, and turned on the air conditioner full blast. While the crisis slowly passed I knew I had let him down – but not he me.

Poor Atlas: so patient and trusting that he allows me to learn on my own, in spite of much bodily risk to him.

Despite the placid, muggy appearance, Marajó's tumultuous history boasts some of the bloodiest indigenous resistance to the Portuguese. It is speculated that the Spanish explorer Vincent Yañez Pinzón made landfall in 1500 several months before Cabral's sighting of Mt. Easter in Bahia, near the town of Joanes named after him. Local legend has it that his treatment – including enslavement, torture, and killing – of the Indians was so cruel that it took a century and a half for the Portuguese to overcome the infamy and make peace with the natives. (Then again, such an apocryphal story could be from our proximity to the Tordesillas line and that old Iberian rivalry.) Only when a Jesuit named Father Antônio Vieira reached the island in the mid-17th century, with permission from the Crown to carry out his missionary work, did the slow process of colonization begin – through proselytizing.[88] (He is the same Father Vieira who, besides pushing through the decree that freed all Indian slaves, once said, "To be born Portuguese, one is obliged to die a pilgrim," with a good Iberian burst of fatalism.) The Amazon region is where the Jesuits gained fame for creating enormous aldeias of ranches and vineyards which, in order to protect them from slavery, were worked by tens of thousands of their charges. When the meddlesome Jesuits were expelled from this productive, hothouse paradise a century later, they took nearly sixty percent of the Marajoara population with them, leaving behind over one hundred thousand confiscated buffalo and horses,[89] among them the Marajoara breed of Arab descent, which is such a hardy breed that it competes annually in a hundred and eighty kilometer swamp-marathon designed for them.

Due to an alluring remoteness only a short boat ride from Belém, the island became a refuge for runaway slaves and free Indians. During the Cabanagem War, Marajó was known for the slaying of foreign visitors,[90] a practice now discouraged by all the "We respect tourists here" signs in hotel lobbies, which show a stick figure tourist in a loud Hawaiian shirt with sunglasses and camera, in the center of a red circle whose horizontal slash has been kindly omitted. The first Brazilian President to touch foot on Marajó, with or without camera, didn't feel comfortable enough to do so until 1975, a date that is still remembered with reverence by the long-suffering locals.[91]

Dogs are not only trusting but quick to forgive. Atlas had sufficiently regained his normally high spirits to join us for an afternoon excursion to a nearby fazenda called Good Lord. On the heels of several cosmopolitan couples, Atlas and I loaded onto the island's only city-sized bus, which had gotten stuck after a sudden downpour in front of our hotel-on-stilts, requiring that it be freed with the help of a jeep in front and a platoon of rubber-booted staff pushing from behind.

Fortunately, Soure's incongruously broad city avenues are ample enough for the wide turns of a mega-bus, and everywhere we went locals shouted "Joãozinho!" and waved, as he is the sole inhabitant capable of navigating the town with such an ungainly monster. Indeed, the only roaming quadrupeds besides our bus-behemoth were beer trucks and buffalo carts, lumbering back and forth among the ubiquitous potholes. On the way to Fazenda Bom Jesus we passed expansive marshlands with wide glassy plates of water dotted by lone trees and grassy mounds: the rainy season's hangover. Along with various white-bodied wood storks and little blue herons, we saw flocks of the gloriously red scarlet ibis, whose startling slash of color comes from a pinkish diet of crab and shrimp.

After taking the obligatory and buffoonish minute long buffalo ride at Good Lord Ranch, we were introduced to Doutora Eva, the owner, who told us about her admirable partnership with Ibama, the national park service. Dr. Eva left a teaching position in veterinary medicine in Belém to live full time at Bom Jesus, where she treats all the injured, mistreated, and illegally captured wildlife that Ibama finds or confiscates on Marajó. She also receives over four hundred children a year to teach them a thing or two about nature. Yet she wasn't taken seriously by locals until TV Globo did a series of televised reports on her work – which sounded similar to Dona Romana's treatment, that is, anything outside the provincial norm is suspect, until proven otherwise by big-wig out-of-towners.

Ushering us into the fazenda's small chapel, only four years old but already filled with sacred art, she explained, "The main problems are humidity and termites." Among the survivors was a sculpture of Saint Francis, who is believed locally to not only be the patron saint of animals but of fazendas as well. Learning this, I asked Dr. Eva if I could let my Labrador out of the bus, which she kindly allowed, impressed not only by Atlas's comportment but by his red booties as well. In an authoritative tone she told me how to diagnose the bicho de pé's tell-tale boring signs in paw pads.

Of Syrian descent, Dr. Eva showered us with hospitality on her portico, offering us "Arab coffee," buffalo milk, and dollops of Arab cheese over toast quarters, along with assai and cupuaçu juice among other tropical elixirs. When I suggested she was spoiling us, she pointed to her eighty year old mother, who had not uttered a word, and said, "She's the one who's responsible."

Since Atlas and I, as a team, had not visited a beach for years, we joined Joãozinho for an excursion to Praia de Pesqueiro the next morning. Put beach and ball within striking distance and Atlas enters nirvana – which I hoped might make up for the prior day's dally with overheating that had disturbed me much more, from what I could tell, than him. Here along the hard-sand shore he could run in hot pursuit for long expanses and, when growing tired, we could either cool off in the waves or, better yet, I could let someone else do the throwing. This is how I got to chat with Meire from Belém and Fabio from São Paulo, after they succumbed to Atlas's charms. Meire, who studies law and works for her father's wood exporting firm, offered that I call her when back in Belém. I wasn't quite sure what to make of Fabio, whom she referred to as "this character" – a fling, perhaps – but realized belatedly that I was getting involved with two out of three of the state's forbidden fruits: women and wood. Yet Meire was by far the friendliest person in our tour group and appeared almost Central American due to her dark brown eyes, oval face, shortish rust-colored hair, full lips, and high noon disposition.

Born in Breves, on the southwestern edge of Marajó, Meire is but one of fourteen children. The family moved for a time to Macapá, the capital of Amapá, the most northern state that lifts a finger up by French Guiana, and then to Xingu, in western Pará. While Meire, in her teens, re-located to Belém for her studies, and is the only one in her family with a degree, a brother still lives in Xingu where he is mayor. (*Paraenses* can be a lot more mobile than the stay-at-home Brazilians lauded by Dona Sonia, another characteristic they share with Paulistas.) Along with attending to the legal, or not so legal, needs of her father's wood exportation business, Meire consults for her brother's electoral campaign, just starting to heat up for the October polls. For this she flies to Xingu once a month, the plane stopping in her Breves birthplace on the way. When Meire told me she travels to Europe for a month-long vacation every year, I asked her what it is like returning to Xingu and what her childhood friends think of her. They complain, she admitted, that she has changed a lot and taken on airs. She struggles with the contrasts and over the years has sought therapy, that big city remedy to the loss of balance big cities bring.

Later, after buying him a freshly top-chopped coconut, I got to chatting with Joãozinho who told me Soure is so safe that I could leave my belongings on the plastic table where we sat, stroll down the beach for an hour, and return to still find them there. While I didn't take him up on the dare, I did rejoice at the thought of returning to a safer and more innocent Brazil, where trust is still endemic. Joãozinho seems to know what he's talking about, as he once lived in Belém in order to save up for a commercial driver's license. There he drove a public bus along the federal highway that heads east from town and passes by the head of the Belém-Brasília, but his bus was so frequently assaulted he soon tired of the job. (A Belém newspaper warns that, on average, five tourists a day are robbed in the city's old center.)[92] Having left his wife and child back in Soure, he gladly returned to the hotel, where after five years he had recently been made a full employee. The Amazon region is arguably a microcosm of Brazil, with Belém, the local São Paulo, its economic magnet.

By now the full mast equatorial sun was at its most intense, though the river and sea breezes didn't make it feel so. In a short while it would be time to move on. Atlas, I was learning, is a better travel companion than anyone could wish for, as he breaks down barriers with the greatest of ease and pulls me out of a gnawing sense of solitude that travel mitigates but does not disperse. What a reliable friend he is to continue the good work even after I put his life at risk, always ready for the next adventure even when it could be his last. How could I not admire him?

After I dried off a rejuvenated, if spent, Atlas with his towel, we boarded Joãozinho's lumbering bus of dreams and rumbled back to the hotel, on a low-lying island afloat in the glittering expanse of the Amazonian delta. Breaking barriers, I realized, is a force as natural as the Amazon's onrushing ability to clear detritus, free blockages, and send it all out to sea.

~ 16 ~

IN THE END THE FERRY CAPTAIN let us return to Belém without hitch, even though the end of July's holidays filled the boat to capacity. Such is the history of Brazil, the thrust of arbitrary rules which don't seem to grasp. Joãozinho had brushed off the captain's insistence on a crate for Atlas and helped me look for a protective muzzle, to no avail, as we couldn't find one. On the day of our departure, he promised to scrounge up some chord or laundry line so I could make a makeshift one myself, but didn't follow through. No need: our luck, a kind of Brazilian dumb luck that everything works out in the end, held out. Or, as a common phrase has it, no need to "heat up your head."

After we found Fofão and our possessions in one piece at the Beira-Rio – along with a rousing welcome, particularly for Atlas – it was time to think about the northern leg of the journey, as reaching Belém had absorbed so much attention that the rest had received nary a thought. No one, I repeat No One, I met had ever heard of someone driving the northern coast of Brazil, as it just doesn't seem to be done. Even Quatro Rodas, in contrast to its several advisories against touring the Belém-Brasília, was silent on the issue. So this much I knew or, more accurately, conjectured: we were to going to return the extra long way, following the endless northern and eastern coasts that makes Brazil the world's most Atlantic nation.

Heading east – that is, the only possible way by car without returning on the Belém-Brasília – the next city is São Luís, the capital of Maranhão. São Luís, like Belém, is an old colonial port town, and was once the capital of a wide swath of the northern colonies, from the furthest reaches of the Amazon to Ceará, an administrative unit called the State of Maranhão and Grão Pará that reported directly to Lisbon. This odd situation came about as it took much longer by boat from São Luís, due to both distance and the prevailing southeasterly winds, to reach Salvador than Lisbon. Needless to say overland travel, which took months, was not even considered. Only a century and a half later, in 1774, did Maranhão and Greater Pará join the Brazilian union,[93] which against all odds remained intact even as Spanish America splintered apart into numerous, unstable shards.

One searches for parallels, for hints of meaning or precedent in history, which made me wonder: would Atlas's and my remaining journey follow the Portuguese or the Spanish model?

True, overland travel has improved in the interim, but not by much. In the dry sertão of northeastern Brazil there are only several highways which take an east-west trajectory from the coast to as far inland as the Tocantins River – which, itself, runs parallel to the old Tordesillas line. Between the first and last national capitals threads BR-20, reaching across Brazil's mid-section from Salvador to Brasília. Further north there's BR-230, which snakes from the coastal city of João Pessoa to Filadélfia on the Tocantins River and was once part of the grand, starry-eyed Trans-Amazonia. And furthest north, though well inland from the roadless, jagged northern coastline, zigzags BR-316, which, with a few number changes and a bit of Brazilian luck, would carry us from Belém to Fortaleza and Natal, from where the coast falls precipitously southwards.

Getting to São Luís, however, would prove even less straight-forward than zigzagging implies. As the capital lies on the eastern edge of the large São Marcos Bay, to get there requires a wide loop south on BR-316, making it an impossibly long stretch for one day, over eight hundred kilometers with much of it in "precarious condition." Meire had recently made the trip for Carnival, during an overnight bus ride that, owing to some dangerous stretches in Maranhão, was done in convoy. That is, her bus had joined a large flotilla of party buses at a pre-arranged point, after which they were escorted by police for much of the night.

On one map I noticed that a state road cuts more directly eastwards towards São Marcos Bay where, presumably, a ferry to São Luís could be found, even though all guide books were silent on the issue, as tourists don't bother to drive in these parts. Meire offered to contact a friend, whom she believed had recently taken the route, and then call me back at the Beira-Rio. She had good news the next day, sharing the ferry service's phone number and approximate driving time to meet it. After getting through to the small port, I reserved a place on the last ferry the following day, our prolonged and welcome procrastination in the City of Mangos coming to a close. Time, once again, to put our fate into the rough, callused hands of Brazilian highways.

August is not an auspicious month for travel in Brazil. Many Brazilians are familiar with the rhyme "Agosto, mês de desgosto," or "August, month of disgust," and stick around home. The curse of August has taken its toll especially among populist politicians, for it was in August of 1954 that the "Father of the Poor" President Vargas committed suicide; in August of 1961 that President Quadros resigned, kick-starting a cycle of instability which led to the military takeover; and in August of 1976 that ex-President, Brasília-founder, and leading opponent to military rule, Juscelino Kubitschek, died in an automobile accident. Yet craziness is not confined to politicians or to lesser humans. As the title of a Brazilian novel *Month of Rabid Dogs* implies, even animals behave strangely in August.[94]

Fortunately I had recently discovered a potential palliative. At the Jesuits' St. Alexandre Church in old Belém, I was introduced to the story of São Cristovão (from the Greek *Christo Phoros*), a large man, almost a giant, who had "spent his life carrying travelers across the deep waters of Lícia, in Turkey." One day a child asked to be lifted across the river and mysteriously grew heavier and heavier, almost making the giant desist when he could bear the weight no longer. Only on the far bank did the child reveal himself as Jesus, after which the giant became known as "the carrier of Christ." From this, São

Cristovão became the protector saint of travelers and, especially, drivers. I found this last of keen interest, and read on:

> One of the oldest popular traditions linked to São Cristovão claims that if you look fixedly at his image for a few moments, you will pass that day without any kind of accident.

But where, oh where, could I find a handy dangling windshield ornament of St. Carrier of Christ in preparation for our eastern plunge?

Atlas, who doesn't give much credence to such superstitions, nudged me awake soon after sunrise. The drive that day turned out to be a series of transitions. With even less traffic than the Belém-Brasília, BR-316 was surprisingly well maintained through most of Pará, until the first crater surfaced just short of three hundred kilometers out of Belém. The vibrant green of the Amazon basin continued practically until the state line, but once in Maranhão everything changed. Even though it was the same federal road maintained, presumably, by the same federal funds, all seemed to fall apart, like Spanish America, into pieces. First, the kilometer postings disappeared from roadside. Then the pothole virus metastasized, pock-marking the road so thoroughly that slalom driving became the norm. The concrete speed rumbles once again deteriorated into jagged, hazardous strips, while the green lushness all but dried up due to Maranhão's deforestation. As if pre-ordained, the parched, dust-ball towns returned in force. In fact, the divide between the Amazonian and Northeastern cultures could not have been clearer or more abrupt: the iconic and hardworking donkeys, as well as the emblematic *carne de sol*, or sun-dried meat, after being absent in Pará, once again became prevalent.

Belém and São Luís, as the two largest ports for a thousand kilometers in any direction, enjoy a certain rivalry. While exports, mostly minerals, are largely mined in Pará, those conniving, ex-colonial masters from São Luís continue to export a majority of it, by truck or train from the Serra dos Carajás, among others, in southeast Para. The

Belém newspaper estimated that within six years Pará would produce over eight billion dollars worth of minerals, including copper, iron, nickel, aluminum, and bauxite, representing nearly a fifth of the state economy. Alarmingly, the Companhia Vale do Rio Doce dominates ninety percent of the sector,[95] which may explain why I heard so many community-oriented radio ads in Belém bragging that the company mining towns are "First World, with everything!" Given that Vale had been nominally privatized in 1997, allowing rapacious foreigners to lay their hands on Brazil's mineral abundance even though the government retains "golden shares" and the right of veto, such aspirational boasts are good politics in Brazil, where foreign pilfering of the nation's jewels is always imminent.

A curious if non-pilfering foreigner himself, Atlas was clearly happy to be traveling again, nudging my shoulder, smelling new smells, surfing the air currents with his nostrils. Not one to avoid a stiff wind, he enjoyed sticking his head out the window and just leaving it there, no matter our velocity. When I looked back through the driver's side mirror, the results were often comical when Atlas's ears flapped madly, his lips curled open, and his eye sockets widened to show the whites of his eyes: in other words, a nutty and hairy professor's face subjected to g-force.

Without unduly anthropomorphizing my dog, I felt a shift in my relation to Atlas. Despite the lighter moments, after our experience in Soure I came to realize what a large responsibility I have to protect Atlas – and not necessarily the other way around. A series of flat tires or a breakdown in the equatorial heat could, in fact, be much more life-threatening to him than to me. Deprived of a good wind or the car's feeble air-conditioning, and faced with a lack of shade along the highway's deforested corridors, Atlas could not walk, as we had in Soure, for very long without grave consequences. And would passers-by or truckers willingly stop to pick up a drooling, dragging dog? I had my doubts.

I had prepared carefully for the trip, with bits of cash stashed around the car and on my person (including the old money belt trick), with credit cards and notarized document copies similarly distributed. One time I lost my passport, traveler's cheques, and all my money (save for a risible amount stashed in my hiking boots) at a remote Zambian border, so I knew what it was like to be stranded and dependent on the generosity of strangers. For this excursion, accordingly, I had prepared more or less for catastrophic loss, for the theft of my wallet and of Fofão and all of her contents – save for Atlas. I could lose just about everything, but would consider risking my life to save my dog's. What else could I do? One must protect the innocent and one's loved ones at nearly all costs – particularly if you placed them in danger in the first place.

When we turned onto the state highway for the shortcut and ferry to São Luís, the road immediately improved, which was a relief, making it look as though we could traverse the remaining two hundred plus kilometers and still have an hour to board the boat. We had left the hotel with two extra hours to spare, but I had gotten lost while trying to leave Belém, which was already slow work due to road construction. (Imminent travel often makes me anxious, causing me that morning to clip one bottomless Belém pothole and then drive through another that was, miraculously, filled with rocks.) The terrain, on our approach to the delta, flattened out and grew lusher again, dotted with the *babaçu* palms that, due to their manifold uses – from edible hearts to cooking oil to myriad construction uses – are the mainstay of the rural Maranhense economy. So if we didn't make the day's last ferry at six, we could always revert to colonial subsistence by building a palm-thatched hut and surviving off of a few babaçus.

That possibility became distinct when, right after a big iguana crossed the road wiping the sandy black top with its tail, the highway deteriorated into scores of sand moguls. I could see the direction we were going in and, sure enough, after St. Helena the road simply gave up the ghost and, shedding its asphalt skin, collapsed into dirt. A well graded dirt track can be a big improvement over deteriorated asphalt, but this was not the case. It was a rough and potholed dirt road that in a former life had once been paved: the worst kind. Neither my map nor the information relayed by Meire had warned of this, so in all likelihood the road had been washed out during the last rainy season, with forty-one kilometers of paving completely destroyed by a few months of flooding – and all of this outside the Amazon region! There was also a complete absence of signs, requiring that we stop to confirm our direction with frequency. My concern was that as our speed declined, to between twenty and fifty kilometers per hour, we would miss the last ferry. It was nearly five o'clock with what looked like – for no map showed the ferry landing – a hundred kilometers to go.

In Pinheiro, where ex-President Sarney was born, an old man assured us the rest of the way was better, and sure enough drivable asphalt returned for a tantalizing brief period, before descending once again through multiple levels of road purgatory, around curves of hope and despair. As the sun also fell, I realized that either we would have to race over the potholes and risk a flat or two, or most certainly miss the boat and spend the night, say, back in Pinheiro. I confess to still acting like a destination-obsessed traveler at times, so that when, as if on cue, a white GM Vectra with São Luís plates passed by at a good clip, leading me to believe he knew what he was doing, I sped up to stay up, even as he flew over gravel stretches, kicking up sand cones. With the low light slowly leeching from overhead, why not give it a yeoman try?

Follow-the-leader, it turned out, was not such a bad idea, for in the end the turnoff to the ferry was marked by a rusty, nearly illegible sign hidden behind a bush, which we would have flown by ourselves, last seen white-knuckle driving in the direction of the wide open Atlantic.

The ferry was late, fortunately, so when we came to a collective stop I thanked the driver of the Vectra, which was filled with day laborers on their way home. I was glad for our reservation as the stand-by line, which the Vectra joined, looked lengthy.

When our turn came, single-file, to enter the small dock area in order to back into the ferry's open hatch, it was nearly dark. An officious-looking sailor, presumably there to help guide us onto the ferry, took one look at Atlas and said, "You'd better roll up that window!" I started to explain that Atlas is a Labrador Retriever, the same breed that leads the blind, succors the ill, etc., etc., but Atlas didn't care much for the looks of the official either and started to growl. This angered the poor fellow, particularly when his fearful reaction caused a number of on-lookers to laugh, so even though I completely rolled up Atlas's windows he decided to remove us from the line and, in an agitated state, complain over his walkie-talkie that there was a dangerous dog in a certain car which he didn't think should be allowed to board. Lowering my voice, I tried to explain calmly that it had been a long drive, that Atlas was only protecting the car as any guard dog would, and that he is a well-trained pooch who wouldn't harm a well-intentioned soul. After making his point as publicly as possible, the official allowed us to board with the admonition that Atlas could not be let out of the car, which was a pity as the enclosed vehicle deck was stifling hot. Then, as we backed up into a spot, the crewman who was assisting us asked something about Atlas, which once again elicited growls through the barely open back window.

It was then that I scolded Atlas – with a sharp "Bad boy!" – for the first and only time of the trip, which I immediately regretted. It may have been his first time on a car ferry, whose dark and belching hold would have scared the likes of Jonas, and clearly I was jazzed up myself, fearful of getting thrown off the last boat.

I promptly apologized to Atlas and gave him one of his favorite treats, the dried tendon of a bull's penis – which is also good for cleaning teeth they say. Yet even after opening all the windows, I continued to feel worse than he did. Although I had already fed him, given him water, and taken him for a pee back at the port, I filled his water bowl again and came down to keep him company, jumping the gate which was locked while we were under way. With the breeze off of São Marco Bay slowly filtering into the engine-clanging hold, the heat became marginally more tolerable, but Atlas, feeling out of sorts, had not even touched his bull tendon. So I stroked his head while telling him everything would be alright.

~ 17 ~

AFTER THE SLOW and rocky ferry crossing, Atlas and I arrived past nine o'clock and still found ourselves eighteen kilometers from São Luís, which occupies an eponymous island jutting out to sea. With the windows fully sheathed, we passed a long low area of wispy sand pines, through which flashed a slightly sagging moon to the north. The smell of dry pine needles flooded the car. Without any road signs to guide us, we followed the flow of traffic through a chorus of welcoming crickets towards the beckoning moon.

Once again I was surprised that a journey, this one the short-cut to São Luís, had been so much more challenging than anticipated. Given that the wide loop of federal highway avoided was largely in "precarious" condition, I had naively thought that our bad driving days would be behind us and that hazardous dirt tracks were a thing of the past, left back around Bananal Island. Instead, the last hour of rushed, all-terrain driving had been among the most harebrained of the trip and had given Fofão, and us, another beating.

While I was not thrilled to arrive in a strange, new city after dark, the translucent glow of São Luís's lights soon replaced that of the low winter moon and our way was assured, to yet another remote, dilapidated equatorial port, the New Orleans of Brazil. São Cristovão took further pity on us when the first seaside hotel we visited not only took us in, but offered a late dinner. In the morning we could go for a long beach run, and all would be well once again. Such are false hopes and old, reassuring habits, along the north border of the South American continent and the slow motion sea that steadily erodes it.

* * *

The Portuguese couldn't have cared less about this coastal backwater until São Luís was settled in 1612 by the Frenchman Daniel de la Touche, who named it in honor of King Louis XIII. De la Touche subsequently built a fort with an eye towards making São Luís the center of French Equatorial colonization. Within three years, however, the prickly Portuguese led by Jeronino de Albuquerque had driven him out and, in a pique, sent Castelo Branco along the coast to found Belém and Feliz Lusitânia the following year. The Portuguese were in turn turfed out in 1641 by the Dutch, who themselves lasted for a mere three years, which gives São Luís the distinction of being the only Brazilian city to have been ruled by – that auspicious number again – three different European empires.[96]

Even though São Luís's political importance declined when it stopped reporting directly to Lisbon, thanks to cotton its economic ascendancy was just blossoming. Cotton production multiplied with the launch of a national export economy in the late 18th century, its share pushing ahead of mighty sugar cane's for a while during the American Civil War, when U.S. cotton sales plummeted. Driven by export wealth, Maranhão for a time became the most prosperous province of Portuguese America. When Emperor Dom João opened Brazil's ports for the first time to "friendly nations" (that is, Great Britain) at the start of the 19th century, the only major ones included were Rio, Salvador, Recife, Belém, and São Luís.[97]

São Luís is now known for its elaborate Portuguese ceramic tiles called *azulejos*, which not only line many a hall, floor, and garden in the colonial center, but also cover many a facade as they provide durable protection against humidity and heat. While the oldest tiles, dating back to the 1750's, are mustard-yellow and like all of them had been used as ship's ballast, the more typical colors are blue or blue-and-white, reflecting the wave-crested sea. As is the case for so many of Brazil's colonial gems, the historical center would not have survived without ample space for development nearby, which dissuaded property owners from tearing down the old and charming to put up the new and cheap. In São Luís's case, across Rio Anil and the José Sarney bridge developed an upscale neighborhood called São Francisco, where everything modern, commercial, and ugly (including my hotel) can be found, while the older parts of town were left to crumble in the Atlantic winds. Only in the 1980's, when the tsunami of relentless modernization and architectural uglification subsided, did the state authorities agree to fix up the colonial center, which subsequently became a World Heritage Site.

Curious and still feeling adrift, I went down to the "Zona," as it is informally called, to stop by the Visitor's Center that first day. There I received the obligatory city map, which more often than not is rough, confusing, and incorrect, and spoke to one of the girls hired, evidently, not only for her connections but for her friendliness.

Lourdes, short, brunette, and bored, could not have been more simpática, detailing all the night spots that São Luís has to offer and, by the end, not only giving me the office number, but that of her cell phone as well, in a wonderfully Brazilian gesture of inclusive trust. When asked about Alcântara, the colonial town across the bay, she showed me some photos until she and her colleague started to laugh. What was so funny, I wondered?

Only then did they introduce me to an Alcântaran friend who had been standing quietly in the shadows all along, whom the local girls started to rib as his town is home to the Centro de Lançamento, a rocket-launching facility built in the early 1990's, where, it seems, everything that can go wrong does go wrong. Five attempted launches failed in the prior decade alone, including the last a few years back (during the month of August no less), when a score of technicians died near the launching pad.[98]

"Tell me when they schedule the next launch," Lourdes joked, "so I can plan to get out of São Luís for my safety!"

Similar to New Orleans's Mardi Gras, São Luís hosts a distinct, home-grown festival called Bumba-meu-boi, a folkloric pageant that unfolds every June. As Alyson, my guide at the Casa de Maranhão, explained, whereas the Spanish like to run *from* the *boi*, or bull, the more sensible Portuguese – who also like to invert things – prefer running *after* him. It all started after the regency of sugar cane but before the reign of cotton, when the ranchers needed a ceremony to assure good pastures and healthy bulls. Soon enough the slaves had transformed it into a celebration of the bull's baptism, using an eclectic mix of Catholic saints and African gods, which, as always, was the slaves' clever means of worshiping their forbidden *orixás* ("deities," in Yoruba), by disguising them as Catholic saints. The Catholic Church – no dummies here – rather than buck the trend moved the bull baptism ceremonies to various Saints' Days in June, including São Antônio's, São Pedro's, São João's, and São Maraçal, even though the last is not officially a saint but, as the local archbishop puts it, "the fruit of popular faith." As a result, every year in every village and neighborhood throughout the land, a bull is re-born in a new outfit with the help of the local Father.

But how does the bull die in the first place? Legend has it that a slave named Catrina, the goddaughter of a local rancher (and therefore part of his panelinha), is overtaken by "the uncontrollable desires of pregnancy" to eat bull tongue, a delicacy, and persuades her husband, Chico, to kill the ranch's prize specimen. When the slaughtered bull is discovered, Chico is tracked down but fortunately has taken refuge with local Indians, through whose spells and incantations the bull is resurrected, leading to the thief's pardon and the reuniting of the young lovers.

In a country where little pretext is needed for a good party, this redemptive tale has motivated thousands upon thousands of celebrations throughout the Northeast, with its impact following the route of the 18th century cattle drives from Bahia through Minas Gerais to São Paulo. A jug of rot-gut wine, for instance, hefted over the shoulder for easy pouring during Carnival in Minas Gerais, is called *sangue de boi*, or "bull's blood." In São Luís, costumed, dancing, and singing bull processions take over the historic center and many a neighborhood over several months, the festivities lasting a full twenty nights per re-born bull. With each troop of musicians and attendant characters – such as the bull in elaborate costume supported by two hunched-over dancers – parading for nearly an hour, six times per night, it all adds up to over a hundred hours of revelry per rejuvenated bull.

As the Casa de Maranhão decidedly put it: "the baptism, then, is the spiritual approval of St. John for the bull to spread happiness throughout the outside world." Amen to that.

In the morning Atlas and I took a cab to the city's boat terminal – which, due to the river's accumulated silt, works only at high tide – in time for an early boat to the missile playground of Alcântara. We were approached by a man in a Brazilian Merchant Marine t-shirt offering us a catamaran ride there, but we declined and went up to the ticket window of N.P. Navegações Pericumã to buy a round trip fare on a good-sized mail boat called the Bahia Star, which was already loading. The ticket girl was about to emit a ticket when a small, stubby man came by and started to complain that he could be sued with a dog on board, the passengers made uncomfortable, etc. I asked him if he was the boat's captain and, after he said no, turned back to the ticket girl, who now refused to issue the ticket.

The captain of the catamaran, nicknamed Louro, or Blondie, said he could take us on board for the same price of ten reals, adding, "That guy's an imbecile. I am sure your dog is more intelligent than he is."

The compliment, though backhanded, pleased Atlas, while the thought of a catamaran ride intrigued me. But then a group of Italian tourists hired Louro's extended services to carry on to the next destination, which meant that we could only sail one way, and would have to depend on the Bahia Star to bring us back.

"Oh, yeah," Louro said, "they'll bring you back, no problem."

"Are you sure of that?"

"Look, there's nothing in the port's regulations saying you can't carry personal pets. You could go up to their offices right now, and they wouldn't be able to show you anything in writing."

While not exactly the reassurance I wanted, I decided to trust

Louro's instincts. How often, after all, do you get to sail a catamaran with your dog over the primordial waters of the Equator?

It was Atlas's first time in a sailboat, which he liked just fine. The Italian girls were pretty and friendly and, to top it off, didn't greatly mind being licked.

During a slack moment I asked Louro, "So what did you say your actual name is?"

"Lindorf. My family is French."

"Were you born here?"

"No, in Rio."

"So you only like cities founded by the French?"

"That's right."

"When did you move to São Luís?"

"In 2001."

"Why, may I ask?"

"Rio's too violent. I had had enough."

"And how did you come to chose São Luís? Were you on vacation?"

"I have relations who live six hundred kilometers inland from here, so I already knew São Luís."

"Not a bad life you have then."

"Not bad at all – work with a view."

At the end of the hour and a half sail, Lindorf kindly warned us that the steel planks of the Alcântara's pier could be painfully hot for Atlas's paws. And then he went out of his way to show us to the town's sleepy ticket office – just a girl behind a desk in an otherwise empty room – where we were sold the return passage without hiccup.

When I asked the girl if there was an open faucet nearby, so I could give Atlas some water, she took us to the restaurant next door where they insisted on finding an old pot for Atlas to drink from. By this time we had already attracted the attention of some locals, including a compact, wiry guide, José, and a young, open-faced boy, Juninho, on his bike.

I don't care much for guides, usually preferring to experience a new place at my own pace, but in the end I was glad to have José and Juninho along. It was José, for instance, who persuaded the employees of the town's small museum to let me tie up Atlas in the central atrium, instead of outside in the sun, even though they feared being reprimanded by their boss. And when one of my inexpensive Brazilian leather sandals fell apart, the sole comically separating to create a noisy flip-flop, José – who is otherwise known as Head-on-Fire due to his unruly and curly yellowish locks – took it to a local *sapateiro* to be glued while I ate lunch. During the meal I taught Juninho how to make Atlas sit, give his paw, and lie down, which provided endless pleasure to the boy, who proudly showed off his control over my black beast to any small acquaintance who would stop and watch for the rest of the day. By the end of the afternoon, we had a dog-wrangling posse of six children.

As Head-on-Fire couldn't take us to the off-bounds Launch Center, I opted to learn more at the local museum. Alcântara, built with the sugar and cotton wealth harvested in the wide delta crescent we had crashed through by car, was once the richest town in northern Brazil, whose former splendor is reflected in the imperial palms dominating the town's bayside profile, as well as the colonial mansions, in various states of ruin, surrounding the central square. If you find São Luís's Zona dilapidated, you only need to visit Alcântara, said to contain the most homogenous set of colonial structures from 17th century Brazil, to see what disrepair really means, with many a tree growing through a roofless building and, other than a sturdy facade, the rest usually rubble. As there is no road worthy of the name to reach town – though, had I missed the ferry turnoff, I might have cleared one – Alcântara is for all intents and purposes an island, which seemed appropriate: yet another mostly abandoned place that time has passed by.

When Brazilian slavery was finally abolished in the 1880's, the town's fortunes declined precipitously, its population falling by half when the wealthy fled to São Luís, leaving Alcântara more or less to freed slaves. Not much happened over the next century – including a

National Landmark designation in the 1940's – until the rocket-launching facility arrived in 1981, dislocating many but also bringing piped water and electricity for the first time to local residents. In a nation of so many contrasts I can think of no better one: with lethargic, charming, and deteriorating Alcântara alongside a space launching pad, which in its full grandiosity is as dependable as soggy fireworks.

A visit to São Luís is not complete without a courtesy call on local royalty. Take ex-President José Sarney, the most famous native son born a hundred kilometers back in Pinheiro, whose story is emblematic of strongmen throughout the history of the Northeast – and all of Brazil. One afternoon while touring the center's Mercês Convent, I stumbled upon the José Sarney Memorial (so called, even though he is still alive), which, along with a gallery-full of cartoons and drawings making fun of his walrus-like features, may or may not attest to the former President's sense of humor. After being elected federal deputy, Sarney got his first break in 1965, a year into the nascent military dictatorship, when he was appointed governor of Maranhão at the age of thirty-five and then managed to rebuild São Luís's main bridge – no mean feat in the corruption-besieged boonies. Within five years he was promoted to Senator under the banner of the military-controlled party, which he eventually led. Then, when Brazil began to open politically after two long decades of military rule, he was asked to join the presidential ticket of Tancredo Neves, a popular Mineiro governor from the civilian opposition party and eventually the first democratically (though indirectly) elected president since 1960 – with Sarney as his running mate, to still the military's itchy fingers. Neves – from my nearby town of São João del-Rei – died tragically before taking office on the anniversary of Tiradentes' April dismemberment, most likely from an infection when the intensive care unit overflowed with concerned well-wishers during his intestinal surgery – dragging poor Sarney into the limelight. Soon faced with Brazil's n^{th} economic crisis, Sarney introduced a new currency, the Cruzado (lopping three naughts off the Cruzeiro), and a new stabilization program called the

Cruzado Plan. This, while successfully advancing his party's interests in the mid-term elections, unraveled soon thereafter, ushering in the wild years of hyperinflation which peaked at 1783% in the late 1980's.[99]

No, that is not a typo, for inflation actually pushed 2000% a year. I recall what it was like, during several internships in Rio, when grocery prices changed daily. Other than governmental incompetence and corruption – for hyperinflation ravages the earnings of the poor but not the rich, who benefit from all sorts of financial instruments – what else can explain such an unwelcome distinction? Brazilians are among the most enthusiastic of peoples, which may encourage them, from time to time, to become the most inflationary.

Despite galloping prices, Sarney managed to ride out the end of his term – no small accomplishment given Brazil's volatile political environment throughout the last century – and, returning to a career in the Senate, rose phoenix-like from the ashes. He then ran for Senator from the northernmost state of Amapá to make space for his daughter Roseana's rapid political rise in Maranhão, was made President of the Senate in 1995, re-elected as Senator from Amapá in 1999, and has recently re-scaled the Senate Presidency. Brazilian ex-Presidents, if they don't die, don't go away.

Which is not to belittle Sarney's major success in nudging Brazil from military to democratic rule, or his more cultured endeavors, including the nineteen books he has authored on display, along with his babyhood bassinet, at his memorial. But his most enduring legacy may well be the semi-feudal political dynasty he created, whose morphological roots reach back to the colonial system of *coroneis*, the Portuguese version of *caudillos*, where loyalty and patronage are all important, the state's or country's interests a distant third. His daughter Roseana has not only continued the family's rule in Maranhão, but also ran for the Presidency under a conservative party's banner in 1998, which she was well positioned to win until the administration of Fernando Henrique Cardoso, at the height of the election campaign, sent a posse of federal police to raid her husband's office, where vast quantities of cash were uncovered. The ploy worked and, after her poll numbers plummeted, she pulled out.

While the Sarneys own a villa in Switzerland and could comfortably retire from public service, in Maranhão, and presumably in Amapá, the good works continue. Alongside the Sarney Memorial was an exhibition on *Visions of Brazil as Paradise*, one of the most comprehensively pedagogical public history lessons I have seen in a nation that lacks much interest in either history or education. I noted from the obligatory guest signing book – which if you try to brush off, an attendant will patiently corral you to sign – that I was the 150,506[th] visitor.

Proving once and for all that power and sentimentality are not mutually exclusive, the memorial included a poem Sarney had written in 1986, his first full year as President in Brasília. It is titled *Love to Maranhão*, and no doubt suffers from translation:

> Maranhão is inspiration,
> It's life, it's nostalgia
> That doesn't stop hurting
> One day, it's a dream,
> It's too much love,
> Maranhão, my land, my passion

The feeling, apparently, is mutual, as old habits – including my own – don't die and never completely go away.

~ 18 ~

ONE EVENING IN SÃO LUÍS, when Atlas and I were returning from dinner and a walk in the Zona, we had another flat. It was night, with all the windows down, so I could hear the pfsssssss of escaping air. We slowed to a stop after a small field where youths were playing soccer. First there was Atlas to unload, then all of the trip's support detritus to pile up on the sidewalk in order to pull out the spare. Around this time a small car pulled over and stopped ahead, the Good Samaritan yelling, "I'm a professional flat tire fixer!" as he approached so as not to alarm us. Even with his help, by the end of the tire change I was soaked with sweat. I gratefully paid him a gratuity, and thanked São Cristovão that the flat had not happened during the mad twilight dash to the ferry in the wilds of the delta bush.

I got around to fixing the tire a few days later, only to find it beyond repair. By chance it was the same tire that had taken the finger-long nail near Bananal Island and, besides the well worn treads, now had a tear in the sidewall. At the surprisingly well equipped tire shop near my hotel, in the ugly if efficient part of town, I bought two new tires (also retiring the questionable spare) and replaced the brake pads. Braking for so many potholes, apparently, had taken its toll. The brake pad warning light had stopped blinking, we now discovered, when the sensor wire had gone from frayed (while jungle-scraping towards Cangaçu) to severed. To celebrate a newly refurbished Fofão, I took her to a car wash where I met a couple from Ceará who assured me that the road between here and Fortaleza was in fine shape. What a relief, I thought, to have the worst of the driving finally behind us. In a winterless land, hope springs eternal.

*   *   *

If the most rewarding *and* accessible parts of Brazil are at the end of long dirt roads, that dissuade most drivers from visiting, this also holds true for newly paved roads, as our next destination showed. The only way to Barreirinhas, according to my several guidebooks, takes over eight tortuous hours by bus, yet by our visit the over two hundred kilometers from the main highway had just been asphalted. Dead-ending at an old fishing village, it is probably one of the remotest stretches of paved road in Brazil: we passed only one truck. Electricity lines are strung between weathered-gray tree posts, and many a standing stick fence has impaled laundry drying in the wind. From the frail houses that appear shell-shocked by life's increasing velocity, children watched intently as we passed – as they often do in villages or outposts throughout the interior. A new and perfect road is too good to be true, which may explain why whenever we crossed a brook or low swamp, the concrete bridge rose so far above the road that the jolt was worse than a speed bump's. Road engineers just can't seem to make smooth bridge to road connections on any secondary road in Brazil. Then, from a hundred kilometers out, an odd mixture of bogs, ponds, and patches of white sand materialized, just as summer-like torrents of rain fell for the first time of our trip, lasting ten minutes before the clouds fled a hot-pursuit sun.

But why all the effort for little Barreirinhas? The village, like São Jorge in Goiás, is the launching point for another national park, here the spectacular Lençóis Maranhenses which encompasses one of the world's rarest and most perplexing ecosystems. The name Sheets of Maranhão stems from the billowy appearance of over 1,500 square kilometers of endless white dunes that end in the sea. Known as the Brazilian Sahara, it is a huge "desert" that is teeming with life, for it is full of fresh water. Product of a unique combination of forces, from sedimentary river flows, waves, and winds, the dunes are raised with fine quartz sand that, after being washed to sea by various rivers, is churned up by the waves and blown back inland by constant on-shore winds. During the rainy months, numerous ponds and lakes accumulate throughout the dunes, with crystalline clear water filtered through the sand traps. And it is this juxtaposition that most startles: white sandy dunes interspersed with endless blue lagoons. It is the least arid desert in the world, riddled with hidden life.

Intentionally, Atlas and I arrived in Barreirinhas towards the end of the day when Dona Iza would have to take pity on us, despite the policy of no pets, for how could she send us four long hours back to São Luís in the dark? Her small pousada on the banks of the sweet-smelling Rio Preguiça had been recommended by our receptionist in São Luís, whom Dona Iza didn't recall, but no matter. The room was plain but clean, with a ceiling fan and a television capable of one unfuzzy channel. Best of all was the sandy river beach where Atlas could dive after his ball in the warmth of the late afternoon sun. As the sunset's saturated multicolors faded, the symphony of crickets, tree frogs, and cicadas tuned up, before taking hold, *multo alegro*, of the riverside jungle. We were headed for yet another isolated patch of Brazil, a metaphorical island unto itself.* What is it about islands that I find so compelling?

Although Barreirinhas is over forty kilometers up Rio Preguiça, or Sloth River, from the sea, sand is everywhere, the town embraced by dunes. And while everything appears rather stable and fixed, it is not. The sands blow and the dunes move, the village's largest, called Ladder Hill, threatening to cut off the main road into town. In the days to come I would visit a tiny aldeia populated by some of Brazil's last nomads, for when the dunes march over their thatched roof huts (as they must), the families move to another open riverbank, starting all over again – with echoes of Hiroshi Teshigahara's fatalistic film *The Women of the Dunes.*

That first morning I found a seat on a large Toyota Bandeirante which crossed Rio Preguiça on a two-car ferry. While the park is

---

* Culturally, Brazil is very much an island in a Spanish-speaking neighborhood, which is mystified by it. The first explorers, indeed, mistook Brazil for an actual island.

without any sort of infrastructure and not officially open to tourists, the local guides and tour companies have come to an understanding with Ibama on where and what can be done. Once we crossed the river, a small sign beckoned us:

> Welcome to the Paradise of Lençóis!
> To Preserve is to Live!
> In this Sanctuary of Life we feel God's Embrace!

On the far side of a tiny village we saw an entrance gate and a small building under construction: the future park entrance. Then, after forty minutes on a rough deep-sand road that felt like riding the swells of a mild sea, we arrived at the edge of the suddenly treeless desert expanse.

According to Wagner, our guide, Lençóis was first comprehensively explored in 1981 by state-owned Petrobras, which, upon finding no valuable mineral deposits, turned it over to Ibama. Both its remoteness and the challenges posed to sustaining life have protected it over the centuries. With little to offer materially, there is little to take. Yet the idea that no one – other than the nomads, presumably – had "discovered" or mapped Lençóis until so recently seemed odd, but Brazilians have historically been a fairly uncurious lot. Only after a foreigner, and an English nanny at that, scaled Rio's Sugarloaf for the first time in 1817, did a Carioca decide, in a fit of pique, to repeat the feat and replace her Union Jack with the Brazilian flag.[100] In recent years world-class Brazilian athletes have shown the sort of stamina and derring-do one expects from a large, sports-crazed country, so perhaps the grit and determination pioneered by the Bandeirantes is returning full circle.

As for Lençóis, new winds are blowing with tour buses arriving daily from São Luís on the wings of asphalt. Wagner claimed that after Lençóis was featured in TV Globo's hit novella *The Clone*, tourism had increased markedly. And even as we spoke, a film called *The Women of the Sands* (mimicking Teshigahara's new wave classic) was being produced on the far side of the park. Clearly, the park service was playing catch up.

Due to Ibama's honor-system restrictions, we parked at the edge of the endless dunes and walked for twenty minutes to the first large lake, Lago Azul. There we swam with sixty-plus other stunned people in the surreal landscape, the white dunes sandwiched between the blue above and the refracted blue below – and nothing else, no trees, no bushes, just a few stick figure tourists. Despite the glaring heat, I jumped at the opportunity to take a guided hike to a more remote lake called Half Moon with only three other people, like the Bandeirantes, all Paulistas.

The rainy season recently past, one only needs to scratch the flat sand surfaces to encounter ground water seeping from the massive sand sponge. More closely eyeing the lake rims, one finds large quantities of isolated grass shoots and wild rosemary, enough to support the half dozen cattle (part of Ibama's honor system?) also wandering through our small corner of the park. The evaporating lakes were full of minnows which, when stranded, turn into easy prey for kingfishers and seagulls.

Intentionally lagging behind my small group, I felt like a child in my own out-sized sandbox. Once safely out of view of all but seagulls and foreign satellites above, I spun around like a top crying Happy Birthday to me!

An August birthday in Brazil might be more hazardous than most, but I was getting used to them: as low key affairs, for I am usually traveling. To celebrate with Atlas, at day's end I gave him a full once-over by inspecting his body for ticks, cleaning his ears with cotton, brushing him down, and, after drying him off from an hour long bath in – where else? – the Sloth River, squirting him with citronella spray against the multitudinous bugs. All of which he took in stride, with the "if you must" attitude of a spa denizen. New guests, we noticed, had arrived in the bungalow across the central grassy strip from ours, including two girls and a middle-aged woman. I tried to converse with one of the girls, who replied with bland pleasantries. Only after Atlas made nice did the mother decide we were safe and strike up a conversation, mentioning a local place for a good fish dinner.

When Atlas and I arrived at the open air restaurant, the threesome invited us to join them at their table. (Coincidentally, the Italians from the Alcântara catamaran were seated nearby and gave Atlas a particularly warm reception.)* The mother, who lives in São Luís, appeared interested in expanding their three-way conversation. The daughter and her French friend were ballerinas for a professional troop in Alsace-Lorraine not far from Strasbourg, and sported their dark hair in tell-tale ballerina buns. Both girls had left home in her early teens to study ballet, with the daughter spending her first two-year apprenticeship in Cuba's Havana. When the local fish dishes arrived, so did Dona Iza and her son, who sat down at a nearby table. So it turned into quite a sociable evening, without anyone knowing it was my birthday – just how I like it. When registering at the pousada I had gone so far as to transpose the first numerals of my requested birth date, placing it back in July. As a precaution. The road lends anonymity, which I prefer to guard at times.

Our last night in Barreirinhas, after Atlas's and my evening walk, Dona Iza invited us to join her, her husband, and son for a coffee on the open veranda. The pousada had emptied of weekend-trippers including the ballerinas, so we had the place to ourselves. A half-moon aided by a dangling low-watt bulb softly illuminated the family scene.

After good-evening pleasantries, I asked them about the Sarneys' dominance of Maranhão politics, which Dona Iza thought positive, while son Hanil expressed his reservations about the ex-President. Given that Dona Iza's family, originally from São Luís, had spent years working in São Paulo, I found this intriguing, as Paulistas pay by far the most into the federal treasury and are usually critical of the wasteful strongman politicians who dominate the Northeast and, due to the region's disproportional representation, are able to block most national reforms. While admitting that the Sarneys had grown rich off of public service, pointing to the infamous Swiss castle, they paraphrased the

---

* How had they gotten here? I doubt by catamaran, so perhaps they flew.

informal campaign slogan of one of São Paulo's native strongmen by saying, "They rob, but they get things done."

Hanil had recently returned home after nearly two decades of working, as a flight attendant, out of São Paulo, yet had nothing but praise for Sarney's daughter, Governor Roseana, saying it was she who got UNESCO to designate São Luís as a World Heritage Site and paid TV Globo to include Maranhão in such a positive light in the most recent novella *The Color of Sin* (whose protagonist, a mulatta affectionately known as Preta, or Blackie, is from São Luís). But it was the governor's love of Maranhão culture that most impressed Hanil, who pointed to her promotion of the Bumba-meu-boi festival with national advertising, and her diligent work to spruce up São Luís's central district. And all of this despite a complicated case of breast cancer, which required repeated treatment in São Paulo.

As the evening was soft and the company relaxed, I joked with Dona Iza that her son had not lost any of his enthusiasm for his home state after several decades away – indeed, that distance seemed to have made his heart grow fonder.

My observation encouraged Dona Iva to recall, with a laugh, how I had interrupted her while she was making a booking for me on the phone, in order to explain I would prefer a Rio Preguiça boat tour with a group of Brazilians, NOT with foreigners. Apologizing for my presumption, I tried to explain that a boat-full of non-Portuguese speakers would have been exhausting, as guides rarely speak any foreign language well. This occasioned Hanil to pay me the compliment, "Why, you've turned Brazilian!" which is a high one, as the family is originally from Syria.

The pousada's parking area hosted a small group of turkeys, whose plump bodies were silhouetted in the dark against the white gravel. During a conversational lull we heard a commotion and saw a small donkey clop back out to the road, having ventured inside the gate to nibble on grass.

"The turkeys scared away the donkey," Hanil pointed out.

"How brave!" I offered.

"Did you see that Mom and Dad?"

"Was it a donkey, or a mule without a head?" his father, Fernando, asked. They laughed.

"Do you know what he is referring to?" Hanil asked me. "*Mula-sem-cabeça* is an old children's fairy tale. She's a kind of ghost, or what happens to the priest's lover, who is transformed into a headless mule. It is her punishment to gallop the entire night, the flames coming out of her nostrils and mouth – even though you don't see the head – the sound of her hoofs heard from far away. You used to believe in it Dad, didn't you?"

"When I was a child," explained Fernando, who once worked as a rubber tapper in Pará. "My parents told me about it, and it used to frighten me, yes." The question had been for my sake, as this was clearly oft-repeated family lore.

"But it was really a horse going by in the dark, wasn't it?" Hanil chided him.

"I was young, how was I supposed to know?"

When arriving at Pousada do Rio, I had found the place a bit too fussy – with regulations on the room door prohibiting "Taking breakfast food on any excursion" and warning that "Visitors are not allowed inside the apartments; on the contrary, an additional charge will be added to the bill after visits of longer than 15 minutes" – but the family had grown on me with time: as warm, generous, and welcoming. Travel's greatest risk, confirmed over and over again, is going too quickly, treading on the quicksand of first impressions.

As Atlas and I pulled out of the driveway the next morning, a chorus of gobbles rose in parting. "The turkeys are saying good-bye," Hanil said from Dona Iza's side.

"Brave *and* polite turkeys!" I called as we left.

While departing Barreirinhas and bumping over the sandy feet of Ladder Hill extending into the road, I recalled the parting message of the park's home-spun sign over the banks of Sloth River, which reads:

Nature thanks you, Return always!

Did you feel the presence & love of God?

I don't know — but maybe. And thanks for asking.

~ 19 ~

THE DEEP POOL of Brazilian folklore and spirituality is like the high water table under the Sheets of Maranhão, just lurking below the surface if you look for it. Such was my experience, only the week before, when Joãozinho introduced me to my first *terreiro*, the worship center for practitioners of the Afro-Brazilian cult called *candomblé*. It was at night, back on the outlaw island of Marajó in northernmost Brazil where, if you listen carefully, you can hear the soft, thrumming echoes of Mina-nagô drums.

With Joãozinho's help, I was introduced to Fatima da Silva, a *mãe-de-santo*, or candomblé priestess, in town. I knew next to nothing about candomblé, which is an African word denoting a dance in honor of the gods, and was curious to see what I could find here, in the heart of indigenous Brazil. While no *batuque* was currently planned, Dona Fatima implied that it was for lack of "materials," the righting of which could motivate a gathering that very night. So I immediately offered to reverse the material-deficit, which was so warmly received that Fatima directed Big João, the association's president, to give me a ride back to the hotel on the back of his bicycle, to facilitate things. There I gave the proffered cash to Big João, who pedaled back into the twilight of adumbrations.

Ominously, a large thunderstorm rolled in overhead that evening, unleashing sheets of rain and several lightning bolts which rendered the air so thoroughly that Atlas, who normally doesn't bother with such things, barked sharply each strike. Atlas was edgy, and I don't blame him for being so, here on a soggy isle adrift in the Amazon's torrential discharge – sixty times that of the Nile.[101] Only when the rain diminished to a drizzle did I leave my hotel for the twenty minute walk to the terreiro, the streets gradually re-filling with pedestrians (as the water ebbed), including one who whistled "Hey! Tourist!" A smell of dusky fertility, unleashed by a million raindrops, permeated the heavy air.

Feeling anxious yet excited by the prospect of, once again, being out of my element, I arrived at the designated hour to find the lights were out all along Fatima's street. Without power it was preternaturally calm, with only the patter of spent rain dripping off of leaves and tiles: *drip, drip, drip-drop-drip*. I was welcomed into a dim reception room where a musty dark blue cover was promptly thrown over the sofa, and where seven or eight people, including several babies, were just finishing a meal scraped from the bottom of a battered aluminum pot by the light of a sole candle. When Dona Fatima came out, she said we had to wait for the power to return.

I was ceremoniously offered a seat on the newly covered sofa, even after remonstrating that I didn't want to interrupt the family dinner, and then one by one the indistinguishable bodies slipped out of the room until I was alone in the near total darkness. Fatima had sent several of her daughters on a hunt for more candles, with none yet to be found. Tiring of my own company, I joined them on the porch where the young band had reconstituted itself and, once again set in movement, kindly offered me space on the bench. Despite the artificial gloom, there was a festive edge to the atmosphere.

A son had been sent off to advise the power company's repairman of our predicament, and then an extra candle was found to add detail to the dark faces around me. I asked one daughter if another, who had been playing with an infant in front of us, was part of the Eco Marajoara dance group (another good name fallen victim to the "eco" trend), which I had seen perform at my hotel the prior night. The show features a troop of boys and girls in patterned shirts and skirts dancing the traditional *Carimbó*, in which the males flit around the inaccessible females, who twirl so quickly as to become whirling dervishes. Yes, Nicole replied, and offered that she, too, is part of the dance troupe.

Soon enough the yellow moon pushed through the dispersing clouds, throwing a pale light over the proceedings as more people and supplies arrived. Moon rays penetrated the porch and kitchen across the way, from where a suspicious neighbor stared back at us. Nicole told me that her mother has been mãe-de-santo for thirty-two years, and that five of her children still live at home.

We waited long enough for the electric company's truck to arrive and the repairman to jack his ladder up one of the nearby poles, after which Tati, the organizing daughter, ushered me into the empty terreiro behind the house as Fatima had decided that, power or no power, the batuque would proceed in the chiaroscuro of candlelight. Tati showed me to a lone bench up front by the spectators' gallery, where she motioned for me to sit. The main area contained a raised dais with a stuccoed balustrade, behind which were arrayed various instruments, including bongos, Mina-nagô drums, and bamboo tubes filled with pebbles. In front of the dais spread a small votive area, with candles, a solitary black hat, various shells, and a painted semi-circle on the polished cement floor. A small urn filled with smoking embers would be stoked the entire evening, creating the most sticky and omnipresent smoke I've experienced since the bowels of Jerusalem's Holy Sepulcher church. In the middle of the shiny polished-cement floor a lonely candle anchored a rectangular design with Arabic writing, while off to a corner gathered some oily-dark statuary, almost Thai Buddhist in their wet sleekness. Behind the spectators' area I noticed several large displays with full-body mannequins, mostly clad in elaborate colonial dress, the dummies with brown plastic skin and mute faces. The play of candlelight seemed to flash in their unblinking eyes.

When the drumming started in earnest, led by Big João behind the tallest drum, a dozen dancing apprentices filled the enclosed area, surrounded on two open sides by a crowd of worshipers, initiates, and neighbors, who at first sign of activity had populated the stands instantaneously, almost without my having noticed. Dona Fatima, transformed into an opulent mãe-de-santo, or literally "saint's mother," in bright red, took the lead in singing and dancing before the drummers and offerings. Nasal-high, female singing rose and tumbled in syncopation with the rhythms of swaying hips. Fatima and most of the women wore elaborate hoop skirts, in satin of various colors with fancy white frills, which spun up and around as they twirled, revealing puffed-up knickers that tapered off to bare legs and bare feet – an effect that looked surprisingly like hen's legs. Fatima's garb was the most elaborate and multi-layered, including a cotton-weave skull cap from which hung a long red scarf and a large quantity of heavy, stabilizing beads hugging her breasts. The men, for the most part, wore baggy silk pants and white open button-down shirts, with prayer beads slung across their chests like spiritual ammunition belts for backland cowboys.

I felt transported back to a colonial Haiti soon after the bloody overthrow of the French. The songs seemed celebratory, at times defiantly so.

One prominent dancer, in particular, caught my attention. She was a proud and austere-looking *cafuza* (a woman of African and Indian heritage), with tautly smooth, black, and perfect skin, whose high cheek bones and penetrating eyes gave her a regal appearance: I could have mistaken her for an African King's daughter or a Nordic Ice princess. She was the most startlingly beautiful woman there. The tallest and thinnest dancer on the floor, she wore a headband with two tall feathers to further accentuate her stature. She danced at Fatima's side while showing constant deference, as though in training to succeed her.

The headgear allowed for more individual expression. Besides the skull caps and headbands, several women wore hard white cowboy hats in a continuation of the Cowboy and Indian theme, which, for all I know, was imported from Hollywood. What stood out were hard leather hats that look like half-Saturns with stilled rings, made famous by the *cangaceiro* Lampião who terrorized the northeastern sertão for over two decades early last century. All that was missing to complete the north coast's cultural array was a Portuguese sailor cap or, perhaps, a Jesuit's hat.

The women had smoked a few joints at the start of the evening's festivities, and some, including the mixed-blood Princess, took drags to smooth their trance descents. After several long dances the batuque had warmed up considerably, with some women dabbing their foreheads with frilly handkerchiefs and others quaffing beer. Fatima's every desire was quickly attended to, if not by Tati then by the Princess, be it an outstretched arm with an empty glass in need of filling or a fat joint in need of lighting or several bead strings to be taken away. After leading for several songs Fatima was the first to get the shakes, her cries accompanied by violent jerks of her body during which the ever attentive circle braced her, as needed, from tipping over. I watched carefully, transfixed, even startled, by the spiritual depths opening before me. If someone had blown smoke in my ears, I might not have even noticed.

Fully transformed into "Ilansa," her mother-of-saint name, my hostess then retired to a small back room to sit out the rest of the evening, while receiving guests with an ever-overflowing glass of beer held like a scepter in hand. Ilansa was thirsty.

The lead position changed from then on, and somehow every dancer had the wherewithal to hand off a hat or some beads to a colleague before succumbing to the shakes. Few, if any, personal objects fell to the ground.

And so it went. At times the reduced crew circled around the central candle and rectangle, or, as energy flagged and surged, those who had rested jumped back in. The drummers and tube-shakers played until spent, when they were replaced by fresh recruits including Nicole and the other young Carimbó dancer-daughters.

Tati looked after me with great care, offering me a homemade drink of guaraná and then inviting me back into Ilansa's inner sanctum. As it was difficult to understand her due to the racket, Ilansa (or was it Fatima?) took me outside for a minute to explain that her birthday was coming up and, if I wanted to contribute to the celebration, that Tati would give me the requisite information on how to make a donation. And that I would always be welcome – presumably with or without material-bolstering funds.

After more bowing and Japanese-like expressions of gratitude, we returned to the terreiro. By now the electricity was back on and the candles were snuffed out – but the energy felt spent. On the dance floor there remained only a few men and some hardy old women, whose shuffling dance could have gone on for ages. It was past midnight when I decided to head back to the hotel.

When the *moto-taxi* arrived, Tati ushered me to the front porch where the evening had begun and, liberally berating the motorcyclist, instructed him to take good and careful care of me on the way back to the hotel. This woman, the organizing daughter, was a wonder to behold. She made me feel like the most worthy guest of the Pasha of Marajó.

I climbed onto the scooter behind the driver, a young man so obviously familiar with the terrain that he wove expertly in the near-total dark through the maze of puddles and glassy full potholes without the benefit of a headlamp. After the smoke-filled batuque, whose thumping cries receded under the calm weight of the sky's stillness, the equatorial night breeze felt like a soft, cleansing spray on my face. He told me on the way to my bay-front hotel that he wanted to marry Tati more than anything else in the world, which I could understand. More than that, I rejoiced. For only in Brazil can you meet someone for a few passing moments and be brought so fully and effortlessly into his or her confidence, sharing life's greatest hopes and desires. It is a nation of quick, jagged, and often uncertain moves, yet also of surprising and unselfish intimacy. (As the historian Sérgio Buarque de Hollanda wrote, one of the defining Brazilian characteristics is the "desire to establish an intimacy.")[102] While over my head, once again, and destined to be the perpetual outsider, I suddenly felt relaxed and part of the group – though which group I'm still not sure.

After dismounting, I thanked the young driver for treating me so carefully and well, and along with the fare gave him a good tip, saying it was for the wedding. Which I am certain will happen if it hasn't already, for in Tati's admonition there was a delicate and knowing upbraiding, the kind that could fill a lifetime. And while it hardly merits mentioning, there did not seem to be the slightest impediment to their union from the pedestrian fact that he is white and she is black – on the outlaw isle of Marajó in northernmost Brazil.

We said our goodbyes and then the low gurgle of the motorbike sputtered away, as the gears slipped progressively through lower octaves into night.

~ 20 ~

THAT PEACEFUL EVENING on Dona Iza's veranda near the banks of Sloth River, Hanil also recounted the story of Saci, the one-legged Negro who likes to scare children. It was a stilled night under a surprisingly strong half-moon, perfect for spinning tales. Hanil described Saci's most distinctive feature – after the missing leg – as a rakish red cap that gives him mysterious, even revolutionary powers. He smokes a pipe, doesn't like to cross water, and announces his arrival with a strange whistling that is difficult to locate and emanates as if from the shadows. Among his various nocturnal habits, Saci likes to tie knots in horse, sheep, and other animal hair (after exhausting the animals in their corrals), scare steer, frighten night-travelers, put out cooking fires, burn stovetop meals, and with some frequency misplace household objects. In other words, he is the source of most domestic conflict, a scapegoat almost as useful as the promiscuous Boto. Outdoors, where he is most encountered, he is often seen as a moving shadow and sometimes transforms himself into a small whistling bird. For one who puckishly enlivens marital disputes, he appears well adjusted at home, accompanied either by a poorly dressed Negress whose own whistling makes a noise approximating his name – *sa-see! sa-see!* – or, at times, by an old Indian woman.[103]

Having crossed the Maranhão border into the Northeast we were, like Saci between wives, transitioning from Indian to heavier African influences, in many ways to the heart and soul of Brazilian culture. Folktales, such as Saci's, are really the story of Brazilian slavery endlessly retold, here with the playfully vengeful ex-slave. In truth, it is a tragic and horrifying story, of roughly four million Africans forcibly brought to Brazil – more, by far, than to any other region in the New World, including North America's four hundred thousand. For those who survived the Atlantic crossing, a short and brutish life awaited them: worn down by physical labor, the average life span of a slave by late 18th century was twenty short years. (For Londoners, in 1800, life expectancy was not much longer, at twenty-three years.)[104]

It was the first governor-general, Tomé de Sousa, who requested the Crown's permission to import African slaves in 1549 to build the new capital Salvador named, without irony, for Our Savior. The Portuguese were well versed in slavery, having explored the African coast from their new Atlantic island possessions in the 1440's and then setting up the first sugar-mill, worked by slaves, on Madeira in 1452. Throughout the 16th century the Portuguese had a virtual monopoly on the Atlantic trade in human chattel. So it is no coincidence that it was the planting of sugar-cane (originally from Asia) in northeastern Brazil that accelerated the human commerce. Only Brazil's first truly lucrative crop could pay for the high costs of imported slaves and required infrastructure. Thus, in the receptive soils of Bahia and Pernambuco, slavery and sugar cane were planted with equal vigor, turning Brazil into the world's leading sugar exporter for a century. When coffee plantations took root further south in the early 18th century, this only multiplied the need for pliable, dependable, and self-propagating labor.

Sousa's arrival also signaled the Crown's fresh commitment to settle the colony, as the system of captaincies had proven too weak to tame the Indians or fend off other European interlopers. A nobleman with experience in India and Africa, the governor-general arrived on a flotilla of boats with one thousand strong, bringing with him the first heads of steer, the first Jesuits[105] and, no less importantly, the first "women of good quality" who were orphans and, naturally, white. But Sousa was up against a force of nature, as the lone-wolf Portuguese felt little compunction in mating with Indian and, eventually, African slaves whenever possible. (Due to the "liberty," as the Pernambucano sociologist Gilberto Freyre put it, "that the European had to choose among dozens of Indian women.")[106] So strong was the Portuguese drive to populate the vast colony that miscegenation was officially encouraged – at least with indigenous women – and even Catholic priests were allowed to have children. (Only much later, during the First Republic, did the diluting of black blood through European immigration become the objective of an official "whitening" policy, in a misguided attempt to compete with their Europeanized arch rival Argentina.) Such was the increasingly magnetic pull of Brazil's promise, that during the 18th century gold rush the Crown had to pass a law discouraging the de-population of Portugal.[107]

Yet this attempt, the first of many to civilize the nascent colony, would end in tears when Sousa, a bastard himself, gave up to return to Portugal after only four years in the fallen paradise, disgusted with the "low-lifes" who undermined the process of colonization and whose growing numbers were like "throwing evil seeds on the land." (It didn't help that among his one thousand frontiersmen were four hundred deportees, who were "horny, criminal and half-insane" according to one early 20th century Rio journalist.)[108] His abrupt departure was paralleled by the apocryphal story of Brazil's first Bishop who, setting sail back to Portugal in 1556 in a huff, was shipwrecked by a storm off of Alagoas and promptly eaten on the beach by the local cannibals – whom he had derided.[109] Cultural assimilation cuts both ways.

The northern coast of Brazil is largely bereft of bishops, journalists, and other tourists. The beaches are generally poor, the shore of difficult access, so roads hew well inland and only intermittently meet the sea at ports or along river deltas. All of which explains why I liked it. The coast, when you can find it, isn't overly developed; the people (like those of Goiás and Tocantins) aren't accustomed to foreign interlopers; the region as a whole feels more buffeted by wind than by change.

Consequently it was a long, meandering driving day, at first along the lengthy road from Barreirinhas back to São Luís, then on the sparsely trafficked BR-316 all the way to the border of Piauí. There were few commercial vehicles other than feeder vans, as long-haul transporters from the Southeast's economic vortex prefer the Belém-

Brasília to the circuitous "coastal" route – which suited us fine. With the windows down, the equatorial breezes passing through the car were a welcome relief from the stifling humidity of stasis. It was good to be on the road again, trying to keep ahead of an accelerating and nearly overwhelming past.

Not surprisingly the "evil seeds" which Sousa condemned did not include the bane of slavery which he first sowed. And well planted it was, as slavery and a slave-based society were widespread throughout Portuguese America by the early 1600's, made up almost entirely of African slaves, with the exceptions of São Paulo and Belém where blacks would nominally replace Indian slaves only a century later.

The African influence on Brazilian culture cannot be underestimated. As the memorial at Belém's Ver-o-Sol explained, "All of us Brazilians are the flesh of the flesh of those prostrated Negroes and Indians." How can you travel in the Northeast, where the blood of millions of slaves saturates the land, and not feel the deeply Afro-Brazilian roots in music, food, dance, and spirituality, all cultural facts which, in a sweet-bitter reversal, dominate the country? Their genius underpins two of the most distinctive Brazilian characteristics: startling creativity coupled with an embracing, sunny disposition – the envy of many an artist.

Which does not deny that the process was tortuous, or that the plight of poor blacks, who contrary to the Brazilian myth of "racial democracy" still face prejudice, is still wretched. Unlike the Indians, who knew the ways of the jungle and could slip with ease into the backlands to escape servitude, blacks were caught between the deep sea and the dense forest, forced to either submit or fight.

The Portuguese, accordingly, lived in mortal fear of slave insurrections. By the turn of the 18th century, only thirty-one percent of Brazilians were considered "European," eight percent indigenous, and sixty-one percent of African or mixed descent, with slaves representing nearly half of the population.[110] So for the colony's first two centuries and more, there were vast regions, including Minas, Rio, and the

Northeast, not to mention major capitals such as Salvador and Rio, where slave populations were a significant majority.

The first durable challenges to slavery occurred far from the coasts, in communities called *quilombos,* made up of runaway slaves braving the jungle interiors. As many as seven hundred isolated towns descended from these African villages still exist. The most famous quilombo, called Palmares in the Bishop-consuming state of Alagoas, was led by the chieftain Zumbi and survived for nearly a century before being wiped out – after five local militia offensives which failed – by a large military expedition of Bandeirantes in the late 17th century, brought in for the kill.[111]

Only later did the much feared coastal revolts, of slaves rising up against their masters, materialize. As shown by the Cabanagem War in Pará, when the ruling white elite divided in a power struggle against itself, uprisings by slaves often followed. The same occurred in the Balaiada Revolt in Maranhão – named after the basket-weaving profession of one of the leaders, as *balaio* means basket – when the rebels occupied the province's second largest city, Caxias, well inland. Among its leaders were the basket weaver who joined to avenge his daughter's rape by a police captain; a cafuso fighter (of mixed blood, like the Candomblé Priestess); and a black leader named Cosme, at the head of a contingent of three thousand runaway slaves. The rebellion was repressed within two years by government troops, with a public hanging, naturally, reserved for Cosme.[112]

Just before crossing the state line into Piauí that day, Atlas and I passed by Caxias in Maranhão's parched interior. While a Brazilian historian in the mid-19th century called it "the city of crime, refuge of criminals, the domain of minor pashas who at their will determined others' lives, [which] was accustomed to seeing murders everyday,"[113] the city now blushingly bills itself as "The Princess of the Sertão." But then within many a princess lurks a more interesting lineage.

Most slave revolts occurred after Brazil's destabilizing independence from Portugal. This came about in 1822, when Dom João VI's son, Pedro I, declared himself Emperor of Brazil with the *cri-de-coeur*

"Independence or Death!," which encouraged post-colonial power struggles among the elites and seeded dreams of liberty among everyone else. (Consistent with most of Brazil's fair-skinned *coups d'état*, hardly one person died in the transition from colony to empire.) Salvador, the old colonial capital, was the center for a number of slave rebellions, including a brief one called the Sabinada Revolt by Islamic African slaves in 1835. Several years later the unbowed rebels re-took the city and tried to compromise on the issue of abolition by promising to manumit native-born slaves. Yet with lower (and darker) class insurrections, there could be no compromise, no peaceful end: in hand-to-hand combat the city was re-taken by imperial troops within two years, leaving nearly two thousand dead and most of the City of Our Savior in flames.[114]

That night Atlas and I ended up in Teresina, the capital of Piauí, that is so fiery hot it is known as "the bunghole of Brazil," according to a Pernambucano software engineer I met in Lençóis. Despite repeated efforts on my part, nothing seemed to work in Teresina – and not only due to the heat.

The two tourist offices I visited (both, at first, found closed during working hours) confirmed that the Piauí Museum was open, when it wasn't. This I discovered by stepping into the museum's cool interior, only to find the furniture and exhibitions covered in sheets, and by naively asking "Are you open?" to a largish woman loitering there.

"No, my dear," she replied. "We closed for renovations. The exhibitions here are all wrapped up, but still haven't gone anywhere."

Morbidly curious, I asked, "So when are you scheduled to re-open?"

"They say three months," she replied with a broad smile, "but the way things are here..."

When I asked at my roadside hotel for directions to a restaurant known for local cuisine, the receptionist turned out to be map-illiterate, at first suggesting the help of a businessman going my way (who agreed to lead me before disappearing), and then giving me rough directions from memory (the map in conflict with her spatial recall), with the advice I ask for directions as approaching. That I did four times, after getting completely lost in the normally dangerous periphery of a strange city after dark, only to learn that the crab restaurant no longer served regional dishes. The waiter, to lessen my disappointment, was a study in hardscrabble and dignified Northeastern reserve, having worked in São Paulo from age eighteen to thirty, where he had "learned a lot." One more example of the Bandeirantes – adopted or otherwise – on the march throughout Brazil. With a big dog of his own at home, he welcomed Atlas and his keeper without hesitation. (This positive experience was the exception to almost all other Northeastern restaurants, where I often sauntered in with a leashed Atlas as if the most natural thing in the world, only to be met by horrified looks from waiters and managers. At one – in Aracaju, the coastal capital of Sergipe – I asked the panicked waiter why well-trained dogs weren't allowed, to which he replied "because of the air conditioning" – implying a dog's germs are dangerously spread that way.)

But the biggest surprise in Teresina was when I learned on TV that the city's federal deputy, named Alfonso Gil, had just been found dead at his home. Although reported as a suicide, everyone, including the spatially-challenged receptionist, suspected murder due to his having uncovered an extortion and assassination racket within the city's federal police. The journalist who first exposed the crime ring had already been killed four years previously, along with a political colleague who had helped Deputy Gil to reveal the underworld scheme, murdered just before the prior election after the racket's kingpin, a Lieutenant Coronel Correia Lima, had threatened their lives from his maximum-security prison cell. (Perhaps the ultimate form of security, in such cases, would be the death penalty, but it is outlawed in Brazil.) The city was abuzz with crime scene details, such as reports that Deputy Gil was locked in his bedroom and drunk at the time of his death, and that there had been not one but two shots – a number not usually congruent with suicide. As, undoubtedly, the only lone alien passing through Brazil's "bunghole" at such an inauspicious time, I became convinced I would be unceremoniously woken before dawn and made to report to the local police station for heated questioning.

Busted! – I could imagine – for traveling while foreigner. Perhaps my luck was starting to run out.

If economic determinism, the demand for self-generating and replaceable labor, fueled the rise and permanence of slavery, it was another sort of economic determinism which caused its downfall. The British – who for centuries had been aligned with the Portuguese, in opposition to the Spaniards or, as during Napoleon's reign, against the French – eventually became Portugal's paymaster, as the fading Portuguese Empire, for a century and more the world's most powerful, slowly degenerated into Western Europe's basket case. Portugal, once the greatest of seafaring nations, came to depend on the Royal Navy to protect its lopsided trade with the Brazilian colony, which was only allowed to purchase processed goods from the jealous mother country. The massive profits from the Royal fifth taken during Minas Gerais's century-long gold rush are said to have not only propped up the failing Portuguese court but also, when turned over to the British as repayment for loans, paid for the Industrial Revolution. (Such was their prevalence that Portuguese gold pieces, on the streets of London, were reported to have outnumbered British ones for a time.) When Brazil achieved independence, the New World's only homegrown empire tried to facilitate the peace and assure open maritime trade by assuming Portugal's debts to Britain, which included costs incurred while fighting against its very liberation. And so began Brazil's long and illustrious history of indebtedness.

The spilling of African blood began to slow in the New and not so innocent World when the United States prohibited the slave trade in 1807, followed sixteen years later by the British Parliament's abolition of slavery in its Atlantic colonies. In the interim the British pressured Brazil, the world's largest slave economy, to sign a treaty outlawing the slave trade within three years. The subsequent Brazilian law, declaring all slaves who reached its shores to be free men, met the same fate: it was not enforced. The cat and mouse game continued – spawning a phrase "for English eyes only" which survives to this day – until the Brazilian parliament categorically banned all such trade, if not ownership, in 1850. Around this time the British were seizing most slave ships headed towards Brazil, over four hundred of them during the prior five years. After the American Civil War, the only remaining major slave states were Brazil and Cuba. As pressure mounted, the Brazilians passed the "Law of the Free Womb," manumitting all children born in captivity. As for abolition itself, it waited for the "Golden Law" of 1888, a total and immediate abolition without compensation. Within a year the Brazilian Empire collapsed and the country's first republic was formed.[115]

Racism in Brazil, as in most other places, is a touchy, bitter subject, that seems to deaden human potential rather than lift it to new heights. Abolition was a start in the direction of human liberty but, as elsewhere, cured little in and of itself. A patronage system coupled with deferring habits allowed serf-like conditions to perpetuate for generations, especially in the Northeast's interior where they still flourish. Freed slaves often became dependent serfs of the large landowners, with the exception of a few places such as Maranhão where they left the plantations and settled as squatters on previously unoccupied land. (A strategy still used by the present day *Movimento Sem Terra*, or Landless Movement, which is known to close highways for hours at a time while pilfering stranded goods.)

The new solution to racial "problems," rather than torture and outright subjugation, rapidly became the old solution already applied to the Indians: miscegenation.[116] Failing all else, sex and procreation resolve most conflicts in Brazil. The whitening of the population became all but official policy, from the encouragement of mixed marriages to the first large disembarkations of European immigrants in over a century. Motivated, likely, by pangs of guilt, all that was by root black and African was, to the ruling elites, shameful.

This myopic attitude began to change after World War I. A central figure in the transition, the writer-sociologist Gilberto Freyre, published a pioneering study of Brazilian social history called *Casa-grande e Senzala* (released in English as *The Masters and the Slaves*), which for the first time celebrated the African roots of Brazilian society and culture. At long last, after the assimilation of millions of Africans into the voluminous confluences of Brazil, was the racial and cultural distinctiveness of the country recognized and praised. Yet along with such overdue recognition came an overly optimistic reading of history called the theory of "racial democracy," claiming credulously that Brazil has long been above racism.

Nowadays, it is still common to hear that Brazil suffers not from racial but from class discrimination and, as blacks tend to be poorer, they just happen to suffer disproportionally from lack of economic opportunity. But in the same way that environmentalism has become a subject of intense interest to educated Brazilians – largely due to the maligned process of globalization (of fads and ideas) – discrimination is now discussed more openly, in the media and at the local bar. Racial quotas have started to make their way into university admissions guidelines, in yet another costly import from the United States, and whatever the merits of reverse discrimination one has to feel sorry for the administrators and bureaucrats who will be charged with implementing them, for the immensely diverse palette of Brazil is extremely difficult to classify, more so than anywhere else in the world. (One household survey turned up 136 different terms Brazilians use to describe their own skin gradations.)[117] Yet Brazil has long been less a meritocracy than a juggling of powerful interests, which leads to the hope that the country, rather than permanently institutionalizing discrimination along racial lines, might assimilate these newly recognized interests with good humor, grace, and compassion.

If only we could always deal with life's challenges that way.

A fate worse than being murder suspects awaited us when we fled up the TransPiauí Highway, the only road linking the state's two largest towns from Teresina to Parnaíba on the coast, and were swallowed whole by our trip's worst potholes that required repelling down before free-climbing back out. Unsurprisingly not much worked in Parnaíba either, a town whose main reason for existence, its port, became inoperable after the river silted up years ago. Twice over two days, a local agency promised boat rides out into the massive delta of the Parnaíba River that fell through, and then the hotel tried to overcharge us after the unctuously concerned manager – who had thankfully been asleep when we checked in – asked if Atlas "wouldn't be more comfortable in the parking lot?"

"No, he's just fine in the room," I answered with a pinched smile, almost adding childishly, "And you?"

I decided that the journey to escape Piauí, instead of returning via the dreadful TransPiauí, couldn't be any more disastrous along the coast – the first feasible coastal driving since Belém – particularly after a gas attendant described the route as much better. Apparently the locals don't get out of town much, as it was much worse, thirty-two kilometers of the most consistently bomb-cratered road of the trip, really wave upon wave of sand traps dotted by elevated islands of asphalt: another wash-out. To make matters worse, when we were lost trying to leave town, a truck, coming in the other direction, charged over a low railroad crossing and splashed up some filthy accumulated liquid from between the rail ruts, not only onto the windshield but through my open window. When I stopped at another gas station to ask for directions and to squeegee the worst splotches off of Fofão, I neglected to wash my hands and, subsequently, while trying to maintain some sanity driving over the inverted moonscape, ate a quick sandwich and apple lunch. Only later, after realizing how smelly my fingers were, did I put two and two together and figure out that low lying brackish water in an otherwise dry landscape could only be sewage, whose bacteria had effortlessly jumped from my fingers to my lips, and that I would certainly fall ill and die within days – as sure as a double-shot suicide.

There is no escape from the past, distant or recently laid down. The curse of August, thanks to Piauí, had struck at last.

THERE IS NOTHING like a good pissy mood when traveling to attract even more mishaps. Don't ask me how, but while we were fleeing Piauí a speeding truck sprayed fresh cow dung all over Fofão's front. I would not have thought it possible, but it is. Sometimes you just have to accept things as they are, which is one of life's harder lessons, including more than a few truths that don't reflect well on you.

Take me, for example. Despite being raised by several German Shepherds, I was not such a dog expert after all – and had a lot to learn. Other uncomfortable truths, dawning as slowly on me as a mountain valley daybreak, included the likelihood I was never a very good husband and am probably not cut out for the marriage racket, preferring instead the deft if perambulatory touch in human relations, the non-stop roadtrip of life. When the road gets rough, or risky for your health, you can always move on.

Yet precisely when it appears nothing more can go wrong while scraping the bassoon-depths of travel, and you're ready to throw away your shriveled pride, give up, and opt permanently for the package tour, is usually the time a little perseverance can bring sudden rewards, of redemptive if fleeting moments to the rescue. Such it was that afternoon, when we drove inland through some of the most enchanting backroads of Ceará, before climbing the Chapada da Ibiapaba up a one lane mountain road to the simply nicest pousada of our trip, called Neblina. When the attentive girl at Mist Inn told me the price of the spotlessly clean and ample room, I joked – as she had already welcomed the presence of Atlas – "And that's for single occupancy?'

"Yes."

"But Atlas doesn't even earn a salary!"

After a chuckle she allowed, "Maybe we can give you both a discount." At thirty-five reals it was the most reasonable of the journey.

The next morning I visited the kilometer deep caves of Ubajara National Park, the country's smallest, which is named after a legendary cacique ("master of the canoe" in Tupi) who came up from the coast to live alone for the rest of time. I could see why, as it is the only place in Brazil where you can gaze from rainforest down onto the Brazilian semi-desert, or the vast ecosystem of the sertão named *caatinga,* by the Indians, for "white forest" – a view spanning the greatest ecological contrast of the country.[118] The Ubajara oasis is what's called an altitude swamp, a mountainous remnant of the Atlantic rainforest that once covered much of the Northeast, before tree-felling and burning created a tortured, sun-scorched landscape of some tragic beauty.

The caatinga is characterized by sparser vegetation than the cerrado, the trees even more stunted, the landscape dotted with varied cactuses (including one, for the world's largest Catholic country, mischievously called Pope's Head) and with numerous bromeliads, whose water-catching properties make them indifferent to lack of ground water. The soil is thin and over-grazed, its parchedness accentuated by rocky outcrops bared by erosion. Annual dry spells are long and irregular, with six or seven rainless months in a row common, lending the landscape a defensive, the-worst-is-yet-to-come look.[119] When the rains do fall, they tend to be torrential, the caatinga bursting into color – including, presumably, the flowering Pope's Head.

We would traverse the austere caatinga most of the following day, nearly completing the last leg of the northernmost east-west highway that starts in Belém and definitively reaches the east coast at Fortaleza, the capital of Ceará. Just when I was certain that the worst driving (kindness of Piauí) was behind us, the relatively benign and idyllic east coast within our grasp, we encountered the worst federal highway conditions of our trip, after Sobral, of over a hundred kilometers completely riddled with trip-breaker potholes. (I should have noticed the bad omen when, upon leaving Ubajara, we were blocked for nearly a hour by an overturned junkyard truck.) The colors of the pothole dirt varied, making it more difficult than usual to gauge depth. We hit many of them, two of them so hard I could hear the painful clang of metal against metal, the shock-absorbers unequal to the beating. Thank São Cristovão the two pairs of tires, new and old, held out.

There is something about such an awning deterioration of public trust along a major federal route that drives otherwise sane humans to distraction. It is as though the wounded spirits of the long-gone jaguars, peccaries, rheas, and giant anteaters that once inhabited the sertão, pre-caatinga, return to infiltrate hapless wanderers with a wild-eyed disbelief. As the afternoon leached away to a twilight gloom, I saw cars, which had earlier navigated the potluck road with relative calm, now fly past us with abandon – no one wanted to be trapped by these hell-holes at night. Even the usually lucid truck drivers were performing hijinks I hadn't seen on Brazilian highways since the good old lawless, each-to-his-own days of the early 1990's, such as one large truck inching past another on a blind curve. (Never mind the illegality of it: an oncoming car would have met a swift death or a prolonged tumble through the caatinga.) I cursed the memory of that young couple at the car wash who had assured me the highway all the way from São Luís to Fortaleza was in "good shape." All is relative these post-modern days, such that if the road had been impassable for most of their lives, then the qualification *good* might even apply, but I ascribe it instead to the delusional suppression of facts in dissonance with the holiday mantra, "We are on vacation and we are having fun!"

Yet as a philosophy of life – even if a kind of pathological upbeatism so common in Brazil – there are certainly worse ones.

Delusional dissonance just about explained my exhausted state of mind as we finally, under cloak of night, breached the coast that runs south for over two thousand kilometers of almost non-stop beaches. Besides one more drive through the sertão between Mossoró and Natal in the state of Rio Grande do Norte, the rest of the trip, principally on BR-101, would more or less follow the spectacular white-beached and palm-dotted coastline of the Northeast, until the last day's inland trek back to Minas Gerais.

But it is the sertão – which while meaning backwoods pertains almost exclusively to the Northeast – that defines the essence of the region, though tourists rarely experience it. Even when clinging to the coastal lushness of our free fall south, we could always sense the sertão's presence, hovering off to the side, a glancing memory never quite out of mind's eye. For Brazilians, the sertão is synonymous with crippling droughts, whose recurring history traces as far back as 1692 when one killed most of the Northeast's cattle. In the 1790's, and then again in the 1870's, a third to a half of the populations of Pernambuco and Ceará perished due to droughts. And the list goes on, including a particularly harsh one in the 1930's when hundreds of thousands of subsistence farmers and laborers died – in part due to the environmental degradation wrought by their own hands. The history of Brazil largely unfolds with the internal migrations from the Northeast to other regions, not only because the young colony started in Bahia and, along with some coastal seeding, spread outwards, but due to the successive flights of economic desperation, to mine gold in Minas Gerais, to tap rubber near Belém, or to hunt material well-being and at times simple survival in the mega-cities of Rio and São Paulo. It is as though the Okies' fateful journeys, depicted in John Steinbeck's *The Grapes of Wrath*, were repeated again and again, without end.

Nordestinos are by definition a hardscrabble people, often of shorter stock with corkscrew hair and wide facial features. They like to keep their own counsel, but also have a sing-songy manner of speech which is both joyful and subversive at the same time. The colonial system began here and in many ways its feudalism carries on, leaving the Northeast's foundation of patronage largely intact. (Such widespread slavery engendered a deep-rooted paternalism, which is both Brazil's burden and history's revenge.) The culture of patronage blithely descended from the strongmen coroneis, those corrupt politicians who along with Brazil's most famous bandits are endemic to the region – and are sometimes one and the same. Such is the local talent for endurance that in places such as Pernambuco, where the Dutch had a three decade crack at running the capital, startling blue eyes still surprise three centuries after the fact.

For me, it was love at first sight visiting the Northeast in the days when the only flights from Rio or São Paulo made mail-stop hops going up or down the coast, touching down at the small capital towns that multiplied as abundantly as rural families.

But this time, for some reason, the bloom was off the desert rose and I felt disappointed. Part of it may be that in comparison with the rest of Brazil (less the steamy fleshpot of Rio), the Northeast was now crawling with foreign tourists, most of them European. During this Brazilian winter, it was the Italians' turn to infiltrate every nook and cranny of the stupendous coast, an invasion which began as far north as Alcântara with my fellow catamaran passengers, and would continue until the rainforest comes crashing off the coastal range and sweeps away the typically flat, palm-fronded Northeastern beaches, somewhere around Holy Spirit state.

Not only Italian tourists, but Italian dentists doing charity work and Italian families purchasing rundown seaside inns and fixing them up. Italy's family-centric capitalism takes well to the region's hierarchical and who-knows-who lifestyle, so if any foreigners can fathom the shifty business opportunities without losing their shirts, they are the Italians. I have often thought of Italy as the most Brazilian nation in Europe, for the exuberance of life that hangs out of windows and fills small alleys with shouts of joy, for its love of family and lapsed Catholicism, for the quick con job done with a pleasant smile. (Or, seen from another angle, the age-old enigma of a Mediterranean versus Northern Europe flourishes in the hothouse of Brazil as its polar opposite, transformed but identifiable.)

So I shouldn't knock the hordes of fun-loving Italians who blend in better than most other nationalities, but the tsunami of tourism, in a country relatively untouched by natural disasters, has had an impact on Northeasterners, who are losing some of their natural charm and disarming gracefulness. A pity – at least for nostalgic travelers like myself.

*　　*　　*

There are many renowned, even charming *sertanejos* who have had national impact, for good or ill. The two most famous ones were born last century in the sertão of Pernambuco. Brazil's best known outlaw, Lampião, was a simple cowboy until his parents were killed by a landowner. He and his brothers took up with the cangaceiros of the back bush, and by 1920 were leading a gang which, unlike those of other bandits at the time, was indiscriminately cruel to all, including the poor. (No Robin Hood romanticism here.) Lampião's name, derived from "lamp," came from the flash of his deadly accurate rifle in battle. Over nearly twenty years he terrorized the interiors of Pernambuco, Ceará, and Alagoas, for the last decade with his wife Maria Bonita at his side, until the Sergipe military police caught up with the lot, killing them all. His fame had grown enormously, with tales and songs of his exploits disseminated throughout the sertão. The entire gang, including Maria Bonita, were decapitated – the Frenchified method of high profile capital punishment long preferred by Brazil – and their heads put on display at the Salvador Medical Institute as curiosities of human cruelty, until given a tardy burial in 1969.[120] But, not to worry, small ceramic figurines of Lampião and Maria Bonita, in the colorful and primitive style made famous by the Pernambucano town of Caruaru, can still be found throughout the Northeast, with funny Saturn hats, farmer's boots, ammunition belts crisscrossing chests, and, for Lampião at least, thick black eyeglass frames, Phillip Johnson-style, that wrap around his face like limp clay.

A native son who has inspired even more than songs and effigies is President Luiz Inácio Lula da Silva, or Lula as he is called in the Brazilian habit of familiarizing the most exalted with one-word nicknames. Born in a shack near Garanhuns during the drought of 1945, he was the seventh child of a family no longer able to sustain itself, his father abandoning them two weeks before Lula's birth to try his luck in São Paulo. By the time Lula's mother, seven years later, put the entire family on the back of a flat-bed truck (locally called a "parrot's perch") and made the thirteen day journey to São Paulo, the wayward husband had already taken up with her cousin to father more children. This didn't discourage his siring of several more with Lula's mother, Euridice, and still others with her cousin, so that by the time of his death he had ten offspring with one and thirteen with the other. Lula shined shoes on the streets of São Paulo as a child, and eventually defied dictators in the 1970's at the head of the Metalworkers Union. At the time his long black hair hung in long curly tentacles; hence the nickname Lula, or Squid, which stuck. (Later he formally added it to his name.) In 1980 he formed the Workers' Party, and on his third bid for the Presidency was elected in 2002 by a wide margin.[121] When the governing party's usual scare tactics failed, Brazil passed a remarkable milestone: not only had it peacefully made the democratic transition from ruling elites to the opposition, it had put in power a have-not, a man whose humble origins, rough clothes, and lack of much formal education (he never finished high school) would have made his rule unthinkable during the country's first five hundred years. As a local historian declares, "The Brazilian government has [often] been misused by a clever elite."[122] And so the old elites finally lost out.

The coastal highway BR-101 that connects Northeastern capitals like a string of Christmas lights, after a briefly calm stretch through Paraíba, descended once again into unadulterated awfulness through Lampião's and Lula's home state of Pernambuco. As this is the only road connecting all six Northeastern economies, the truck traffic increases the further south you fall, attracted like bits of loose iron towards the magnetism of Southeastern Brazil – which encompasses Rio, Minas, and São Paulo, or nearly two-thirds of the nation's output. Like Euridice and her seven children atop the neighbor's parrot's perch, we were beginning to feel its pull as both potholes and truck traffic multiplied. Since BR-101 is a simple two-laner, like every other highway of our trip, and whatever climbing or breakdown lanes there were had long ago been rendered useless by encroaching vegetation or sand pits, the growing parade of kamikaze trucks and wild-cat buses made the potholes ever more treacherous to navigate.

Exhausted, we finally reached the state capital of Recife in the late afternoon, and only after a handful of attempts, while circling back and forth, could we find the way to Olinda, the famous (if unsigned) colonial town just north. I had spent a week in Olinda during Carnival some years before and thought I knew the place, but either urban sprawl or the lack of Carnival revelers disoriented me – or could it be that the locals just don't care?

Back in Barreirinhas I had met an Olinda native named Marcelo, who suggested I give him a call once in town, which I did. And good thing too, as Atlas and I would have a particularly tough time finding a place to take us in that night. We rendezvoused with Marcelo, a burly computer technician, in a small square by the house where he lives with his parents and grandmother, and after greetings all around he gave us suggestions on where to stay, including Pousada D'Olinda across the square. Our arrival also attracted the attention of a young hustler in blue cut-off pants, ragged t-shirt, and flip-flops who hovered around the car until he got Atlas to bark. He offered his help to find a place, which I declined, explaining that I already knew Olinda and would do fine on my own.

As evening faded into night, few places had rooms and none of them accepted dogs. When we returned after six or seven failed attempts to the Pousada D'Olinda – whose looks I hadn't really liked – Blue Pants was on our trail again, offering to show us the pousada just ten paces from where I parked the car. I explained that Marcelo had already told me about the inn, and thanked him anyway. He nevertheless followed me into the courtyard, which I didn't resist, thinking it better to have Blue Pants inside rather than outside riling up Atlas.

The receptionist showed me an available room reached through a labyrinth of turns on the far side of a laundry area, whose every wall was sooted with mold up to waist level. The room was hardly any better, but we were without options. I decided to tell Abdelilah about Atlas only when filling out the registration form, by commenting that I had a well-trained dog, which shouldn't be a problem, as he has his own bed and can sleep in the bathroom if need be, and breakfast is included, isn't it?

Abdelilah had almost acceded to the fact that having a polite, well manicured, and intelligent dog along for the ride was the most natural and sensible thing in the world, when Blue Pants decided to intervene.

"This dog of his is aggressive."

I looked at Blue Pants in disbelief before telling him to stop bothering us and, for good measure, to get out of my sight then and there. When it looked like he was staying put, I asked what had motivated him to tell such lies about my dog. Had I been less tired I might have noticed that Blue Pants seemed to be enjoying himself.

Meanwhile, Abdelilah stepped outside to make a call from the public phone. Only when he returned to the reception balcony, where I was back to filling out the registration form, did I learn that he had just spoken to the owner. Whereupon he apologized that they, in fact, could not accept my dog.

I nearly went ballistic. "You mean that just because this street urchin calls my dog aggressive, you call the owner?"

He tried to deny it, but there it was: things as they are. I nevertheless berated Abdelilah, saying that I was upset and surprised by his inhospitality and, for good measure, was thinking of leaving Olinda on the spot.

As I walked in a huff back to Marcelo's house, another young hustler tried to offer me his services, poor thing, which prompted me to shout, "Leave me in peace, will you?"

Marcelo was understanding, saying they were probably just having a "bit of fun with a foreigner," and offered that Atlas sleep in the small kennel in his backyard that night. Upon inspection, we found the concrete floor dirty and damp due to a leaky lean-to roof. He apologized for its roughness, saying that he would let Atlas stay on the back porch with their three dogs, but as several of them were jealous it wouldn't be feasible. I gratefully accepted his offer and, as a modest thank you, suggested that the three of us dine out together.

What struck me most during dinner were Marcelo's tales of

increasing violence in and around Recife. He confessed, for instance, that he would very much like to bike the twenty minutes to and from work in Old Recife, but knows that if he did his bike would promptly be stolen from underneath him. Riding in large groups is the only way to go – but even that isn't fool-proof. There's a good bike loop in a town park, he told me, which had become a favorite training routine for bicyclists until one bright day when thieves relieved everyone of their bikes at gunpoint and drove away with a pickup-full. (Recife was once known as the "Calcutta of the Western Hemisphere.") Most amazingly, Marcelo doesn't walk the streets of Olinda alone at night – that is, in the very town where he grew up. (Good thing we two strapping men had brought Atlas along to protect us after dinner.) Both he and his grandmother cautioned me to be constantly on the alert, even though daytime nuisances, such as Blue Pants, are relatively minor.

To say this was a sad state of affairs, with urban Brazil spiraling into a passionately cold cycle of violence, is an understatement. While I once witnessed – from an apparently safe distance – a gun fight during Carnival in Olinda, and had a checkbook pick-pocketed from a fanny pack while stuck in a sweaty mass of partiers, these were, fortunately for an obvious outsider, the only brushes with an endemic violence that threatens to overwhelm a traditionally easy-going society. Yet for a local and street-smart male to fear walking at night in the heavily touristed town where he grew up, just boggles the mind. (That year President Lula's home state replaced Rio as Brazil's most murderous.)

After the rockiness of Atlas's and my welcome, Olinda would have a difficult time swaying me again with its many charms, but in the light of day, the jade sea hovering beyond the white gingerbread colonial homes, it made a yeoman attempt. It is a townscape reminiscent of out-island Greece, only more rectangular, with sharper edges and more articulated tiled roofs. A highpoint was when the Franciscan convent allowed both Atlas and me to wander through its cool ceramic-tiled interiors, where I heard a layperson murmur, "St. Francis always looked kindly upon animals." If only local innkeepers were so charitable.

*   *   *

And what of Lula, whose fairytale rise to power from the rocky subsistence of the Pernambucano sertão to the extravagance of the Niemeyer concrete of Brasília is almost beyond comprehension? It is early to judge, though many of my Paulistano friends who once supported him have felt profoundly disappointed by the cronyism and constant scandals of the Workers' Party in national power for the first time. Does power corrupt or do the perks of high office seem inalienable to newcomers? And what of the political shift, from the previous center-left administration to a definitively left wing one? While Lula has admirably avoided scapegoating others, including the imperialist North, for the country's ills, and pursued the very same orthodox economic policies that he inveighed against as the opposition candidate, in foreign policy there are more ways than one to skin the socialist cat, and his behavior has been erratic at best. In this regard, Lula is but a modest symbol of a Latin America disenchanted with the promise of Instant Capitalism, who has discovered, like Mitterrand in 1980's France, the economic realities of the world while rhetorically railing against the injustice of it all. Lula, during his many overseas journeys, has not met a dictator he didn't like if there was some opportunistic business to be done, and has spent many a trip cuddling up with the rear-guard of illiberal Hispanic America, the Castros and Chavezes of an old and despotic populism. One can explain it as a sop to the unreconstituted left of the party, bitterly disappointed with his domestic pragmatism, but it also reflects the prickly nationalism of a proud and sometimes bewildered people.

Contradictions abound, such as when Lula attempted to expel a New York Times reporter for claiming that he, the Squid, was a drunkard. The last time a Brazilian leader had tried to gag and banish a journalist was during the military dictatorship that Lula had so consistently and honorably opposed. So how to explain such strange behavior, that can hardly classify as the sins of the fathers when within the same person, other than imbibing too deeply from the wells of power?

* * *

The subject of violence came up again when visiting a friend of a friend, a Paulistano who had moved to Maceió to run a sugar processing business called Leão Irmãos. It was a fitting visit near trip's end, as Brazil's long dalliance with extractive economics had first flourished with the mighty sugar cane of the Northeast. Cezar was one last example of the revenge of the Bandeirantes, venturing out to minister to the administrative needs of the country. I called him up after only the seventh hotel along Maceió's beachfront deigned to take Atlas and me in, and he came by for a few *choppes*, or draft beers, on the sea-breezed sidewalk across from an uninviting beach.

Cezar has an exacting way of having his needs met, such as when he berated the waiter about our plate of fried sardines. "I asked for dry and crunchy, and it didn't come dry or crunchy. Tell the chef, as the next time I will complain."

When I told him about Marcelo's tales of increasing crime and violence in Recife, Cezar's response was just as concise and clear. "You know what the problem is? Lack of punishment. These guys can rob and kill, rob and kill, and are back on the streets in no time. Lula's Justice Minister just said that the jails are too crowded, so he's going to reduce the prison population. Great! More thieves and murderers on the street!"

"So why is there so little punishment?"

"Well, along with the human rights stuff after the military government came too much concern about prisoners' and criminals' rights – poor things! Admittedly there was some good reason for it too, as the police here in Alagoas, for instance, used to kill thieves on the spot, which kept crime low but, hey, if you can execute bad guys that way, what's to stop you from doing the same to anyone?"

I wondered whether the country is overreacting to its most recent, decades-long period of military rule, when the police were reviled and feared, and the joke was, "Help! Call a thief!"

"The entire judicial system is in shambles," Cezar explained. "There are laws for everything, but few of them work in practice."

Many of my Paulistano friends, I pointed out, would argue that lack of education and jobs is at the root of so much violence.

But Cezar was adamant. "That's rot," he retorted. "Of course that will help in the long run, but the problem right now is lack of punishment." Or perhaps the same kind of avert-your-eyes, wishful do-goodism that once allowed New York City to spiral into a haven of crime.

Brazil used to be known as a pacific place, untouched by wars on its own soil, and far removed from the lunatic eruptions of European violence that killed tens of millions this last century alone. Yet this line of thinking only goes so far, for with a country so large and expansive, there are always exceptions and contradictions. Brazil, for instance, was the only Latin American country to send troops during World War II, to fight for the liberation of Italy.[123] In recent years, Brazilian soldiers composed the majority of the United Nations peacekeeping forces trying to avert bloodshed, all over again, in Haiti. (Cynics point out they only want a permanent seat on the Security Council.) At the same time stories of inhuman cruelty have a long pedigree in Brazil: of slaves thrown alive into furnaces and flogged to death for minor infractions. Or, more recently, a gang of renegade military policemen in Rio who, the year after my trip, gunned down thirty innocent bystanders on a rampage through the poor neighborhoods of the Fluminense Lowlands,[124] an area once made uninhabitable by malaria and yellow fever, now made unlivable by humans. And so on, until you realize that beneath the easy-going, happy-go-lucky exterior, there lurks a sudden capacity to explode into violence – urban or roadside.

Which, for some unknown and inexplicable reason, had yet to touch us despite my accent and looks that yelled *gringo!*, my foreign-born purebred dog who epitomized exotic, and my ragged, scratched, and abused possessions, including my station wagon – all of which continued to attract as much attention as an armful of watches. Up to this point, apparently, we had simply lucked out.

~ 22 ~

WHO, REALLY, CAN BLAME the Northeasterners for a reputation of charming indolence, when, at least for those early coast-dwellers, they truly had found an earthly paradise? Imagine what it was like: a year-round tropical climate, with abundant water and available food that started out easy and sustainable and soon enough became dependable and varied. Within five decades of Brazil's discovery, the New World was rapidly transforming into a cornucopia of abundance. Sugar cane – based on its success in the Atlantic islands – was spreading rapidly, assuring both the colony's future and a never-ending supply of cachaça; plantations of orange, banana, grape, figs, and quince were introduced; steer were shipped to Bahia; and African staples such as coconut milk, dendê oil, black beans, okra, and chili pepper were becoming popular. By the centennial, the Bandeirantes were spreading indigenous food and cooking habits, such as manioc, corn, and methods of stewing meats, throughout the interior.[125] Cutlery, other than plain knives and homemade cooking spoons, didn't make landfall for another century, in the early 18th, but no one went hungry for lack of them.* Brazilian cooking, after all, is richer, more interesting, and – from diverse roots to everyday sacramental meals – even spiritual.

Once the agreeable coasts were seeded with sugar cane, crops, and slavery, then the myriad river systems, such as the mighty São Francisco whose mouth we ferried across at the Alagoas and Sergipe

---

* Cutlery, after all, only came into use in London starting in the 1690's, according to "Nationhood and mutton pie," *The Economist*, 8/16/2008, p.82.

state line, were conduits for cultivation into the forbidding interior. Those first oxen and cows, brought by Tomé de Sousa, spawned the cattle industry that accompanied the sugar cane plantations' spectacular growth, supplying many of the sugar workers' needs for meat, butter, and clothing, and in turn created the cowboy culture that continues to thrive – where else? – throughout western Brazil. After river-sleuthing came cattle drives through the vast interior, that are still seen in places like Mato Grosso where history repeats itself along the moving frontier.

Brazilians have never liked work for the sake of work, that is, if it can be avoided. Such lethargy stems, in part, from the Portuguese *ancien régime* that divided the population into nobility, clergy, and peasant. A practical consequence, according to one Brazilian historian, was "At least until the time that masses of European workers came to central and southern Brazil, manual labor was socially scorned as 'something just for the blacks.'"[126] Another factor, forwarded by some Brazilians, is the Catholic emphasis on the delayed gratification of the after-life – so why overly stress in this one?

Yet the tropical dislike of hard labor had many compensating charms, particularly in the Northeast, including a sweet, laissez-faire disposition that makes way for the mysterious and human. What has been written of Cariocas also applies to Northeasterners: they have "a more aristocratic sense of living,"[127] especially along the fertile coasts. They may not have all the money in the world, but they know how to live, with an ebb and flow of joy, sociability, and consideration.

I had a few such aristocrats to look up in Maceió, the parents of a friend in Tiradentes who hadn't ventured home in years and was glad to send me as an envoy. When I telephoned Senhor Nilson, a retired pilot, I doubted the efficacy of his directions – which were to follow the coast north for twenty-three kilometers, pass Fisherman's Village, turn right at the House of Construction, and ask anyone where "Socorro's house" is – but they worked perfectly, and I was welcomed at the gate by Socorro herself, the maid, whose name reassuringly offers *help!*

Senhor Nilson and his wife Dona Dinoràh are just about the nicest couple I have met in Brazil, which is saying a lot. Not only was I made to feel an honored guest, with Socorro serving me juice, desert, then coffee and biscuits on the austere veranda overlooking the ocean, and given a tour of the spectacular and uncluttered grounds facing the sea, but soon felt enveloped in a generous warmth as steady as the afternoon sun's. I was introduced to two live-in grandchildren, in their early twenties, who were treated as dotingly as children. (Their father, from different marriages, had died six years back.) The boy, named Nilson *Neto* – for "grandson" – despite digestive problems was studying law in Maceió. His elfish half-sister, Barbara, was also a student, whose lips curled impishly in amusement at my foreign accent and mannerisms. Enveloped by a sweet, briny smell, the low thunder of waves on rocks were rhythmic and constant, as if the arterial musings of the earth's expansive, pulsating heart. Later when their diminutive and eccentric great-aunt Aparecida appeared and told me with a wide smile that my friend, her nephew, was her favorite person in existence – that is, along with Nilson Neto (and, as an afterthought, Barbara) – I almost got down on my knees to give her a proper hug. Where else in this world can one brush with the divine in the form of a gracious spinster? Just meeting Aparecida and delivering my friend's embraces nearly made my trip complete. Atlas and I left before sundown, nearly feeling refreshed.

Maceió, of course, is the languid capital of the small state of Alagoas, with a backwater feel despite its perch over the glorious, palm-stuttered coast. Alagoas is notorious for a national soap opera of its own, with the meteoric rise and flame-out of native son Fernando Collor, in no small part due to the influence of TV Globo, the world's fourth largest private network. At first mayor of Maceió during the military's ascendency, and then state governor, the telegenic Collor was plucked from a wide yet shallow field of candidates in 1989 – the first direct Presidential elections in almost thirty years – to defeat the openly socialist Lula, in part due to his celebrated anti-corruption campaign to fire *maharajahs*, or paid Alagoan state employees who had not once showed up to work. The well-dressed and athletic Collor – the Brazilian Kennedy as he came to be known – received glowing treatment from Globo, while Lula – looking disheveled in his frumpy suits and tussled hair, especially during the last televised debate – appeared uncomfortable, the sweaty Nixon. As added measure, the Collor team paid for Lula's former mistress to come forward and claim that Lula had offered her money to abort the child she was then carrying.

Collor won by only five points, yet soon embarked on a quixotic economic rescue program, brought on by yet another crisis of overspending, which included his government's freezing (i.e. confiscation) of all personal savings accounts for one year – public thievery on a federal, near continental scale. But the lesson for the presidency was less to avoid economic incompetence and chloroform statism, for generations part of the country's genetic code, than to be careful what you promise, which in Collor's case was to be as clean as a whistle.

In a story with overtones of Cain and Abel, it was Collor's younger brother, Pedro, who brought the president down, justifying the fratricide in part due to Collor's attempt to seduce his wife. When Pedro went public – and this, too, reads like a soap opera synopsis – Collor had the family's matriarch fire him from his position running the family business. This only made Pedro produce more revelations, most of which centered around Collor's *éminence grise*, who had fleeced millions during and after the campaign to pay for Collor's (and his) exalted lifestyle, extravagant even by Brazilian standards. Surfacing later was how the First Lady's well-publicized charity institute had speculated on truckloads of water taken to drought-stricken disaster areas and even – a first – on children's coffins.

All of this might have been treated as business as usual if not for the fine coincidence that TV Globo was then airing a novella called *The Rebel Years*, an idealistic look at the Brazilian counterculture of the Sixties under the theme song of Caetano Veloso's *Happiness, Happiness*, which inspired a new generation of youth to spill onto the streets in protest. When *The Rebel Years* showed clips of Haight-Ashbury hippies with flowers painted on their faces, the very next day the protestors, as if with one voice, took to the streets with painted, florid faces. Only then did Globo, which had brought Collor from the obscurity of a small, backwards Northeast state to national renown, turn against him.[128] And in a tropically warm country where household incidence of televisions is higher than that of refrigerators, what Globo says matters.

After less than three years in office Collor was impeached, turning the reigns over to his incompetent and populist vice president whose name Itamar, if slightly mispronounced, means "Aiy! What a mess!" No doubt a coincidence, but Brazil had consumed its first democratically-elected President in three decades, a young man from the state where home-grown cannibals had dined on the country's first Bishop.

I will always remember my delightfully random visit to the elusive Museum of the Sergipe Man hidden away in the state's capital, Aracaju. The Museum had deserted its old address and only the fourth passer-by – most of them surprised to learn that a museum had ever been there – could tell me where to find it, a few blocks away. There the museum had been re-inaugurated and then, due to water infiltration, disassembled, in its present condition four months after the grand re-opening. But a little persistence can pay off in such circumstances, which is what happened when I took a languorous look at the lone exhibit on Sergipe ceramics, whose content was less intriguing than the person who, delighted by a visitor, came by to explain.

Notwithstanding the lack of a museum, Socorro (that name again) was the best museum guide I have ever encountered. A short, wiry woman, her energy was enveloping, her openness and enthusiasm boundless.

"So you are American?"

"Yes I am. But I live in Minas Gerais."

"Came to Brazil and fell in love with it."

"That's right."

"Became impassioned with the culture."

"You bet."

"And never wants to go back to the United States!"

"Well, I wouldn't go that far..."

"From Minas, you said? That's a heavily Catholic state, like Sergipe, with lots of tradition."

"It is."

"Ninety percent Catholic I believe. No, that's not right. I'm thinking of all of Brazil. Ninety-percent Christian, sixty percent Catholic, the other part Protestant. The Protestants don't have so many festivals or saints, do they?"

"No, I don't think so."

"Some, but not as many."

"Yes, that would be difficult..."

When Socorro offered to show me pictures of local folkloric traditions from the archives upstairs, I accepted right away. After escorting me to the one-room library, she brushed away some clippings from the top of the sole desk and suggested I sit in the one chair. When she pulled out three stand-up archival boxes full of photographs, I sat on the bench to the side and insisted she take the seat. One by one she pulled out old photographs from envelopes marked with the date, subject, and the stamp of the University of Sergipe, and told a story around each photo. Such was her enthusiasm that she sometimes stuffed photographs back into the wrong envelopes, but I couldn't bring myself to interrupt a flow so magnificent that it was difficult to keep up with her. Most wondrous of all was when she started not only to sing the song associated with the costumed *bloco* or parade, but got up, to my surprise and delight, to dance a representative part, a lovely little jig on the floor by my side. Invariably it was while showing me a few dance steps that a broad grin, that can only be called beatific, spread across her face – the face of Brazil that I have known and loved, smiling down upon me.

The days were starting to cool down again, the southern winter creeping back with the slatternly light. Due to the false change of seasons as we tumbled south, I could feel a powerful itch to move on, my reservoirs of travel stamina rapidly diminishing. In the end I would fly through Bahia, which, it is true, I have visited a handful of times before – but that is no excuse. I didn't visit Salvador, I barely tasted the food, I didn't listen to the music, or lie in a hammock by the sea. In other words, I ignored all that is good and great about Bahia. Had I been carrying the handgun urged on me by so many Brazilian friends, I would have had to shoot myself then and there and be done with it.

In truth, I was growing weary of my journey's chosen logistics and especially the prejudice, dissembling, and, at times, ritualized hysteria relating to Atlas – the seven stops in Aracaju to find lodging were indicative – which began to make me irritable, the bane of any traveler. Things began to look up when I discovered that nearly a dozen pousadas in Bahia were classified by Quatro Rodas as pet-friendly, which was truly a bounty after only a feeble pair had been so labeled since Belém. Alas, after the canine luxury of Belém's Beira Rio, such promise was bound to disappoint, with the heavily touristed Bahian coast becoming less welcoming to one and all, tourists and foreigners, furry or not.

In Arembepe, north of Salvador, a seaside hotel was listed as dog-friendly, but when we arrived the woman said they had changed their policy. She showed me where the low, earthen kennel had been by the side of the road, and said that passing locals had tormented the caged pets so much that they had to put a stop to it. I had to confirm the existence of Atlas's bed, among the usual assurances, before she took pity on us – for which we were grateful, as it afforded us a good number of runs, walks, and swims by the lovely, coconut-bombed beach. Since we were the only guests, in short order the owners' children were marching Atlas around on the tall, grassy knoll buffering the hotel and road from the beach. One evening before bed, Atlas and I stood at the pool's edge where the on-shore breeze was so warmly consistent that Atlas's ears lifted and stayed aloft, a benediction of the African winds. By the end of our short stay the owner, who had started out so suspiciously, insisting needlessly that I pay for potential damages, told us we were welcome back any time. So close to old and increasingly violent Salvador, she has good reason to be careful.

We drove in a half circle around the old capital and quickly got lost in the Rencôncavo, the lush Portuguese plantation zone that surrounds All Saints' Bay and, in former times, was vibrant green with sugar cane wealth – so prosperous that it paid for much of Salvador's colonial architecture. Only when we found Santo Amaro, where Caetano Veloso grew up, could we find our bearings and continue south.

In Ilhéus, made famous by native novelist Jorge Armado and his creation *Gabriela, Clove and Cinnamon*, the sugar cane fields gave way to the *zona de cacau*, from where two-thirds of Brazil's cocoa is still produced. Our hotel, just south of town, was also listed as dog-friendly, but the new Italian owners hadn't gotten around to informing Quatro Rodas of the change in policy. In the end only a dilapidated kennel was offered out back where one good rain storm would easily soak Atlas, but at least my room's back window was just forty paces away. When I took Atlas and his bed there at day's end, we passed a small junkyard where some animal had possibly met a terrible fate, for Atlas took one smell and became the most agitated I have seen him, crouched close to the ground on all fours, crawling minutely forward for a quick sniff before sudden retreats. What danger lurked inside? I would have dismissed it as a small, furtive mammal in his lair, but in place of the usual tail-wagging and *what-fun!* attitude was the most fearful reaction I've witnessed from Atlas, the gunnel-scraping off Boto Velho magnified a few times over. I had no choice but to sit down inside the kennel with him for some time, telling him that it was alright, that what had happened in the junkyard would never happen to him. (What is meaningful travel about, after all, other than overcoming the fears and hesitations that besiege us outside our comfort zones?) Atlas barked plaintively when I returned to my room, from where I spoke to him in a normal voice over the dark and violent history, telling him I would always be there for him – which, in reality, was not the case.

As best as I could, I was trying to give Atlas the parenting and support I never received, through divorce and distraction, as a child – an awning, lingering neglect which helps to explain the disjointed and peripatetic life I have chosen, not overly tied to person, place, or thing. Dogs, in their humble ways, can lead us to basic truths with far less polemic than human co-conspirators. It is as though their sensory abilities, despite millennia of years of cooperation with over-developed humans, are more attuned to the natural order of things, leading us to fetch and retrieve old worlds of wisdom lost somewhere within.

At Trancoso, in southern Bahia, I had some friends from São Paulo with a lovely and not overly sophisticated pousada, where I was looking forward to a day or two of uneventful rest. I didn't warn them of our arrival and just showed up. When I explained to the reception girl that both Atlas and I had stayed here before, she took us in after a quick call to one of the managers.

Although the manager's two Labs had the run of the place, along with my friend Aline's year-old Basset Hound, Atlas was not really welcome in the end. To make matters worse, due to my patchy memory, I had erred: Atlas had never visited Trancoso before, but had come close when Mom, Dad, and dog spent New Year's in Cumuruxatiba on the other side of Mt. Easter, where Cabral first sighted Brazil.

Nando, Aline's husband, was diplomatic about it, telling a story about how some old friends from São Paulo had once visited with their dog, but had called before to ask for permission, had brought presents for the manager's Lab with whom their pooch would share a kennel, and then had even sent photos of the dog-frolic afterwards. This is clearly the polite and considerate way to travel with your dog in Brazil, a lesson I half-learned belatedly, even if the length of our trip made such niceties unrealistic. In any case, I could have offered to checkout then and there, but was feeling too frazzled, selfish, and defensive to do so. Sometimes, after learning a thing or two, you just have to move on.

Aline, an embracing blond formerly from an advertising agency I used to work with, had made the transition from big city to village with aplomb, and was not only helping Nando with the pousada and restaurant, but had opened her own home decoration shop where I ended up buying too many knickknacks for my small and already crowded house. Sensing her concern for the condition of our suite at one point, I assured her that Atlas and I would leave the room cleaner than we had found it. This didn't deter her from saying, when I thanked her at checkout for so kindly taking in Atlas and me, "It wasn't me," and pointing to the receptionist, "it was her." I was trying, not very well, to make the best of a bad situation I had created.

One morning I woke up to find Atlas tangled in the draping of my four-post bed's large mosquito net – something that only Saci, the tormentor of domesticated animals, could have arranged. Evidently Atlas had sidled up to say hello in the middle of the night and, without a whimper of complaint, had wrapped himself up so thoroughly that, while able to lay down, he had become immobilized and decided to wait patiently for my morning assistance.

He was exhausted in a good way, for both days we had visited the magnificent town beach, where the green aquamarine sea glitters like a shifting bed of emeralds – the gem which had attracted so many 16th century Europeans to the New World in the first place. Although Atlas is more a fresh- than a saltwater dog, he was quickly learning how to approach crashing waves while in hot pursuit of a tossed tennis ball. Unlike ground games, where he can burst out running in the direction of my throwing arm, here he learned to wait and see where the ball, after re-entering the earth's atmosphere, made ocean-fall before charging the battalion of waves. Patience, that ancient if neglected virtue, has many rewards.

I realized on our final sea-spray day that this would be our last beach outing for some time, until the next loopy journey into the achingly kind hinterlands and coastlines of Brazil. So, naturally, neither of us wanted the moment, the outing, the confirmation of companionship and loving care to end, as I threw the lazy ball one more time into the same Atlantic of Atlas's Labrador Sea ancestors.

"This will be the last ball, okay Atlas?"

"OK, this is the very last one, got it?"

"So this is the final one, understood?"

"One last time, Atlas my boy, and that's all."

"Well, if you insist..."

It would take two days of straight driving, divided by one night in the coastal range of Holy Spirit state, to reach my humble house in Tiradentes, and I have to admit that upon entering Minas Gerais I felt the greatest relief, an overwhelming sense of security, as if returning to the height of civilization after a foray into the trembling unknown. I breathed easier for the first time in months, and nearly got out of the car to kneel and genuflect in the musky earth. Minas, for me, will always be associated with the smell of *capim doce*, or "sweet grass," that seems to greet me whenever I cross the state line – but this felt like the sweetest, fullest welcome of all.

So Brazil had done it again: just when I thought that I had become impervious to her charms, resistant to her spells and tricks, she had up and broadsided me once again. It was a journey that so many had said shouldn't be done, was too risky, too indulgent, too childish, too this or that – and in the end it was none of those things. Brazil is a magical and very large, yet startlingly intimate, place – a nation of so many warm panelinhas on the low burner of a long afternoon.

As for Atlas, he began to stick his head out the side windows with greater frequency as the air cooled and the mustier smells multiplied – of the old and diminishing cerrado in the misty, dry grasp of its winter hibernation. His ears flapped, his eyes widened, his nostrils flared, and his jowls rolled upwards showing the smooth determination of his teeth. Undoubtedly, with a dog's sixth sense he already knew the way, and, with a much better notion of direction than I could muster those final days, was pointing the way home.

And so it came to pass, for a dog born in Costa Rica and brought to Brazil at the tender age of one, that Brazil was now his home as it would always be. As for me, that is another story whose outcome is not yet told, as home continues to be the last place where I feel welcome.

Then we arrived, and everything changed. Now, if someone would only throw the ball again.

Epilogue

≈

L OOKING BACK, I can see more clearly that I was more exhausted than I have ever been after a journey, bar one. While Atlas and Fofão held up reasonably well, the trip had extracted more than a pound of flesh, reducing me to a sad sack of nerves those last days. Seventeen thousand kilometers and one million potholes had taken their toll, and I would feel a certain fatigue, an echo of tenseness, buried deep within muscle and bone for months to come.

Such was my stunned relief and contentment to be home once again that I fell into the deepest of slumbers, with Atlas curled at the foot of my bed guarding my dreams and looking over me with his usual care and attention, for most of a week. Then it was time for him to return to São Paulo.

But don't get me wrong. I like Brazilian roads, despite the fact that half of them are classified in awful shape by a Brazilian bureaucracy now and then on truth serum. Potholes, seen from a different perspective, are actually bracingly efficient tools to avoid traveling on the surface of things.

When driving, by comparison, on one of those perfectly smooth, gently curving, wonderfully signed and maintained super-highways of the developed world, I pay less attention and get drowsy, which makes them far more hazardous for me. In Brazil you have to fix your gaze steadily on the here and now, always waiting for – no, expecting – a new turn with fresh obstacles just ahead.

In memory of Atlas
– who died in my
lap a year
after
our return
from rat poison
left out by a farmer
in the hills of Tiradentes

Acknowledgments

≈

BRAZIL IS A BIG, GENEROUS country, where many deserve my sincere thanks. For early encouragement, Fernando Moreira Salles stands out, as do John and Anna Maria Parsons. For detailed readings, to correct Portuguese errors and misunderstandings common to strangers traveling in a strange land, my deep gratitude goes to Cristina Catunda and Elaine Mello. (All remaining misunderstandings are fully my own.) I also wish to recognize the countless kind people, mostly nameless, I met en route who carried me aloft in the palms of their hearts.

The process of writing, while solitary, is sustained with the help of many, most of whom go unrecognized. For their full or partial readings at important junctures, I would like to thank Anna Stein, Lesley King, Carolyn Carlson, Molly Batchelder, and Leslie Dunton-Downer.

As always, Mary Rhinelander's and Marieclaire Bizzarro's artistic contributions were far above what I deserve or can repay. Lastly, in the adventure called publishing, timely support and input from Lesley King, Tim Batchelder, Oakes Plimpton, and Roger Ullman underline what friendship is all about.

About the Author

≈

BEN BATCHELDER has traveled extensively on American and Brazilian backroads.

Nothing in his background, from a degree in Visual & Environmental Studies at Harvard to an MBA from Wharton, adequately prepared him for the experiences. Nevertheless he has published two books on his New World journeys, that map the inner and exterior geographies of meaningful travel, with plans for more.

Having grown up in Cambridge, Mass., he currently leads a bi-hemispheric life, as a mountain man in the hills of Minas Gerais, Brazil who comes down to the sea at Miami Beach, Florida.

For more about the author, visit www.benbatchelder.com.

≈

To continue the journey, subscribe to www.backroadsbrazil.com or www.facebook.com/backroadsbrazil.

Bibliography

≈

Bishop, Elizabeth and The Editors of LIFE. *Brazil.* New York: Life World Library, Time Inc., 1962.

The Brazil Reader: History, Culture, Politics. Edited by Robert M. Levine and John J. Crocitti. Durham: Duke University Press, 4th printing 2004.

Burton, Richard F. *Explorations of the Highlands of the Brazil, Vol. I & II,* 1869. Chestnut Hill: Elibron Classics, 2005.

Câmara, Ibsen de Gusmão, *Megabiodiversidade Brasil.* Rio de Janeiro: GMT Editores, 2001.

Caminha, Pero Vaz de. "A Carta de Pero Vaz de Caminha," 1500, in *A Carta de Pero Vaz de Caminha.* Edited by Jaime Cortesão. Rio de Janeiro: Livros de Portugal, 1943.

Cardoso, Fernando Henrique. *A Arte da Política: A História que Vivi.* Rio de Janeiro: Civilização Brasileira, 3rd edition, 2006.

Carpenter, Geoffrey Paul. *Pilgrim of the Sublime.* Bloomington: Xlibris, 2003

Cascudo, Luís da Câmara. *Dicionário do Folclore Brasileiro.* São Paulo: Global Editora, 10th edition 2001.

Castro, Ruy. *Rio de Janeiro: Carnival under Fire.* Translated by John Gledson. New York: Bloomsbury, 2003.

Cleary, David; Jenkins, Dilwyn; Marshall, Oliver. *The Rough Guide to Brazil.* London: Rough Guides, 4th edition 2000.

Cruz, Tomaz Barbosa da. *Marajó e suas histórias*. Belém: Lugráfica, undated.

Dos Passos, John. *Brazil on the Move*, 1963. New York: Paragon House, 1991.

Holanda, Sérgio Buarque de. *Raízes do Brasil*, 1936. São Paulo: Editora Schwarcz, 26th edition 2004.

_____ *Visão do Paraíso*, 1959. São Paulo: Editora Brasiliense, 6th edition 2002.

Fausto, Boris. *A Concise History of Brazil*. Translated by Arthur Brakel. Cambridge, UK: Cambridge University Press, 1999

Fernandes, Caloca. *Viagem Gastronômica através do Brasil*. São Paulo: Editora Senac, 5th edition 2000.

Fleming, Peter. *Brazilian Adventure*, 1933. Evanston, IL: Northwestern University Press, 1999.

Freyre, Gilberto. *Casa-Grande e Senzala*, 1933. São Paulo: Global Editora, 49th edition 2004.

_____ *The Mansions and the Shanties: The Making of Modern Brazil,* 1936. New York: Alfred A. Knopf, 3rd printing 1968.

Grann, David. *The Lost City of Z: A Tale of Deadly Obsession in the Amazon*. New York: Doubleday, 2005.

Guia Quatro Rodas, *Brasil 2004*. São Paulo: Editora Abril, 2003.

Guias Philips. *Parques Nacionais Brasil*. São Paulo: Empresa das Artes, 1999.

Guia Unibanco. *Brasil*. São Paulo: BEI Communicacão, 2006.

Kane, Joe. *Running the Amazon*. New York: Vintage Departures, 1990

Lonely Planet. *Brazil*. Melbourne: Lonely Planet Publications, 5th edition 2002.

Mann, Charles C. *1491: New Revelations of the Americas Before Columbus.* New York: Vintage Books, 2006.

Meade, Teresa A. *A Brief History of Brazil,* 2004. New York: Checkmark Books, 2nd edition 2010.

Page, Joseph A. *The Brazilians,* Cambridge, Mass: Da Capo Press, 1996.

Parker, Richard G. *Bodies, Pleasures, and Passions: Sexual Culture in Contemporary Brazil.* Boston: Beacon Press, 1991.

Rocha, Ana Augusta; Linsker, Roberto. *Brazil Aventura 2.* São Paulo: Terra Virgem Editora, 2nd edition 1995.

_____ *Brazil Aventura 3:Ilhas.* São Paulo: Terra Virgem Editora, 1996.

_____ *Brazil Aventura Guia Ilhas.* São Paulo: Terra Virgem Editora, 1996.

Roosevelt, Theodore. *Through the Brazilian Wilderness,* 1914. New York: Cooper Square Press, 1st edition 2000.

Shoumatoff, Alex. *The Capital of Hope.* New York: Coward, McCann & Geoghegan, 1980.

Skidmore, Thomas E. *Brazil: Five Centuries of Change.* Oxford: Oxford University Press, 1999.

Travelers' Tales. *Brazil.* Edited by Annette Haddad and Scott Doggett. San Francisco: Travelers' Tales, 1997.

Veloso, Caetano. *Tropical Truth: A Story of Music ad Revolution in Brazil.* Translated by Isabel de Sena. New York: Alfred A. Knopf, 2002.

Notes

≈

Editor's Note: Road conditions cited are from 2004 and are subject to change. Likewise, most statistics mentioned are from 2005 or earlier.

1. Thomas E. Skidmore, *Brazil: Five Centuries of Change,* 1999 (Oxford University Press), p.23.

2. Guia Unibanco *Brasil* guidebook, 2006 (BEI Communicacão), p. 230.

3. Boris Fausto, *A Concise History of Brazil,* 1999 (Translated by Arthur Brakel, Cambridge University Press), p. 26.

4. Sérgio Buarque de Holanda, *Visão do Paraíso,* 1959 (Editora Brasiliense, 6th edition 2002), p.122.

5. "Steel Samba School," *The Economist,* 16/10/2004, p.58.

6. Boris Fausto, *Op. cit.,* pp.9-10.

7. Ana Augusta Rocha & Roberto Linsker, *Brazil Aventura 3:Ilhas,* 1996 (Terra Virgem Editora), pp.7-8.

8. As quoted by Sérgio Buarque de Holanda, *Visão do Paraíso, Op. cit.,* p.41.

9. Lonely Planet *Brazil,* 2002 (Lonely Planet Publications, 5th edition), p.287.

10. Thomas E. Skidmore, *Op. cit.,* p.9.

11. *Ibid.,* p.10.

12. As quoted in, *Ibid.,* p.15.

13. Pero Vaz de Caminha, *A Carta de Pero Vaz de Caminha,* 1500 (Edited by Jaime Cortesão, Livros de Portugal, 1943), pp.210-212.

14. Ibsen de Gusmão Câmara, *Megabiodiversidade Brasil,* 2001 (GMT

Editores), pp.83-84.

15. *Ibid.*, p.78.

16. Ruy Castro, *Rio de Janeiro: Carnival under Fire*, 2004 (Translated by John Gledson, Bloomsbury), p.23.

17. Lonely Planet *Brazil*, *Op. cit.*, p.412.

18. Luís da Câmara Cascudo, *Dicionário do Folclore Brasileiro*, 2001 (Global Editora, 10th edition), p.226.

19. As quoted by Sérgio Buarque de Holanda, *Raízes do Brasil*, 1936 (Editora Schwarcz, 26th edition 2004), p.107

20. Annette Haddad and Scott Doggett, editors, *Travelers' Tales Brazil*, "Brasília the Beautiful," by María Cristina Jurado (Travelers' Tales, Inc.), p.206.

21. Thomas E. Skidmore, *Op. cit.*, p.148.

22. Ruy Castro, *Op. Cit.*, p.11.

23. Thomas E. Skidmore, *Op. cit.*, p.155.

24. Alex Shoumatoff, *The Capital of Hope*, 1980 (Coward, McCann & Geoghegan), pp.19-20.

25. Theodore Roosevelt, *Through the Brazilian Wilderness*, 1914 (Cooper Square Press, 2000), p.181.

26. As quoted by Sérgio Buarque de Holanda, *Visão do Paraíso*, *Op. cit.*, p.66.

27. *Travelers' Tales Brazil*, "Brasília the Beautiful," by María Cristina Jurado (Travelers' Tales, Inc.), *Op. cit.*, p.207.

28. Lonely Planet *Brazil*, *Op. cit.*, p.408.

29. Joseph A. Page, *The Brazilians*, 1996 (Da Capo Press), p.18.

30. Ana Augusta Rocha & Roberto Linsker, *Brazil Aventura 2*, 1995 (Terra Virgem Editora), p.161.

31. *Ibid.*, p.156.

32. Guias Philips *Parques Nacionais Brasil*, 1999 (Empresa das Artes), p.188.

33. Roberto Linsker, *Brazil Aventura Guia Ilhas*, 1996 (Terra Virgem Editora) p.183.

34. *Brazil Aventura 3:Ilhas, Op. cit.*, p.139.

35. Thomas E. Skidmore, *Op. cit.*, p.166.

36. Lonely Planet *Brazil, Op. cit.*, p.663.

37. Roberto Linsker, *Brazil Aventura Guia Ilhas, Op. cit.*, p.183; Roberto Linsker, *Brazil Aventura 3:Ilhas, Op. cit.*, p.139; Guias Philips *Parques Nacionais Brasil, Op. cit.*, p.30.

38. David Cleary, Dilwyn Jenkins & Oliver Marshall, *The Rough Guide to Brazil*, 2000 (Rough Guides, 4th edition), p.432; Roberto Linsker, *Brazil Aventura Guia Ilhas, Op. cit.*, p.192; Lonely Planet *Brazil, Op. cit.*, p.663.

39. Teresa A. Meade, *A Brief History of Brazil*, 2004 (Checkmark Books, 2nd edition 2010), p.130.

40. Lonely Planet *Brazil, Op. cit.*, p.17.

41. "'Lost towns' discovered in Amazon," BBC News, 8/28/2008, http://news.bbc.co.uk/go/pr/fr/-/2/hi/science/nature/7586860.stm July 2014

42. Thomas E. Skidmore, *Op. cit.*, p.14.

43. *Ibid.*, p.10.

44. As summarized by Sérgio Buarque de Holanda, *Raízes do Brasil, Op. cit.*, p.125.

45. *Ibid.*, p.126.

46. Paul Raffaele, "Out of Time," *Smithsonian*, 4/2005, p.65.

47. "Tribe's plight highlighted," *The Miami Herald*, 5/3/2008.

48. "Sem Fé, Lei ou Rei," *Veja*, 4/28/2004, p.49.

49. Vanessa Thorpe, "Veil lifts on jungle mystery of the colonel who vanished," *The Observer*, 3/21/2004.

50. As quoted by Sérgio Buarque de Holanda, *Raízes do Brasil, Op. cit.*, p.132.

51. Gilberto Freyre, *Casa Grande e Senzala*, 1933 (Global Editora, 49th edition 2004), p.161.

52. Boris Fausto, *Op. cit.*, p.169.

53. Paul Raffaele, *Op. cit.*, p.65.

54. Lonely Planet *Brazil, Op. cit.*, p.79.

55. *The Rough Guide to Brazil, Op. cit.*, p.432.

56. Roberto Linsker, *Brazil Aventura Guia Ilhas, Op. cit.*, p.196.

57. *Travelers' Tales Brazil*, "My Maravilhosa Career," by David George, *Op. cit.*, p.319.

58. Larry Rohter, "Diamonds' Glitter Fades for a Brazilian Tribe," *The New York Times*, 12/29/2006

59. "Sem Fé, Lei ou Rei," *Veja*, 4/28/2004, p.48.

60. Boris Fausto, *Op. cit.*, pp.30,42.

61. *Travelers' Tales Brazil*, "Ancestor Worship in the Deep, Deep South," by Jack Epstein for *U.S. News & World Report, Op. cit.*, p.273.

62. Elizabeth Bishop and The Editors of LIFE, *Brazil*, 1962 (Life World Library, Time Inc.), p.148.

63. Caetano Veloso, *Tropical Truth: A Story of Music and Revolution in Brazil*, 2002 (Translated by Isabel de Sena, Alfred A. Knopf), pp.291-292.

64. Ibobe, May 2005 poll, www.renctas.org.br/pesquisa-renctasibope/ July 2014

65. Alex Shoumatoff, *The Capital of Hope*, 1980 (New York), p.56.

66. "Dorothy Stang: A martyr for the Amazon," *The Economist*, 2/19/2005, p.36.

67. "The future of the forest," *The Economist*, 6/13/2009, p.28.

68. "Preso suspeito de assassinato de freira," *O Estado de S.Paulo*, 2/20/2005, p.1.

69. "Madeira ilegal dá lucro bilionário," *O Estado de S.Paulo*, 2/29/2005, p.1.

70. "The Brazilian Amazon: Asphalting the jungle," *The Economist*, 7/24/2004, p.34.

71. *The Rough Guide to Brazil, Op. cit.*, p.335.

72. Boris Fausto, *Op. cit.*, p.45.

73. Lonely Planet *Brazil*, 1996 (Lonely Planet Publications, 3rd edition), p.577.

74. *The Rough Guide to Brazil, Op. cit.*, p.335.

75. Sérgio Buarque de Holanda, *Raízes do Brasil, Op. cit.*, p.90.

76. Boris Fausto, *Op. cit.*, pp.90-91; Lonely Planet *Brazil*, 2002, *Op. cit.*, p.630.

77. Boris Fausto, *Op. cit.*, p.90.

78. *Ibid.*, p.176.

79. Lonely Planet *Brazil*, 2002, *Op. cit.*, p.624.

80. Boris Fausto, *Op. cit.*, p.176.

81. Lonely Planet *Brazil*, 2002, *Op. cit.*, pp.26,667.

82. *Travelers' Tales Brazil*, "Where the Sun Dines," by Diane Ackerman, *Op. cit.,* p.160.

83. Sérgio Buarque de Holanda, *Raízes do Brasil, Op. cit.*, p.129.

84. Boris Fausto, *Op. cit.*, p.45.

85. Roberto Linsker, *Brazil Aventura Guia Ilhas, Op. cit.*, p.31.

86. Lonely Planet *Brazil*, 2002, *Op. cit.*, p.643.

87. Tomaz Barbosa da Cruz, *Marajó e suas histórias,* undated (Lugráfica), p.23.

88. Roberto Linsker, *Brazil Aventura Guia Ilhas, Op. cit.*, p.31.

89. *Ibid.*, pp.31-32.

90. *The Rough Guide to Brazil, Op. cit.*, p.346.

91. Tomaz Barbosa da Cruz, *Op. cit.*, p.5.

92. Luiz Flávio, "Turismo envolve prazer e perigo na Cidade Velha," *Diário do Pará*, 7/25/2004, p.4.

93. Lonely Planet *Brazil*, 2002, *Op. cit.*, p.624.

94. Larry Rohter, "The Devil Take August. In Brazil, It's Just Too Scary," *The New York Times*, 8/5/2004.

95. Raimundo José Pinto, "Pará deve produzir US$8,3b em minerais," *Diário do Parà*, 7/25/2004, p.1.

96. Lonely Planet *Brazil*, 2002, *Op. cit.*, p.606.

97. Boris Fausto, *Op. cit.*, pp.59,65.

98. www.en.wikipedia.org/wiki/Alcântara_Launch_Center, Feb. 2014.

99. Thomas E. Skidmore, *Op. cit.*, pp.192-194.

100. *The Rough Guide to Brazil*, *Op. cit.*, p.92; July 2014, http://www.summitpost.org/p-o-de-a-ucar-sugar-loaf/153880

101. David Grann, *The Lost City of Z: A Tale of Deadly Obsession in the Amazon*, 2005 (Doubleday), p.18.

102. Sérgio Buarque de Holanda, *Raízes do Brasil*, *Op. cit.*, p.148.

103. Luís da Câmara Cascudo, *Op. cit.*, p.610.

104. "Economic history: The merits of genteel poverty," *The Economist*, 8/18/2007, p.74.

105. Lonely Planet *Brazil*, 2002, *Op. cit.*, p.18.

106. Gilberto Freyre, *Casa-Grande e Senzala,* 49th edition 2004 (Global Editora), p.84.

107. Boris Fausto, *Op. cit.*, p.51.

108. Azevedo Amaral (1881-1942) as quoted by Gilberto Freyre, *Op. cit.*, p.82 – although Freyre quotes Amaral in order to dispute him.

109. Richard F. Parker, *Bodies, Pleasures, and Passions: Sexual Culture in Contemporary Brazil*, 1991 (Beacon Press), p.16.

110. Thomas E. Skidmore, *Op. cit.*, p.57.

111. Lonely Planet *Brazil*, 2002, *Op. cit.*, p.20.

112. Boris Fausto, *Op. cit.*, pp.91-92.

113. Robert M. Levine and John J. Crocitti, editors, *The Brazil Reader: History, Culture, Politics,* "Uprising in Maranhaõ, 1839-1840" by Domingos José Gonçalves de Magalhães, p.72.

114. Boris Fausto, *Op. cit.*, p.91.

115. Thomas E. Skidmore, *Op. cit.*, pp.54-55, 69-70.

116. *Ibid.*, p.78.

117. "Brazil: No black and white matter," *The Economist,* 7/17/2006, p.38.

118. Guias Philips, *Op. cit.,* p.162.

119. Ibsen de Gusmão Câmara, *Op. cit.*, pp.87-91.

120. Lonely Planet *Brazil*, 2002, *Op. cit.*, p.28.

121. Barry Bearak, "Poor Man's Burden," *The New York Times Magazine*, 6/27/2004, pp.35,50; Teresa A. Meade, *Op. cit.*, p.175.

122. Boris Fausto, *Op. cit.*, p.335.

123. Thomas E. Skidmore, *Op. cit.*, p.121.

124. "Brazil's trigger-happy police: Law-enforcers on the rampage," *The Economist*, 4/7/2005.

125. Coloca Fernandes, *Viagem Gastronômica através do Brasil*, 2000 (Editora Senac), pp.13-23.

126. Boris Fausto, *Op. cit.*, p.28.

127. *Travelers' Tales Brazil*, "Once upon a Time in Ipanema," by Edward A. Riedinger, *Op. cit.*, p.21.

128. Thomas E. Skidmore, *Op. cit.*, pp.217-221.

Made in the USA
Middletown, DE
17 May 2016